MANAGING AMBIGUITY

EASA Series

Published in Association with the European Association of Social Anthropologists (EASA)
Series Editor: Aleksandar Bošković, University of Belgrade

Social anthropology in Europe is growing, and the variety of work being done is expanding. This series is intended to present the best of the work produced by members of the EASA, both in monographs and in edited collections. The studies in this series describe societies, processes, and institutions around the world and are intended for both scholarly and student readership.

MANAGING AMBIGUITY

How Clientelism, Citizenship, and Power Shape Personhood in Bosnia and Herzegovina

Čarna Brković

berghahn
NEW YORK · OXFORD
www.berghahnbooks.com

First published in 2017 by
Berghahn Books
www.berghahnbooks.com

Library of Congress Cataloging-in-Publication Data

Name: Brkovic, Carna, author.
Title: Managing ambiguity : how clientelism, citizenship and pow-
ershapes personhood in Bosnia and Herzegovina / Carna Brkovic.
Description: New York : Berghahn Books, [2017] | Series: EASA series |
   Includes bibliographical references and index.
Identifiers: LCCN 2017013750 (print) | LCCN 2017025651 (ebook) |
ISBN 9781785334153 (e-book) | ISBN 9781785334146 (hardback : alk.
paper)
   Subjects: LCSH: Bosnia and Herzegovina--Social conditions. | Bosnia
and Herzegovina--Social life and customs. | Bosnia and Herzegovina-
-Social policy. | Patron and client--Bosnia and Herzegovina. | Political
sociology.
   Classification: LCC HN639.A8 (ebook) | LCC HN639.A8 B76 2017
(print) | DDC
                                              306.0949742--dc23
LC record available at https://lccn.loc.gov/2017013750

British Library Cataloguing in Publication Data

A catalogue record for this book is available from the British Library

ISBN: 978-1-78533-414-6 (hardback)
ISBN: 978-1-78920-841-2 (paperback)
ISBN: 978-1-78533-415-3 (ebook)

To Ksenija, my sister

Contents

Figures and Tables

Figures

Table

Acknowledgements

This book is the result of a lot of wandering, in a conceptual as well as an ethnographic and physical sense. The work on this book started at the University of Manchester, where I initially wanted to look at how the links between statehood, borders, body, and power are played out in the everyday life of welfare recipients in Bosnia and Herzegovina. Ethnographic fieldwork brought to light the questions about favors that I have engaged with ever since. The first draft of this book was written in Budapest, in the productive atmosphere of the CEU Institute for Advanced Study (CEU IAS). The final version was written in Regensburg, with generous support from the Graduate School for East and Southeast European Studies (GSOSES). Over the years, many different institutions and people provided support for this research in various ways. I will not be able to thank them all.[1]

I am deeply grateful to people from my fieldsite for sharing their experiences and letting me learn from them. I particularly want to thank Stef Jansen for his intellectual guidance and support in research and writing. My sincere gratitude goes to Sarah Green for encouraging me to engage with issues from the fieldwork which were socially and politically effective, yet difficult to get a stable hold on. Paul Stubbs supported my approach to Southeastern Europe as a space of political and intellectual originality, for which I am very grateful.

I had an opportunity to present versions of chapters 2, 3, 4, and 6 during seminars at the London School of Hygiene and Tropical Medicine, CEU IAS, Centre for Southeast European Studies in Graz, and Centre for Women's and Gender Studies in Belgrade. I am grateful for the feedback I received there, which led me to sharpen several key points of this research. Elissa Helms, John Clarke, Jonathan Mair, Soumhya Venkatesan, Frances Pine, Vanja Čelebičić, Andrew Hodges, Dunja Njaradi, Marina Simić, Ivan Rajković, Andre Thiemann, Ainhoa Montoya, Deana Jovanović, Lisa Reidner, Laura Jordan, Goran Dokić, and Marek Mikuš commented on early versions of the chapters, and I wish to thank them for this. I thank Ulf Brunnbauer and Heidrun Hamersky from the GSOSES Regensburg for their support, and also Ger Duijzings, who offered constructive and generous comments on the last draft of the manuscript. At the CEU IAS, Gina Neff and James Brophy taught me some of the intricacies of book proposals as a genre of writing, for which I am grateful. I also want to thank the three anonymous peer reviewers, and Eeva Berglund for her precious editorial guidance.

Personally, I wish to thank my family—Danilo Martinović, Ksenija Brković, Dragana Kršenković Brković, and Tomislav Brković—for everything. My parents never quite learned how to deal with ambiguities of life in former Yugoslavia, and I am grateful for that.

Notes

1. Parts of chapter 2 were included in: Brković, Čarna. 2015. "Brokering the Grey Zones: Pursuits of Favours in a Bosnian Town." In *Ethnographies of Grey Zones in Eastern Europe,* edited by Ida Harboe Knudsen and Martin Demant Frederiksen, 57–72. London: Anthem Press. Parts of Chapter 4 were included in: Brković, Čarna. 2016. "Flexibility of *Veze/Štele*: Negotiating Social Protection." In *Negotiating Social Relations in Bosnia and Herzegovina. Semiperipheral Entanglements,* edited by Stef Jansen, Čarna Brković and Vanja Čelebičić, 94–108. London and New York: Routledge. A version of Chapter 5 was published as: Brković, Čarna. 2015. "Management of Ambiguity: Favours and Flexibility in Bosnia and Herzegovina." *Social Anthropology* 23(3): 268–82. Parts of Chapter 6 were included in: Brković, Čarna. 2014. "Surviving in a Moveopticon. Humanitarian Actions in Bosnia and Herzegovina." *Contemporary Southeastern Europe* 1(2): 42–60.

Notes on Transliteration

Bosnian-Croatian-Montenegrin-Serbian (BCMS) language standards are phonetic, which means that each letter of the alphabet represents one sound. Their Latin scripts are almost identical to the English alphabet; however, there are some small differences. BCMS uses certain letters of the English alphabet (q, w, x, y) only infrequently, and there are letters that do not exist in the English alphabet, which usually have diacritic marks and/or are digraphs.

The basic rules for pronunciation are as follows:

The letter *c* is pronounced as "ts" or "tz."
The letter *j* is pronounced as a *y* (Jugoslavija is "Yugoslavia" or "Yugoslaviya").

The letters with diacritic marks are:

ć is pronounced as soft "ch" or as "tj," like the "ci" in Italian word *ciao*.
č is pronounced "tch," like the "ch" in *check* (harder than ć).
š is pronounced "sch," like the "sh" in *she*.
ž is pronounced "zh," like the "s" in *leisure*.
đ is pronounced "dj," like the "g" in the Italian name *Giorgio*.
dž is pronounced "dj," like the "j" in *joy*.
lj is pronounced "ly," like the "ll" in *million*.
nj is pronounced "ny," like the "n" in *tenure*.

I use anglicized forms for place names, as these are in common usage (e.g., Belgrade instead of Beograd, Bosnia and Herzegovina instead of Bosna i Hercegovina). For persons and relatively unknown places, I use the original spelling, including diacritics.

Introduction

The "Pathological" Relationality of Clientelism

Zoran, a man in his thirties, had to call emergency services for an ambulance because his father suddenly became very ill.[1] The man who answered the phone said that the ambulance was on its way. Twenty minutes later it had not arrived. Zoran's flat was only a four- or five-minute ride away from the hospital so he called them again. The same man answered the phone. Zoran started yelling at him: "Where is the ambulance? Do you know who I am? Do you have any idea what I can do to you? I can get you fired!"

This time, the call was successful; the ambulance arrived fifteen minutes later. Zoran told me in a confessional tone that he had lied during the second phone call, because he had no real influence over anyone's job at the hospital. Why did Zoran make false threats? He claimed that his father would not have had to wait more than half an hour if he had had powerful *veze* (literally: "relations, connections"; singular: *veza*) and *štele* (literally: "relations or connections that had to be fixed"; singular: *štela*). Zoran's story illuminates the importance of *veze* and *štele* for the organization of life in one border town in Bosnia and Herzegovina (BiH).

Perhaps the ambulance was late that night because it had been swamped with calls. Perhaps it had arrived at Zoran's place as quickly as possible. Then again, perhaps the paramedics had decided to first respond to a call from someone they knew personally or someone they considered more important than Zoran and his family. Maybe they did a favor for a friend or for someone who, unlike Zoran and his family, could help them in the future. There was no way of knowing why the ambulance was late and, considering how often things got done through *veze* and *štele* in the Town, Zoran's false threats sounded to me like a reasonable reaction.

Veze and *štele* constitute an important dimension of politics and everyday life in BiH. Almost anybody who has lived and worked in BiH knows that *veze* and *štele* exist and affect sociopolitical and economic life, although how and why exactly they are pursued in everyday life remains somewhat unclear. After the 1992–95 war in BiH, many different international and local actors attempted to transform and "modernize" the state.

Perhaps it is more accurate to say they invested efforts into remodernizing it. From 1945 to 1992, BiH was one of the six federal republics of the Socialist Federative Republic of Yugoslavia (SFRY), which developed its own version of socialist modernity. Since the end of the war in 1995, postwar reconstruction of the country has gone hand in hand with postsocialist transformation, whereby various agencies and actors have invested a lot of effort into peace building, fighting clientelism and corruption, and transforming the postwar remnants of socialist statehood into a (neo)liberal democracy. Despite such efforts, *veze* and *štele* have not gone away. According to a United Nations Development Programme (UNDP) report (Nixon 2009), 95 percent of more than 1,600 Bosnians who were asked thought that a *štela* was required to access welfare, especially healthcare and employment.

In numerous popular accounts, *veze* and *štele* are presented as a form of clientelism and BiH is described as "captured" by this presumably predemocratic practice. The prevailing assumption is that it would dissolve once there is a fully functioning neoliberal democratic state. Clientelism in Eastern Europe is often discussed in a benevolent manner, as an understandable and expected, even inevitable, response to large-scale societal transformations:

> As other forms of social organization did not exist when communism collapsed, it was both obvious and inevitable that clientelist networks would survive and become the core for future relations, notwithstanding the inefficiencies of the resulting give-and-take that corrupts the morale of democracy and the logic of the market. (Sajo 2002: 9)

Such a, largely benevolent, interpretation has less benevolent consequences, since it prevents "an understanding of clientelism as a field of relationships of political struggle" (Stubbs and Zrinščak 2011: 4).

The benevolent interpretation has a strong paternalistic overtone, because it does two things that relieve political actors in Eastern Europe of responsibility for their own actions. First, it identifies the causes of clientelist relations in the tumultuous past and places the "solution" in a neoliberal democratic future. Displacing, or rather "distiming" (Jansen 2009b: 55), clientelism as a predemocratic phenomenon means approaching it as something similar to a childhood disease: it should go away as the country grows up and becomes more mature. Second, this understanding of clientelism impoverishes the political imagination by reproducing an image of Western Europe as a discrete entity that is in the position of a nurturing parent helping Eastern European states to overcome challenges on their road to becoming fully democratic, marketized, and modern countries.

Sajo (2002: 2) assumes that the rule of law in postsocialism is not implemented properly because it is "alien to most of the local political cultures, acquainted as they are with only the primacy of surviving by mutual social favors." This suggests that once members of these local political cultures are taught how democracy and the market work in Western Europe, they will be able to ensure a convergence of their countries with Western European states. When Bosnians are seen as people who "interpret life in terms of corruption" (Hrelja 2002: 27), it makes sense to teach them new ways of reasoning about life. Bosnians are not expected to develop political imagination in order to envision contextually sensitive forms of struggle and alternative foundational principles for their polities and economies, since all they have to do is implement a series of recommended techniques for becoming "properly" European.

This book suggests that clientelism and contemporary globalized forms of flexible governance are not contradictory to one another but often mutually constitutive. Indeed, Shore (2000) demonstrates that clientelism and patronage have a well-established place in the very heart of Europe: the European Commission (EC). Lack of procedures that would make the EC accountable to the elected representatives of national governments and the absence of democratic control led to the development of an ambiguous system "based on patronage, cronyism and fraud," which was tolerated because it functioned: "from the point of view of the Brussels elite, it [the system based on patronage and clientelism] was the oil that made the machinery of bureaucracy work in practice" (Shore 2000: 215).

In the Town, somewhat similar things took place: neoliberal restructuring of social protection did not introduce procedures and legal obligations for any particular actor. Instead, they reinforced ambiguities over responsibilities and thus encouraged the patterns of clientelist relationality. During my fieldwork, it was profoundly ambiguous which private or public actor had what role and responsibility in social protection, if any. *Veze* and *štele* offered people a way to navigate this ambiguity—and sometimes to manage it. Clientelism in social protection was not backwardly unruly but fit right into the growing expectation of flexibly and proactively managing social relations within a community.

In BiH, a benevolent-cum-paternalistic understanding of clientelism was reinforced through two powerful discourses: one, the hegemonic view of the Balkans as perpetually ambiguous and, two, a therapeutic approach to the postwar reconstruction of the country. The Balkans is hegemonically perceived as a region of ambiguity and permanent transformation (Todorova 2009) and as a place where everything appears to be fractally and monstrously related to everything else: "The Balkans always seem to generate ambiguous and tense connections that ought, in modernist terms, to be clearly resolved separations" (Green 2005: 129).[2] Since clientelism is largely understood as the creation of personal relationships where there should be none, it fit all too well into the Balkanist discourse.

The therapeutic approach to the postwar reconstruction of BiH also strengthened the benevolent interpretation of clientelism, by framing war-affected populations as in need of mass therapeutic interventions due to the experiences of a mass trauma (Hughes and Pupavac 2005). The therapeutic approach legitimizes the role of the international presence in the country, denying Bosnians the ability to govern themselves. As the political philosopher Husanović writes, "Therapeutic politics ... transforms us [Bosnians] all into victims, passive and politically irrelevant subjects who do not have a right to a voice" (2011: 269). Indeed, almost two decades after the 1992–95 war in BiH, the internationally introduced Office of the High Representative (OHR) still plays an indispensable role in the maintenance of the current political setup of the country.[3]

The result of such discursive merging of Balkanist and therapeutic perspectives may have been an attempt to use UNDP resources for "diagnosing the national pathology ... which requires radical surgery if the patient [BiH] is to be restored to health" (Kolstrup 2002: 3–4). The call to *surgically* remove problems such as clientelism and corruption fully follows the hegemonic idea that the solution for "too much" relationality in the Balkans is simply to "put a stop to it" (see Green 2005: 140). From this perspective, clientelism introduces unpredictable and, therefore, ungovernable relationality in places where people should be linked through bureaucratic indifference. As we will see throughout the book, Bosnians seem to place the sociality of kinship, friendships, and patronage in contexts that are imagined in discourses of development as properly governed only by reason.

That various kinds of social relations "sneak" into bureaucratic practices becomes interpreted as pathological because it is perceived as hard to anticipate and control. However, on the one hand, the rule of reason is not opposed to sociality, but is socially produced following "the same logic and symbolism as that of (for example) the supposedly backward peasant of non-industrialized Mediterranean lands" (Herzfeld 1993: 9). On the other hand, the Balkans is not isolated from transnational processes, which means that ethnographic and historical research of this region "should reconstruct the relevant spatial dimensions of the relevant matters, and not start by a given spatial—be it national or regional—'container'" (Brunnbauer 2011: 78). Clientelism could be approached as a part of transnational, globalized processes rather than as an "ill" firmly located within a particular country.

Theoretical Perspectives on Favors

The anthropological responses to clientelist relationality have included attempts to understand everyday forms of economic and moral reasoning that entice people to engage in such semiformal and informal relations. From an ethnographic point of view, there has to be a meaningful, contemporary reason for people to persistently pursue favors and engage in shady bureaucratic and economic practices, which has nothing to do with "primitivism," "backwardness," "mentality," or the inability to shake off the chains of a socialist past. In studies of Eastern European politics, one such reason has been found in a perspective I will call "systemic."

The intrusion of informal sociality into state arenas has been interpreted as a response to the problems of postsocialist transformation (Ledeneva 2006). The systemic perspective suggests that "it's not the people," but rather the new state apparatus, the market economy, and a young democracy still in transformation that perpetuates the need to pursue favors and clientelist relations. In this view, clientelism and favors persisted after the fall of socialism in Eastern Europe because the socialist economy was and the postsocialist economy is flawed, although in different ways. The problematic underlying assumption of systemic perspective is that once Eastern European countries are "properly" transformed—modernized, democratized, and neoliberalized—clientelism and favors will disappear.

Another such reason for engaging in shady crossovers between the formal and the informal has been found in morality and emergent studies of the good. This "moral perspective" is largely based on Laidlaw's (2002) suggestion that morality should be distinguished from sociality, because it depends on freedom to choose what kind of a sociohistorically grounded self one wants to pursue. Moral perspective demonstrates that practices that developmental actors may label "clientelism" or "corruption" actually provide the material from which people constitute themselves as moral persons. Thus, Humphrey (2012) asserts that when striving toward moral personhood, people in Russia and Mongolia willingly choose to engage in "veering" practices. They prefer veering to the official way of getting things done, because this gives them a sense of pride and self-worth and confirms their goodness. Whatever developmental experts may claim, a "good deed is not a crime" (Henig 2017; see also Pine 2015: 25). This book takes something from both of these approaches and leaves something aside.

This book argues that *veze* and *štele* became strikingly relevant for welfare for three related reasons. First, similarly to Humphrey's interlocutors in Russia and Mongolia, *veze* and *štele* offered Bosnians a way to reproduce personhoods. However, my interlocutors did not quite choose or prefer to pursue them. People do not need to like the social strings that shape them in order to be shaped by them. For most of my interlocutors, obtaining a resource through a *veza/štela* was something to be confessed and justified in a low voice, rather than something to boast about as a moral act of a "normal hero" (see Humphrey 2012). *Veze* and *štele* reproduced social personhoods, rather than moral ones.

Second, the persistence of *veze* and *štele* was not conditioned by the flaws in the postsocialist and postwar transformations of the country but by the global structural changes that inserted individual ethics and compassion into the heart of the organization of welfare. In other words, *veze* and *štele* were not results of a transition and a flawed statehood, but of global tendencies to blur boundaries between state and society. For instance, the introduction of ethical citizenship (Rose 2000) into BiH positioned "local community" as the key framework for social protection. The main duty of the government was to create legislature, while everything else—planning, organizing, and delivering social protection—was defined as the responsibility of a local community. This created an ambiguous understanding of social protection as both a citizenship right and a gift of compassionate persons within a local community. My interlocutors used *veze* and *štele* to navigate this ambiguity; they pursued *veze* and *štele* to incite others within a local community to help.

The third reason for the persistence of *veze* and *štele* in BiH can be found in their role in the reproduction of power relations. While most users tried to navigate ambiguous position of welfare as both a right and a gift, there were some people who could manage this ambiguity: decision makers and providers of social protection could decide if a certain welfare support was more of a professional duty or more of a personal favor. They actively shaped the ambiguity of social protection in a certain direction—increased it, decreased it, or transformed it into a clear professional duty/compassionate gift. Furthermore, those who held multiple positions in public and private institutions could serve as a *veza/štela* to many people for various things. By managing the ambiguity of social protection across public and private arenas, they provided favors that could not be reciprocally repaid. Through keeping while giving (Weiner 1992), such persons increased their influence and power. Let us go through these three arguments in more detail.

Personhood

Veze and *štele* stemmed from a local form of sociality that could be called *svijet* (literally: "a world," here: "social world"). *Svijet* was mostly created and reproduced by gossiping and retelling stories about other people. What their *svijet* thought of them was extremely important for many of my interlocutors; it was a strong regulator of behavior, especially for women (Brković 2010). In the sociality of *svijet,* personhood was shaped by connections and relations to other people, similar to what Alexander (2002) found in Turkey. For instance, when my interlocutors wanted to find out who someone was, they often asked questions about who this person knew. They determined what kind of a person a new acquaintance was or what could be expected from her or him by determining who this person knew and in what capacity. My interlocutors also developed a form of knowledge called "knowing by sight" (*znati iz viđenja*), in which "knowing someone" meant being familiar with their personal stories and having a connection to them through someone else.

Veze and *štele* emerged out of such local forms of knowing and being. In Leach's (1993) terms, these were metaphoric relations that helped people to translate expectations across social orders. In enabling people to translate across languages of citizenship and of society, *veze* and *štele* presented a certain kind of sociality "with a purpose," in which it was impossible to clearly distinguish a pragmatic attempt to obtain something from skillful navigation of social relations. My interlocutors used *veze* and *štele* in their encounters with public institutions to translate across the bureaucratic language of citizenship and the language of personalized relations and vice versa. Through them, people made claims to welfare as persons embedded in the social fabric of the Town and as citizens listed in the administrative databases.

When Zoran angrily asked, "Do you know who I am? Do you have any idea what I can do to you? I can get you fired!" he suggested that he was entitled to the ambulance not just due to his father's urgent medical need or by virtue of his citizenship but also because of who he was as a social person. In another example, Sanja (pronounced Sanya) wanted to access better psychiatric treatment for her daughter. As a member of the Sun—an organization I volunteered with in 2009 and 2010 that works with children with disabilities and their parents— she turned to the other parents from the organization for help. As we will see in more detail in chapter one, a famous psychiatrist in the Town had already examined Sanja's daughter and prescribed her medications. However, he was tactless and rude during the examination, and he did not order any tests, so Sanja did not believe this doctor did his best. She wanted her daughter to be examined again, by someone else—someone to whom Sanja would have a personal connection.

The parents from the Sun readily shared their personal knowledge of and connections to the doctors with Sanja. Sanja thought that the first doctor was rude and unprofessional because, to him, she was a "nobody" (*niko*). She was living with continuous financial struggles, because the basic social provision was ridiculously low,[4] and she could not look for a job, because there was no one else who would take care of her daughter. By asking other parents from the Sun for help, Sanja demonstrated that, despite such problems, she was a "somebody" (*neko*): she had her social connections, her *svijet*, to turn to. The parents provided Sanja with *veze* and *štele* to doctors, helping her to make claims to better healthcare treatment as someone's friend, a mother, and a citizen—all at the same time.

The contours of this "sociality with a purpose," enacted through *veze* and *štele*, are also reflected in an emic conceptual conflation of connections and relations. Unlike in English, there is no conceptual difference between "connections" and "relations" in BiH. For instance, *veza* refers to a romantic relationship (*ljubavna veza*) as well to an Internet connection (*internet veza*). Similarly, *štela* refers to obtaining a service through a close friend or through a chain of previously known and unknown persons. Separating out the instrumental dimension of favors from their longer, more profound social and emotional investments is not just impossible but also analytically unnecessary. In order to understand the social logic and political effects of *veze/štele,* their instrumentality should not be distinguished from their social and affective dimensions.

Veze and *štele* were, thus, locally meaningful ways of relating that merged the social with the instrumental. They reproduced a sense of self as a social being as well as a certain material benefit (for instance, a healthcare treatment). They were also targeted by various international actors in the country as a form of corruption. A classic anthropological move would be to critically evaluate and counteract the powerful discourses of development or Europeanization by illuminating the internal logic, everyday routines, and meanings of this contextually specific form of practice.

Ethnographically outlining the effects of *veze* and *štele* on personhoods and society, I could try to challenge dominant Western developmental notions of what counts as corruption by contrasting them with emic ideas about friendship, personhood, or goodness. Postsocialist contexts may have been "an important rubric for critiquing fundamental concepts in western social science," such as the state, market, or corruption (Rogers 2010: 13). However, my intention in this book is not to explore how BiH practices of *veze/štele* challenge Western developmental categories. Part of the reason for this is that Bosnians did not cherish *veze/štele* as a locally meaningful, morally imbued practice that was endangered by development and Europeanization. Instead, they often criticized the structural inequalities *veze/štele* reproduced and the limitations they reinstated.

Just as Zoran did, my interlocutors perceived the redistribution of resources through *veze/štele* as unfair, and often infuriating, while trying at the same time to inscribe themselves in it. For this reason, I follow the reasoning and the arguments of my interlocutors who often, openly and loudly, condemned *veze/štele,* while simultaneously being engaged in them. Similar to business *guanxi* in China (Ong 1999) or patron-client relations in the Mediterranean (Li Causi 1975), *veze* and *štele* re-created particular forms of social inequality — and people in BiH were critical of this. For instance, during the two rounds of public protests in 2013 and 2014, BiH citizens articulated very strong criticisms of the fact that ethnonationalist politics, personal relationships such as *veze* and *štele,* and bribery affected the work of public administrations.[5]

Some of this was mirrored in the words of my interlocutors in the Town, who, in 2009 and 2010, claimed that in a "normal state" there is no need to depend on *veze* and *štele*—and thus on someone's personal good will or compassion—in order to live comfortably, earn a wage, or get healthcare treatment. Similar yearnings for a "normal life" and a "normal state" are expressed by people throughout Bosnia (Jansen 2015). I take their criticisms seriously. Since compassion, personal morality, and goodwill increasingly perform regulatory functions in the West as well as in BiH—although admittedly in very different ways—I think the main target of the criticisms my interlocutors articulated was less BiH and more the global transformations of the welfare state.

Instead of presenting local ways of being and knowing (*svijet,* or *veze* and *štele*) as a form of resistance to the globally powerful discourses about the state and the market, this ethnography follows how they were implicated in one another, jointly creating particular forms of power and inequality. I argue that neoliberalization converged and merged with clientelism in a postwar, postsocialist context; that is, neoliberal restructuring of the state responsibilities for survival and well-being and the related insistence on local community, flexibility, and self-responsibility were translated into clientelist modes of relating and back, and this has produced particular ways of gathering power through ambiguity.

In doing so, I rely on the term "favors," rather than "clientelism." Clientelism is a term under which many different practices are placed together. Part of the historical accounts of ancient Rome (Saller 1982), the term is nowadays used to mark many different types of social exchange that do not fit into the Weberian model of modern rational redistribution of resources. In other words, clientelism is a term that makes a negative definition; with respect to BiH, it explains what things *are not* rather than what they *are*. There are many important differences between *veze/štele* in BiH, *blat* in Russia (Ledeneva 2006), *znajomości* in Poland (Dunn 2004; Wedel 1986), *guanxi* in China (Yan 2003), and so forth. Whether all of these should be lumped together in the box labeled "clientelism" and, if so, under what conditions, is a matter of analytical choice. Furthermore, the terms *veze* and *štele* refer to a wide variety of relations and connections. This means that it is fairly difficult, if not downright impossible, to make the same interpretative claims about all *veze/štele* in contemporary BiH.

The ways my interlocutors personalized the educational system, high-level politics, and business, or access to rare goods, might not have been the same as the ways they negotiated healthcare and social protection.[6] Therefore, this book is not concerned with all forms of *veze*, but only those that were important for the organization of the politics of survival and well-being in the postwar, postsocialist BiH.

The word *klijentelizam*—a direct translation of *"clientelism"* from English—is not widely used in everyday talk among speakers of the Bosnian/Croatian/Montenegrin/Serbian (BCMS) language standards.[7] Instead, what my interlocutors discussed at length were *veze* and *štele*. Since there is no fully corresponding translation of *veze* and *štele* into English, the book more often relies upon the term "favors," which is integral to the anthropological vocabulary of semiformal relations in postsocialist countries. The terms "clientelism," "favors," *and* "informality" are tied up with particular conversations in social sciences. In order to clarify when a certain conversation is relevant for understanding *veze/štele*, I will occasionally refer to different terms in different places. For instance, I will use the term "clientelism" only when discussing how the everyday practice of *veze/štele* relates to the dominant, developmental, benevolent understanding of clientelism.

When ethnographically discussing how "things got done" regarding social protection in BiH and situating this in anthropological discussions, I will refer only to the terms *veze/štele* or favors. The term *usluge* (favors) does not quite overlap with what is denoted by *veze/štele*. *Usluge* are oriented toward the result of a particular relationship, while *veze/štele* emphasize the relationality that precedes the practical outcome. Furthermore, *usluge* refers to a whole set of *uslužne djelatnosti* that could not be subsumed under the meaning of *veze/štele*. (*Uslužne djelatnosti* literally means "service occupations," and they include any kind of work done for others, from cleaning computers and working in a restaurant to detective work.) Despite these differences, there is an important similarity: *usluge*, like *veze/ štele*, conflate instrumental, temporary, and fleeting connections with enduring, socially, and morally imbued relations.

Ethical Citizenship

In pursuits related to social protection, *veze/štele* present a locally meaningful way to make claims to support as both a citizen and a socially located person—as someone's friend, mother, or teacher, for example. However, that access to welfare is ambiguously defined as a right of citizens *and* a compassionate gift of socially located persons is not a BiH specificity. Neoliberal restructuring has repositioned elements of welfare arrangements as a matter of personal compassion, ethics, and morality in various places throughout the world, including the West. By "neoliberalization" I mean a global dissipation of stable frameworks for organizing lives.

The exact contours of this dissipation differ: such stable frameworks may have been provided by the state or by working places, such as factories and universities, or in some other way. Also, their dissipation seems to regularly entangle the market and flexibility, albeit in various ways. The important thing for me here is that, during neoliberalization, relations between the state, society, and citizens have been moving away from welfare state models and toward something else. As Fink, Lewis, and Clarke suggest:

> The thread suturing the relation between state—people—welfare ... came under sustained and systematic attack through the convergence of a fiscal crisis related to the sharpened contradictions of global Fordism and the coming to power of New Right political parties in many countries of Europe and the USA. The result was a shift in the filaments suturing the people to state and welfare away from rights and towards the idea of duty and responsibility. (2001: 3)

This increased relevance of duty, responsibility, and morality was both productive and oppressive for various groups of people in various ways (see Kalb 2009; Montoya 2014). The term "neoliberalism" has acquired so many meanings that it has become effectively an empty signifier (Clarke 2008). Yet, I keep it in this book because it serves as a strong counterpoint to the visions of postsocialist Eastern Europe as a place that has yet to catch up with the West. Postsocialist transformation presents a form of neoliberalization and "the 'transition' from communism to capitalism in ECE [East Central Europe] represents perhaps one of the boldest experiments with neoliberal ideas in the world today" (Stenning et al. 2010: 2; see also Makovicky 2014). Furthermore, multiple and heterogeneous meanings of contemporary neoliberalism in critical social theory are perhaps not just a reflection of an analytical blind spot. They may stem from profound ambiguities and uncertainties created by the dissipation of stable structures supporting life.

Analyzing debates about the Third Way in politics in Britain and the United States, Rose notices "the emergence of a new politics of conduct that seeks to reconstruct citizens as moral subjects of responsible communities" (2000: 1395). The idea of the "social state that underpinned welfare regimes in the 20th century" is increasingly being challenged by "another image of the state [that] is coming to the fore: that of the facilitating state, the enabling state, or the state as animator" (ibid.: 1400). In this view, the state is supposed to encourage a community—consisting of ethically inclined individuals, firms, organizations, schools, parents, hospitals, and so forth—to take a portion of responsibility for welfare: "Ethical citizenship and responsible community [are] fostered, but not administered by the state" (ibid.: 1398).

Similarly, Muehlebach (2012: 6) argues that the Italian state "has in the last three decades sought to mobilize parts of the population into a new voluntary labor regime—a regime that has allowed for the state to conflate voluntary labor with good citizenship, and unwaged work with gifting." Simultaneously with cutting down and privatizing social services for the elderly and the unemployed in northern Italy, the state encouraged volunteers to care for the "dependent citizens." In this way, it aimed not just to alleviate the effects of its own withdrawal but to insert "the fantasy of gifting into the heart of neoliberal reform" (ibid.: 6–7). Ethical citizenship is not inherently opposed to but is, in a certain form, indispensable to the neoliberal logic of the market order. By permitting personal compassion (and prejudice) to affect what used to be state bureaucratic responsibilities, these new forms of governmentality in Western countries appear to have substantial similarities to the BiH administrations imbued with different forms of sociality.

Part Two, "*Citizenship*," demonstrates that neoliberal transformations of social protection rely on a concept of a "community" and produce particular forms of sociality. Neoliberally informed restructuring is not a "politics of failed sociality" (Giroux 2011), because it has reorganized forms of relating to others in a way that makes favors practically indispensable for survival and well-being. The translation of policies (Lendvai and Stubbs 2009) of social protection from the so-called developed countries into BiH redefined citizenship as an ethical category. Large-scale transformations meant that welfare services and provisions shrank and that many former Yugoslav boarding institutions for social protection were shut down, and the change in legislation left more than 20 percent of BiH citizens without healthcare insurance (Salihbašić 2008).

While the state's institutions are responsible for charting the social protection legislation, everything else is defined as the shared responsibility of a "local community": the financing, organizing, and delivering of social protection is imagined as a joint duty of municipalities, civil associations, nongovernmental organizations (NGOs), private donors, international organizations, and self-responsible users. New policies affecting the Town prescribe that a local community present the framework for meeting the majority of citizens' welfare needs, especially in social protection. The members of a local community are supposed to be ethical citizens who would step in and help develop new welfare arrangements, in line with their personal inclinations and abilities. Social workers in the Town called this a "social model of social protection."

While it may have sounded good to many people in BiH, this shift in policy discourse made it profoundly ambiguous who exactly had responsibility for social protection and in what way. The parents from the Sun had no way of knowing what sort of support their families were entitled to and who in a community would help them to make it happen. For instance, the very basic forms of support, such as a day-care center for children with disabilities, had yet to be constructed in the Town. The parents felt entitled to it, but they had no way of knowing when or where it would be constructed, what services it would provide, and with whose money. Instead of knowing their citizenship entitlements and how to realize them, the parents were expected to "manage social relations"—to proactively look for opportunities, forge alliances, and negotiate prospects as they presented themselves. They sometimes did exactly this, by pursuing *veze* and *štele.*

The parents from the Sun recounted to me how, several years prior to my fieldwork, a privately owned bus company introduced free rides for children with disabilities and their parents, but only on one line, from a nearby village to the Town and back. This initiative was something like a small-scale case of corporate social responsibility and an example of collaboration between the municipality and the third sector, but in a specific manner. How did the initiative take place? One parent from the Sun knew the bus driver personally.

For some reason, the bus driver felt the need to ask the company owner to allow free rides for this woman from her village to the Town so that she could take her kid to the Sun regularly. The owner agreed and introduced free rides for all children with disabilities and their parents, but solely for this line. Most of the parents from the Sun, who lived in other villages or distant parts of the Town, had no use for this, and they criticized the arbitrariness of this initiative. It contributed to the well-being of children with disabilities and their parents, but only those who happened to live close to this line.

Such unpredictable and random forms of support seem to proliferate in neoliberal welfare arrangements that place responsibility for social protection on a local community. In the Town, they usually took place because someone knew someone else who was compassionate enough. There are numerous similar examples demonstrating how personal moral sentiments and chance affected the organization of survival and well-being in the Town. Since there was no legal obligation or procedural script for any particular civic or private actor to engage in social protection, they were supposed to participate on moral/ethical grounds—because they were personally motivated to do so, for whatever reason. By placing primary responsibility for social protection on the local community of ethical citizens, the developmental reforms created ambiguity about who should be responsible for providing what, to whom, and on what grounds.

Favors often provided a way to motivate actors within a local community to step in and provide a portion of support. I argue that *veze* and *štele* helped people to navigate social relations within their local community (or *svijet*), which was expected from them by the developmental reforms. The intrusion of sociality with a purpose into the distribution of welfare does not hinder neoliberal developmental visions of BiH. On the contrary, sociality with a purpose fit right into the neoliberal developmental demands for weakened boundaries and new partnerships between the state and society. My interlocutors used favors to ambiguously present themselves as both citizens and socially located persons under the strains of developmental politics and economic globalization, and they reproduced wider social inequalities in doing so.

Power and Ambiguity

Some common pursuits of *veze/štele* are examples of reciprocal exchange: the parents from the Sun helped Sanja to take her daughter to another doctor, expecting her, or someone from her social world, to conduct a similar favor for them in the future. However, *veze/štele* were sometimes entangled with other, less egalitarian, forms of managing social relations. Their reciprocity was one element within the wider reproduction of power and hierarchy.

The ways in which favors are implicated in the reproduction of power pose certain challenges to the prevailing ideas about ambiguity in anthropology. The quality of being open to more than one interpretation, or of being inexact, is most often understood as a threat to the modernist categories of ordering the world and "seeing like a state" (Scott 1998). This is because, as Augé argues, ambiguity carries a potential to imagine the world otherwise (1998: 31). Augé differentiates ambiguity from ambivalence, whereby ambivalence is an expression of plurality of the existing possibilities: "Ambivalence implies perceiving the coexistence of two qualities, even if, in the domain of truth judgments, ambivalence is due only to a change in point of view or scale" (ibid.: 30).

Ambiguity, on the other hand, means affirming that something is neither one nor the other, from whatever point it is looked at. Ambiguity means "to put in negative form—the form considered at a given moment to be the only one possible—something positive that cannot yet be qualified. It is to postulate the necessity of the third term" (Augé 1998: 31). In other words, ambiguity indicates that the world needs to be altered in order to make something new intelligible. Furthermore, ambiguity is understood as a quality of everyday practice that simultaneously challenges and reproduces categories that appear to be firm and stable. Herzfeld (2005) approaches ambiguity in Greece as a part of a productive tension between official national rhetoric and everyday knowledge about fissures within national identity. The result of this tension is resolved differently in different situations, and while sometimes it reinstates a sense of Greek national belonging, "it is ambiguity that most threatens the ideal order of the state" (Herzfeld 1999: 133).

While I largely agree with such interpretations of ambiguity, I argue that ambiguity does not inherently have the potential to imagine the world otherwise or to challenge the ideal order of the state. In the Balkans, for instance, "ambiguity can be as hegemonic and subject to disciplinary regimes as clarity" (Green 2005: 12). Under certain conditions, ambiguity may be manipulated to reproduce a position of power. As we will see in more detail in the third part of the book, *"Power,"* ambiguity can be managed—and, indeed, the ability to make ambiguous the responsibility for a welfare provision is linked with influence and power.

It is the more powerful people—decision makers and providers of social protection—who are able to influence when and how much a particular service is a matter of their professional duty and when and how much it is a matter of their personal goodwill to do a favor. If neoliberal restructurings position social protection as both a citizenship right and a social gift, there are (powerful) people able to increase and decrease this ambiguity and to decide in what direction it will be resolved, if at all. When someone offers access to a public resource through a favor, he or she decides how much this is a public, civic responsibility and how much a personal, moral one.

The case in point is Ratka, a woman with many public and private roles in the Town, who provides favors to many different people for many different things. Once she gave KM 200 (EUR 100) to Magdalena, another parent from the Sun, to send Magdalena's son's medical test results to Norway and Sweden for special analyses. Magdalena was not sure—and did not particularly care—where the money had come from. Ratka did not clarify in what capacity she provided this support. As the right hand of the Town's mayor, maybe Ratka provided the money from the municipal budget for individual humanitarian needs (over which the mayor had discretionary power). Maybe Ratka provided it from the budget of a religious charity over which she presided. Or perhaps the money had come from some other place, since Ratka was also the head of municipal committees and working groups for social protection and a former member of the local Red Cross and Red Crescent office.

For the parents, this money was ambiguously positioned as Magdalena's entitlement *and* as Ratka's personal gift. The parents interpreted gaps in social protection (and the ensuing need for someone's personal, compassionate support) as indication of BiH's "backwardness," rather than as effects of the new developmental emphasis on a local community and ethical citizens. In the parents' view, if Magdalena were living in a "normal state," she would not have had to worry about such expenses. Thus, in the parents' eyes, this was simultaneously a provision Magdalena should have had a right to, as a citizen, and a personal gift of a caring person who helped to close the gaps of a transforming, "backward" state.

By failing to explain in what capacity she had helped Magdalena this time, Ratka managed ambiguity of this entitlement-cum-gift and confirmed her importance as the person able to help when no one else could. In other situations, Ratka was very clear about what she, or the institutions she was affiliated with, could and could not provide. Her religious charity registered a "humanitarian telephone number"[8] during a humanitarian action for Marko's son, who had to travel to an experimental clinic and possibly receive surgery in Moscow. Humanitarian actions (*humanitarne akcije*) presented a grassroots form of humanitarianism, in which money was raised for an individual medical treatment abroad (see chapter six). Through this humanitarian number, around EUR 3,400 was raised for Marko's son from the people who called the number. A few weeks later, when Marko asked the municipality to financially support this trip, he was told the funds from the municipal budget for individual humanitarian needs were spent for that year and there was nothing anyone could do about it at that moment.

Thus, Ratka's charity helped Marko to raise money from the community, but she did not help him to obtain humanitarian support from the municipality. By deciding when to keep ambiguity between a personal gift and a civic entitlement (as in Magdalena's case), when to provide private charitable support, and when to invoke bureaucratic indifference (as in Marko's case), Ratka managed ambiguity of social support.

Importantly, by providing ever more varied forms of help to ever larger numbers of people, Ratka gained official political influence, similar to the paradox of "keeping while giving" (Weiner 1992). Chapter five will outline in more detail how reciprocity of *veze* and *štele* is intertwined with the reproduction of political hierarchies. People like Ratka, who skillfully navigated multiple public and private arenas to grant favors to others, elevated their sociopolitical status: my interlocutors described Ratka as "a goddess," "a caring person," and "someone who can do what no one else can." By raising their sociopolitical status, such people were also able to step into the world of local politics and gain official political power.

Their power stemmed from the ability to move between and negotiate across various official and unofficial positions, expectations, allegiances, and claims. In a sense, people like Ratka were similar to what Wedel calls "flexians": people working in contemporary international politics, consultancy, and development who generate power by managing ambiguity of boundaries "between the state and private sectors, bureaucratic and market practices, and legal and illegal standing" (Wedel 2009: 15).

The ambiguity recursively appeared on different scales of welfare—from the mutual relations between social workers and users of social protection, to the state behaving as a humanitarian donor and paying hundreds and thousands of euros for a single person's medical treatment abroad during humanitarian actions, to the municipal plans and promises for construction of new social protection institutions, such as a day care center. My interlocutors claimed that without *veze* and *štele* it was difficult—if not downright impossible—to access various public and private services and resources. They suggested that "everybody" pursued favors to get things done. By claiming that "everybody does it" (*svi to rade*), they represented favors as not just inescapable but also egalitarian.

Yet, the bottom-up perspective of the parents from the Sun differed from Ratka's. Most people who needed support could not manage ambiguity of social protection. Instead, they had to navigate it, often by asking for favors. They had to keep moving through their social worlds and state institutions, trying to get various actors to see them, that is, to recognize their need. The case in point is those who initiate humanitarian actions. Chapter six discusses how families in Marko's situation managed to raise thousands of euros from different actors in their local community: during a humanitarian action, hundreds of people, NGOs, private firms, schools, and municipal and state institutions donated small amounts of money. *Veze* and *štele* were of paramount importance in this humanitarian assemblage: most donors either personally knew the family members or knew someone who knew someone else who knew the family.

Marko and other organizers of humanitarian actions went from one office to another and from one acquaintance to the next, increasing the visibility of their personal family problem within their local community. Not knowing who may help them raise money for medical treatments abroad, they pursued favors in all possible directions and attempted to respond to various questions and expectations that different donors placed upon them along the way. Thus, if Ratka and other powerful persons could manage ambiguity of social protection, those who depended on welfare support had to find their way through it and adapt to different expectations of multiple actors in different moments. In brief, some people could manage ambiguity and others had little choice but to navigate it.

An Exceptional Case?

As I was presenting pieces of this research to different audiences, I was regularly asked, "How is this need to pursue personal relations specific to BiH?" It is not. It is similar to many other places and practices. However, similarity—not being quite the same as something else—is a form of difference (Green 2005). By placing a discussion of *veze* and *štele* in a conversation with works that explore links between neoliberalism, morality, and sociality, my goal is to move away from certain exceptionalism in the studies of BiH and to offer a critical conceptualization of ambiguity as intricately related to power relations.

BiH is often taken as an exceptional case of developmental challenges because it has been undergoing a postwar transformation *alongside* a postsocialist transformation over the past two decades. It also has a fairly unique political and administrative structure, which I will describe in the next section. As Blagojević (2009) notes, such "exceptional" places in social sciences oftentimes serve as a point of comparison with more "regularly" organized contexts. In the case of former Yugoslavia, these could be post-Soviet countries without a recent war or postconflict countries with an experience of colonialism rather than socialism or Western states. However, the conjunctures between multiple social processes in such "exceptional" places may shed light on various, seemingly negligible, elements of more "regular" political practices.

In order to illustrate this and to follow the ethnographic convention of providing readers with a map of the researched place in the introduction, I turn now to an artistic installation: *551.35 Geometry of Time* by Lana Čmajčanin, a BiH artist (Figures 0.1 and 0.2). Čmajčanin selected thirty-five maps that show the territory of Bosnia and Herzegovina over the past 551 years, placed them one over another, and lit the background. In this way, as Jelena Petrović writes, "Overlapping on a lit background, instead of showing distinct and clear borders, these maps evidence their shifts, deviations and instability caused by colonial, imperial, conquering, migrational, martial, as well as 'peace-keeping' redesigns."[9]

Čmajčanin presents the shifts and contestations of the territorial integrity of BiH, not as the reflection of a weak or failed statehood but as an indication that state borders and territories are inherently unstable and historically contingent (Reeves 2014). Thus, instead of speaking about the presumable exceptionality of BiH, this work visually illuminates that borders as such can be understood as tidemarks: "Traces of movement, which can be repetitive or suddenly change, may generate long-term effects or disappear the next day, but nevertheless continue to mark, or make, a difference that makes a difference" (Green 2012: 585).

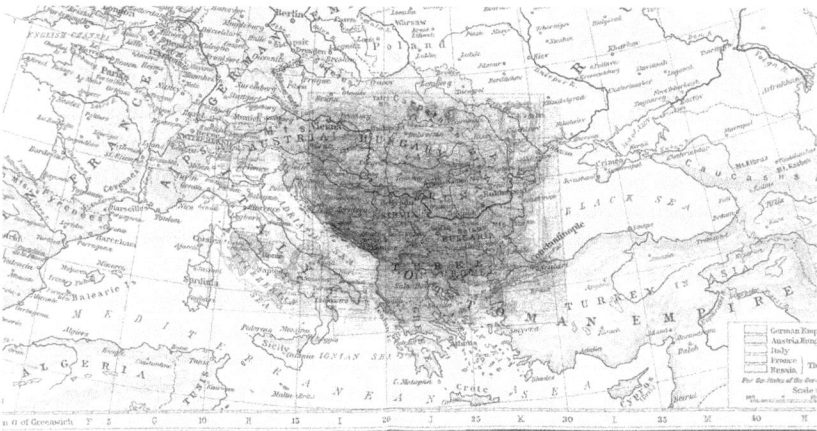

Figure 0.1. *Lana Čmajčanin:* 551.35 Geometry of Time, *video still, 2014, reproduced with the artist's permission*

Figure 0.2. *Lana Čmajčanin:* 551.35 Geometry of Time, *installation view at Garage Museum of Contemporary Art, Moscow, 2014, reproduced with the artist's permission*

Ethnographically grounded research in the past twenty years, similarly critical of the presumable exceptionality of BiH, has fiercely criticized the dominant identitarian understanding of politics and personhoods as based upon distinctive ethnonational, cultural differences, suggesting that senses of belonging to a nation, gender, or any other identity are the result of continuous practice (Helms 2013; Jansen 2011; Kolind 2008). It has also demonstrated that, far from being an expression of a unique obsession with issues of nationality and ethnic belonging, the events in the former Yugoslav countries during and after the 1990s followed the globally dominant logic of organizing people, territory, and culture to its extreme:

> Put bluntly, in the post-Yugoslav context, "ethnic cleansing" of one form or other was the extreme but not illogical outcome of attempts to enforce a mosaic-like national order on a particular slab of territory. While many of the actual events were outrageous in their brutality, the underlying ideas were not out of line with the principle of national self-determination, enshrined in the United Nations charter. (Jansen 2005b: 61)

The focus of ethnographic research has also been on everyday struggles and differentiations that were founded in new socioeconomic patterns that are largely made invisible by the identitarian-based understanding of politics. As in many other places, the post-1990 struggles in former Yugoslav countries "are not between 'classes' but between 'cultural groups,'" reflecting a global "shift in the political imaginary, especially in the terms in which justice is imagined" (Fraser 1997: 2). Attempting to articulate a new language for the new "grammar of claims-making" (ibid.), various social scientists have turned the discourse of transition and development upside down: "What if we posit that, in the present moment, it is the so-called 'Global South' that affords privileged insight into the workings of the world at large" (Comaroff and Comaroff 2012: 114). From this perspective, the socioeconomic experiments tried in the Global South were later applied in the Global North, thus representing the future, rather than the past, of neoliberal transformation.

Whether or not, or how much, the former Yugoslav and other Eastern contexts belong to the Global South is debatable. The parallels between the former Second and the former Third World are uneasy at best (Chari and Verdery 2009). As Blagojević argues, the former Second World can be seen as a sort of semiperiphery that always "lags behind" the core and needs to be "updated," while it also seems to be "'too white,' too industrial, too developed and it does not share the colonial experience, at least not in the sense of how the concept is dominantly used when referring to the 'South'" (2009: 38).

Different historical trajectories create an "awkward relationship" (cf. Strathern 1987) between the East and the Global South. Still, the problems made visible by the 2008 economic crisis were "very much visible from [the] semiperiphery from the beginning of the 90s, because of the extremely high, and unnecessary human costs for the transition" (Blagojević 2009: 184). The changes that took place during social, political, and economic restructuring in so-called Eastern Europe may also help to understand future processes in other geopolitical constellations.

Instead of seeing Eastern Europe as catching up with the West, we could think of it as a region that points to possible global futures. For instance, Ledeneva's (2006) insight—that markets are inseparable from moralities and that economic rationale depends on certain forms of sociality in postsocialist, neoliberalizing Russia—could be taken as an entry point for an analysis of increasingly globalized forms of governance that transform the relationship between the state and society.

In post-Fordist Italy "the state marshals unremunerated labor by publicly valorizing sentiments such as compassion and solidarity" thus "attempting not only to mediate the effects of its own withdrawal, but to craft an anticapitalist narrative at the heart of neoliberal reform" (Muehlebach 2012: 8). There may be important similarities here to the restructuring of welfare in postsocialist Russia where personal care has to go hand in hand with "bread"—that is, meager material support—in order for welfare programs to be seen as meaningful (Caldwell 2004). The politics of life are increasingly becoming regulated through compassion, personal kindness, and care, both in the East and the West, and this has serious implications for contemporary understandings of citizenship (Dunn 2012; Du Gay 2008; Fassin 2005; Muehlebach 2011; Ticktin 2006).

Yet, in postsocialist countries, the increasing ambiguity of whether life and well-being ought to be protected because of personal moral duties or because of state obligations to the citizens has often been understood as a country-specific or region-specific issue that would be resolved during postsocialist development. The ways in which neoliberal transformations have intertwined morality with the economy and citizenship with care have often been interpreted as specificities of particular nation–states and as remnants of their socialist legacies, rather than as a part of wider social transformations of state–citizen relations across the world. It remains to be seen whether sociopolitical processes in the former Yugoslav countries—and the ambiguities and tensions they produce—illuminate the futures of other spaces. At the very least, they reflect some of the globally present concerns, such as the intersections between "sociality" and "personal interest" that characterize neoliberal transformations well beyond BiH and Eastern Europe.

Recent History

As I have mentioned, during my research the main duty of the government was to create legislature regarding social protection. However, by "government" I do not refer to a governmental body that encompassed the whole territory of BiH—because there was no such body. Instead, I refer to the government of the BiH entity in which the Town is located, the Republic of Srpska. BiH has thirteen different governments that regulate various administrative units: its two entities (called the Republic of Srpska and the Federation of BiH), one entity-neutral unit called Brčko district, and ten cantons in the Federation of BiH.

State sovereignty is further fragmented by the role and influence of the international community personified by the OHR, which also has governmental functions. Such a redistribution of state sovereignty across various levels creates complex issues, some of which will be discussed in chapter three. Despite the complexities, all these different governmental levels jointly constitute BiH as a state. Thus, whenever I mention the "government" or "state run" in the book, the state I refer to is Bosnia and Herzegovina.

BiH is commonly described as a consociational democracy, due to its labyrinthine administrative structure and three constitutionally recognized peoples: the (primarily Muslim) Bosniaks,[10] the (primarily Catholic) Croats, and the (primarily Orthodox) Serbs. Its constitution is an annex to the Dayton Peace Agreement that ended the 1992–95 war in BiH. According to the last population census, carried out in 2013, BiH has a total of 3,531,159 inhabitants, of whom 50.1 percent declare themselves to be Bosniaks, 15.4 percent Croats, and 30.7 percent Serbs.[11]

After the war, the Federation of BiH has a Bosniak and Bosnian Croat population as a majority, while the Republic of Srpska has a Bosnian Serb population as a majority. About half of the prewar BiH population, more than 2,100,000 people, was displaced during the war (Bougarel, Helms, and Duijzings 2007: 5).[12] Approximately one half of the displaced population relocated as internally displaced persons to other places in BiH, where "their" ethnonational group constituted a majority, while more than a million people fled abroad as refugees. More than 100,000 people are estimated to have died during the war.

The 1992–95 war in BiH can be understood as a monstrous effort to unmix ethnic groups (Duijzings 2003) and disambiguate multiple senses of belonging that were interwoven in the socialist Yugoslav polity (Sorabji 1995; see also Hayden 2007). This process followed what Malkki (1992) calls the "national order of things," a vision of the world divided into discrete nation–state units. One of the most powerful tools of disambiguating senses of ethnonational belonging has been ethnic cleansing, that is, the violent expulsion of ethnonationally defined populations from and to ethnonationally defined territories.

Another tool has been the genocide in Srebrenica, where an estimated 8,000 men and boys marked as Bosniaks were killed in the course of several days by Bosnian Serb armed forces under the command of Ratko Mladić (NIOD 2002).[13] Thus, during and after the war the above "national numbers" (Jansen 2005b) as well as their meanings were changed. War violence had a "constitutive" role (Bowman 2003), for it had reconfigured places not only through the expulsion of populations but also through transforming known and familiar places into new places of terror (Sorabji 1995: 92; see also Maček

2007; Jouhanneau 2016). The war can also be understood as a particular (violent) way of initiating and enacting postsocialist changes in the country (Duijzings 2002).

The efforts of the international community[14] to rebuild BiH further contributed to the fragmentation of its statehood. The international community played an integral part in the war, constituted through a wave of actions that "gave a rhythm to the development of internal war configurations" (Bugarel 2004: 39). The international investments in the post-Dayton development of BiH occurred in several stages. Initial efforts were dedicated to peace, reconciliation, psychosocial support of the war survivors, and minority return. Such efforts were interspersed with projects dedicated to building the state, democracy, and civil society.

Postconflict reconciliation initiatives were coupled with the reconstruction of destroyed property, the dismantling of the remaining elements of Yugoslav socialism, and the introduction of the principles of the rule of law, democracy, and the neoliberal market economy (Baker 2014; Bieber 2006; Coles 2007; Gilbert 2006; Hayden 1999; Helms 2006; Jansen 2006). Later, the international community focused on grooming BiH as a potential EU member state, fighting corruption, and, most recently, advocating austerity measures (Majstorović 2015; see also Kurtović 2015).

Field Site(s)

Many may consider my decision to conduct ethnographic research in a particular BiH entity (the Republic of Srpska or the Federation of BiH) to be motivated by political reasons. The very existence of the two postwar entities is a strong reminder of the nationalist logic of the Yugoslav wars. In post-Dayton BiH, the entity of the Republic of Srpska:

> exists as a product of the nationalist project, but at the same time it carries the stigma of that project. Although constitutionally equal with the Federation, it is still perceived as the "dirty backyard" of Bosnia-Herzegovina, a safe haven for war criminals, and a place where political and economic activity is enmeshed with the criminal underworld. (Armakolas 2007: 84)

Therefore, it is somewhat unsurprising that a disproportionately small number of ethnographic studies of BiH for an English-speaking audience has been conducted in the Republic of Srpska or with Bosnian Serbs (but see Armakolas 2001, 2007; Duijzings 2007; Kostovicova 2004; Stefansson 2006, 2010; Wagner 2008; Jansen 2003).

When I was preparing for this fieldwork, my reasons for conducting ethnographic research in the Town were practical. It was the only town I found where two things relevant to my study intersected. First, it was a border town and, second, several humanitarian actions were taking place there at that time. My research was a part of the project Transforming Borders: A Comparative Anthropology of Post-Yugoslav Home led by Stef Jansen. Within the framework of the project, two Ph.D. scholarships were granted to people who would work on two BiH borders (for an account of how young people and retirees conceived their lives at the BiH-Croatian border in 2009 and 2010, see Čelebičić 2013). While I was preparing my research proposal and myself for fieldwork, I frantically searched for humanitarian actions organized in BiH border towns—and the Town popped up first.

In the Town, the war resulted in a massacre in 1992 and the forced expulsion of persons marked as Muslims as well as a large influx (throughout and after the war) of displaced persons marked as Serbs. The Human Rights Watch report from the year 2000 states that in 1992, the Town "came under attack by Serbian and Bosnian Serb forces and fell victim to the policy of 'ethnic cleansing' … [organized mostly by] paramilitaries belonging to [Željko Ražnatović] Arkan's Serbian Volunteer Guard, a.k.a. the 'Tigers,' together with other paramilitary forces."[15] After the war, the Town received a large number of Serb refugees, and a village in its municipality has had a very high percentage of Bosniak (Muslim) returnees.

Later on, I reflected upon my decision. Choosing not to conduct research in the entity of the Republic of Srpska, despite the Town perfectly fitting my required parameters (it was a border town and it had multiple humanitarian actions going on at the time), would have been a decision founded upon nationalist logic. People who live in the Republic of Srpska live in BiH, whatever one's political opinion may be concerning the existence of the two entities. Regardless of the personal or professional opinions of nationalists, "internationals," or social anthropologists on how the BiH state should be organized, its current administrative setup (which includes entities, cantons, and the district) is something that shapes the lives of Bosnians today—as it did during my fieldwork. This administrative setup structures people's lives in ways we should not discard just because they do not coincide with our political hopes.

To assume that I should have conducted ethnographic fieldwork in the Federation of BiH because it is somehow a "proper" BiH context, as I have been told once or twice by colleagues in academia, would have been a nationalist view. Similarly, to assume that I should not conduct ethnographic fieldwork among the residents of the Republic of Srpska because they are somehow, presumably, less Bosnian, would have been a very problematic and nonethnographic way of thinking. Ironically, this view would have been easily supported by Bosnian Serb nationalists in their struggles for the independence of the entity (see Kostovicova 2004). Thus, I decided to ethnographically learn and think about the Town, rather than make assumptions in advance about what kind of a place it is, and I found myself living there from September 2009 to September 2010, exploring several different domains and actors.

I was interested in how people raised tens of thousands of euros for medical treatments abroad through humanitarian actions and, more broadly, in how people cared for one another through official and unofficial channels. There were three families who initiated humanitarian actions in the Town during my fieldwork year (see chapter six). These families took a variety of different paths in raising money for medical treatments abroad, turning to social worlds they inhabited for help, which included the state institutions and civil society organizations. My ethnographic engagements were shaped by the paths they took.

The members of these three families, like many other people in their situation in BiH, turned to state welfare institutions and pursued favors within them in order to receive financial support. I therefore followed how they submitted formal applications and researched how other people in the Town negotiated access to state-run healthcare and social protection. I became a frequent visitor at a number of state institutions, such the local Center for Social Work (CSW) and the Public Fund for Child Protection.[16] I interviewed the officials who worked in these two institutions and attended their public meetings as well as nonpublic official routines, and sometimes I was allowed to look through their documents and observe their professional interactions with the users of social protection programs.

Furthermore, the families received various forms of financial and social support from local civil society organizations, so I paid attention to how and when this happened. I volunteered in two such organizations, the Sun and Holy Mother, because at least one of the families got help from at least one of them during humanitarian actions. The Sun worked with children with developmental needs and their parents and I attended their meetings from December 2009 to September 2010. Holy Mother was a religious charitable organization whose members I accompanied on a number of birthday visits to the homes of children with developmental needs from September 2009 to January 2010.

Finally, the families organized many different humanitarian events over the course of their humanitarian actions with the help of their friends and acquaintances. I attended the majority of these humanitarian events and explored the reasoning and practices of the humanitarian donors and organizers. In brief, over the course of a humanitarian action, all three families pursued *veze* and *štele* throughout their social worlds. This led me to follow how favors served as a technology of translation that allowed people to move across the boundaries of the "state" and "that which is not the state" (Gupta 1995: 393) and to explore the work of favors in multiple public and private arenas simultaneously.

Anthropology at Home in a Post-Yugoslav Town

Because I was a citizen of Montenegro, many of my interlocutors perceived me as, in some sense, a native. The question of whether or not I was doing native anthropology or to what degree points to some of the problems inherent in the concepts of "native anthropology" and "anthropology at home." These concepts immediately raise the issue of what constitutes an appropriate frame of reference: native to what—a country, a nation, a language, a culture? What does "at home" mean (Peirano 1998; Ryang 1997)? An understanding of anthropology at home as primarily anthropology conducted in one's own country, or nation, is an example of methodological nationalism—"the assumption that the nation/state/society is the natural social and political form of the modern world" (Wimmer and Glick Schiller 2002: 301).

Before my fieldwork I had not spent more than two weeks in total in BiH. However, the changing forms of statehood in the (post-) Yugoslav region meant that I used to be a citizen of the same country as many contemporary inhabitants of BiH were before the war—the Socialist Federal Republic of Yugoslavia. Today, I share with my interlocutors a kind of parallel post-Yugoslav citizenship and a long-term experience of living in a post-Yugoslav country. Furthermore, while today Montenegro and BiH are two different countries, they share many similarities, including sociohistorical, economic, and political (post-)Yugoslav heritage, language varieties, and geopolitical positions.

In terms of nationality, there were two other reasons I was not a native. First, although I hold Montenegrin citizenship, personally I do not have a sense of belonging in the Bosnian, Bosniak, Montenegrin, Serbian, Croatian, or any other, (ethno)nationality. The distinction between citizenship (understood as a relationship of mutual responsibility and entitlement between a person and a state apparatus, materialized in a passport) and nationality (understood as an intimate sense of belonging to a particular group and its way of life) is important to keep for various political reasons, not just in former Yugoslav countries (see Vasiljević 2012; Jansen 2005b). The national order of things is far from a desirable framework for thinking about the relationship between people, their cultural practices, and the territory in which they live.

Second, I was not working with nationally defined communities. My analytical and research focus was on exploring not how Serbs (or Bosniaks or Croats) gain access to healthcare and the welfare they need, but how people who live in the Town do so. I worked with people who navigated through the healthcare and welfare systems and those who managed their ambiguities. The majority of these people considered themselves to be Serbs, but some considered themselves Bosniaks, or Croats, or Bosnians, and there were also people who did not see themselves as belonging to any particular nation, just like me. Ethnographic research in and on BiH has illuminated the *relative* importance of nationality in various contexts (Hromadžić 2011; Palmberger 2010; Sorabji 2006; Kurtović 2011).

Similarly, nationality was not *the* most important "power vector" for the pursuit of *veze* and *štele*: nationality often became very relevant, but like gender, age, profession, and other vectors of power, it was sometimes relevant and sometimes not. Therefore, I took nationality into account as much as it was relevant to the topic of my research. When it became ethnographically important, I included it in the description and analysis; when it was not, I let it sink into the background. In other words, instead of seeing people as already nationalized subjects, I paid attention to *when* and *how much* people behaved as nationalized subjects or differentiated others on nationalist grounds. I approached my interlocutors as people shaped simultaneously by multiple vectors of power and I followed when and how their multiple social positions enabled them to do certain things and prevented them from doing other things.

Except for citizenship and nationality, I perceived myself as being at home in many other ways. My first language is the one spoken in the Town (this would be a polycentric language that includes Bosnian, Croatian, Montenegrin, and Serbian language standards, see footnote 7). My experiences with the health care system and the education system before conducting fieldwork were similar to those of my interlocutors. Furthermore, during our conversations both my interlocutors and I regularly used the terms "our language" (*naš jezik*), "our spaces" (*naši prostori*), and "our politicians" (*naši političari*), which suggests that I was—at least somewhat—perceived as a local.

Also, when getting to know somebody, people usually located me within the Town's network of relations through the people I spent my time with, as well as through the part of the Town in which I lived. All of this suggests that I developed a shared "intimate affinity" (Narayan 1993: 671) with the field. This intimate affinity does not mean that the relevant frame of reference for "home" and "nativity" is citizenship or nationality—and this was not the case with my research. However, given that home and nativity are not essentialist possessions, but categories of practice resulting from the intersection of various shared social positions, my research presents a form of anthropology at home/native anthropology.

Navigating and Managing Ambiguity

Let us go back to navigation and management for a moment. I argue that, in neoliberal transformations in the Town, power and socioeconomic status were reflected in a difference between navigating or managing ambiguity. A great majority of people had little choice but to navigate their social worlds to survive and/or maintain well-being. Navigation refers to an attempt to get somewhere. On a ship, navigation means answering questions, such as:

> Where are we? and If we proceed in a certain way for a specified time, where will we be? Answering the first question is called "fixing the position" or "getting a fix." Answering the second is called "dead reckoning." It is necessary to answer the first in order to answer the second, and it is necessary to answer the second to keep the ship out of danger. (Hutchins 1993: 39)

Thus, navigation includes two things. First, navigation requires determining a location—of a ship, of oneself, of others. As we will see in chapters one and two, my interlocutors invested efforts to "fix the position"—that is, locate themselves and others—by exchanging stories about their local social worlds. Second, navigation means going forward to make something happen—to reach a certain destination, to keep the ship out of danger, or to access social provisions, a particular doctor, and money for surgery. It is a pragmatic, goal-oriented pursuit that can be controlled only up to a point.

Navigation provides a useful metaphor for describing how people try to make things happen in the midst of ambiguous, uncertain, unsecured environments, whatever the reasons for ambiguity and uncertainty may be. For instance, developing navigation as an analytical concept, Vigh (2009) traces how young men navigated war and poverty in Guinea Bissau. Bear (2015) demonstrates how various people navigated austerity policies and fiscal crisis along the Hooghly River in India. As we will see in chapters three, four, and six, people who needed welfare support had little choice but to navigate their way through their changing social worlds, hoping to stumble upon the right person to help them.

However, a few people can manage neoliberal ambiguities of welfare. Unlike navigation, management marks efforts to organize, plan, and direct something in order to reach a certain objective. Management evokes much greater control in achieving a goal than navigation. It is a useful metaphor for conveying that some people can do something with ambiguity of social protection as both a gift and as a right. Chapter five explores practices of persons who were able to manage, rather than just navigate, ambiguity—they were able to intensify, reduce, or resolve it in a particular direction. For them, ambiguity was not a quality of social relations that potentially illuminates alternatives to the modernist organization of the world; neither was it an unforeseen byproduct of translating welfare policies in an unstable country. Ambiguity was the product of neoliberal restructurings of welfare that could be actively managed, while its management was inextricably linked with reproduction of power.

Notes

1. This book is the product of my ethnographic imagination and practice, and all the personal names and some biographical details throughout the book were changed to fully protect the anonymity of my interlocutors. I refer to my field site as "the Town," rather than by its name, for the same reason.

2. BiH is often represented as the Balkans' epicenter—a multiethnic, multicultural bridge between East and West (Helms 2008). Similar claims are often made about other Balkan countries, including Croatia, Serbia, Macedonia, and Bulgaria, although sometimes instead of a "bridge," the country in question is represented as "the last line of defense" of the rational and civilized West from the dangerous and backward East (Norris 1999).

3. The OHR is an international institution established after the 1992–95 war to oversee the implementation of a document that marked the end of the war violence: the "General Framework Agreement for Peace in Bosnia and Herzegovina" (also known as the Dayton Agreement). The OHR can perform a number of governmental functions in the country: it can introduce new laws and remove elected officials from state positions.

4. The basic social protection provision in 2009 and 2010 was approximately EUR 20 (Džumhur, Jukić, and Sandić 2010: 45), while the average net salary was almost twenty times as much, approximately EUR 385. Gross salary was approximately EUR 600 (Republički zavod za statistiku Republike Srpske 2011: 437–38).

5. For instance, the 2013 protests were provoked by the story of a baby who needed to travel beyond Bosnian borders for a bone marrow transplant but could not do so because of a political-administrative glitch: BiH politicians could not agree whether the last digit of the citizens' personal identification number (*jedinstveni matični broj građana,* or JMBG) should indicate the entity they live in or be a random number. As a result, all children born from January to August 2013 in BiH were left without any personal identification documents, including travel documents (Armakolas and Maksimović 2013).

6. I use the term "*social protection,*" rather than "*social care*" or "*social security,*" because it is the literal translation of the term *socijalna zaštita,* which is used to name this field in BiH. I also occasionally refer to "healthcare and social protection" together, mostly because it was under the jurisdiction of the same ministry in the entity: *Ministarstvo zdravlja i socijalne zaštite* (Ministry of Health and Social Protection).

7. Bosnian, Croatian, Montenegrin, and Serbian are four standards of a polycentric language that was called Serbo-Croatian during the SFR Yugoslavia. After the dissolution of the SFRY, the languages in the post-Yugoslav republics were renamed and new language standards were introduced (see Kordić 2010; Hodges 2016). Despite this, the speakers of all four standards are perfectly able to understand one another. In BiH, the official language standards in use are Bosnian, Croatian, and Serbian.

8. A humanitarian telephone number was a service provided by the local telecommunications company (see chapter six). An organization would register this number for a humanitarian purpose. All calls to this number had the same price, between EUR 0.5 and 1.0. The callers would hear a recorded message thanking them for their humanitarian donation. The

amount of money raised through the calls during one month was transferred to the organization and then the organization was supposed to transfer the money to the family for whom the humanitarian action was organized.

9. Petrović 2014.

10. The term *"Bosnian"* (*Bosanac, Bosanka*) refers to all residents of BiH, while the term *"Bosniak"* (*Bošnjak, Bošnjakinja*) is an ethnonational category encompassing Bosnian Muslims. *"Bosniak"* replaced the older Yugoslav term, *"Muslim"* (*Musliman, Muslimanka*), as an ethnonational category in 1993.

11. Agency for Statistics of Bosnia and Herzegovina 2016.

12. According to the census carried out in 1991, before the war, BiH had a total of 4,377,033 inhabitants, of whom 43.5 percent declared themselves to be Muslims, 31.2 percent Serbs, 17.4 percent Croats, and 5.6 percent Yugoslavs (Agency for Statistics of Bosnia and Herzegovina 2011).

13. Mladić was the highest military commander of the Army of the Republic of Srpska during the war. His trial at the International Criminal Tribunal for the former Yugoslavia in The Hague is ongoing. He is accused of genocide, crimes against humanity, and violations of the laws and customs of war in relation to several war events, including the Siege of Sarajevo 1992–96 and the genocide in Srebrenica in July 1995.

14. Helms notes that "the international community" signifies all foreign governments and agencies involved in relief aid and development but is most often used to refer "more narrowly to the group of supranational bodies and major aid agencies charged with implementing the Dayton Peace Agreement which ended the war in late 1995" (2003: 17).

15. Human Rights Watch 2000.

16. Centers for Social Work in the state of BiH are state-run institutions that provide social protection services. Because BiH has a complex administrative structure, Centers for Social Work are under the jurisdiction of the two entities and relevant ministries.

Part I
Personhood

Chapter 1

Creating Knowledge about Others

Locating, Knowing "by Sight," and Ethnography

Time Has to Pass to Get to Know the World

Nikola, an upholsterer, came to my apartment one day to repair a sofa. While working, he asked me whether I was from Slovenia. This was a question I frequently was asked. The first questions people usually asked me concerned where I was from and what my last name was. I replied with my standard answers: I said I was born in Belgrade (Serbia), which is where I lived until I was seven, when my family had to move to Podgorica (Montenegro). Ten years later, after finishing high school in Podgorica, I moved to study in Belgrade, and then I moved to study in the United Kingdom. As I revealed pieces of information about my own life, Nikola would interrupt with a different story each time. My Montenegrin citizenship led him to reminisce about prewar Montenegrins in the Town:

> Oh, there were, there were many Montenegrins. My friend and colleague Predrag, who was a carpenter, and his wife who worked in a department store. They moved back to Montenegro in the early nineties, and he died a couple of years later. Then, it was … where … we call him Pero, I can't remember his name … His house is right there [*pointing*], his wife was a teacher. He was married to a woman from [a village in the Town's municipality]. He lived here for a long time. His last name was Popović, he was from Cetinje. Popović … he had a brother, Milan, a doctor. He died too … there are probably many more, young people, it's just that I don't know them. I know the ones who came before, older people … A time arrives when a man does not know "the world" [*svijet*], some left, others have come. Time has to pass for a man to get to know these new ones.

Nikola continued describing the lives of older Montenegrins in the Town before moving on to discuss the years he spent working in Germany. He came back to the Town in 1996, after the war had ended, a couple of months before his wife died. He then asked whether I was married and whether I had children. After I replied no on both counts, he told me about a couple named Mitar and Zora, who had lived in my building.

> *Nikola:* Mitar, they had one son, he and Zora. And they [Mitar and Zora] organized his marriage to Nina's daughter. Miro and Alma. And they [Miro and Alma] could not be together; they argued and fought here and there, and in the end, he [Miro] killed himself. He took a gun. And it was all because of his parents.
>
> *Čarna:* When did this happen?
>
> *Nikola:* This was in '83. Miro hadn't had kids with Alma. He had a house and the daughter went back to her parents. Zora, and Mitar, since they couldn't be together, they sold the house and split the money. Zora separated from Mitar. There, right in front of the hospital, see those old buildings, across from the Chinese shops—she owns the first floor now. Zora is there. And Mitar, he married a woman from [another village in the Town's municipality], he sold everything, he only kept some cattle. He took his things and an apartment for himself, Zora took one for herself, and so … no children … He was in Serbia, he used to work in transport. Zora worked in a store, and now she is retired. Both are retired.

Similar conversations often occurred throughout my research, performing two local knowledge practices that I call "locating" and "knowing by sight." First, Nikola tried to locate me into his *svijet*, his social world. He did so by looking for a point of intersection between me and people within his own social networks who I might know. Once it became obvious that our social worlds did not intersect, he poignantly noted that social worlds have changed in general and that it takes time to create new ones. Nikola then started telling me personal stories of the people he perceived to be in some ways similar to me—those from Montenegro and without children. I did not explicitly provoke Nikola into storytelling: I participated in the conversation, but the drive to tell me about these people aged sixty or over, who had been living in the Town before the war, came from him. By retelling stories, he was teaching me about the social fabric of the Town he was familiar with, increasing my chances of getting to know people like Zora and Mitar by sight in the future.

In this chapter, I argue that personhood in the Town was largely constituted from connections and relations to other people. Personhoods, as "culturally specific constructions of the embodied self" (Alexander 2002: 20), were shaped not just by gender, religion, sexuality, ethnonationality, or class but also by who people knew and in what capacity. Locating and knowing by sight were some of the means of creating such connections and relations, and thus of personhood. The personhood made of connections and relations to others reflects the well-known anthropological insight that identity (the issue of who someone is) is in fact the product of social relations (the issue of where someone is located in relation to others). Efforts to ascertain how a new acquaintance relates to other people—locating efforts—constitute an attempt to find out *who* this person is.

The way of doing personhood through connections and relations to others coexisted with another idea: that of an "individual," and his or her interest, as clearly distinguishable from social relations. This idea was put forward in different places, including nongovernmental organization (NGO)–based social activism of people living with disabilities, suggesting that people first had to develop personal skills and only then to connect with others to lobby for shared goals. From the perspective of an individual, sociality started at the point where a person ended. Yet, this idea did not resonate so well with everyday life, in which my interlocutors practiced a certain kind of "sociality with a purpose."

The socialities that have a certain purpose are not a rare occurrence: ethnographic and historical works demonstrate that they have been practiced in one form or another across very different contexts. Sociality with a purpose seems to be crucially important in various contemporary capitalist settings. The case in point is the global music industry, in which artists "are involved in relational labor, by which I mean regular, ongoing communication with audiences over time to build social relationships that foster paid work" (Baym 2015: 16). Investing in an effort to connect with your audience on a daily level can entail "all the complex rewards and costs of personal relationships independent of any money that comes from them [and yet] the connections built through relational labor are always tied to earning money" (ibid.). In a quite different social context, the privatization of the oil industry in Argentina was predicated upon "neoliberal kinship," that is, upon familial relations that enabled former state workers to remake themselves as small business owners.

Maintenance of already existing kinship bonds offered former state workers "the best chance for survival in the reorganized circuits of the global oil industry" (Shever 2012: 74). Yet, this very re-incorporation into the global market left them living in uncertainty and sharing "in the losses ... but not in the profits" (ibid.). In the Town, as in most such cases, the sociality with a purpose was not an ironic endeavor in which people behaved *as if* they were interested in mutual connectedness, while *actually* being invested in completing a pragmatic goal: earning money, saving a job, or obtaining a welfare provision. Making relations and connections, while obtaining a benefit, was often one and the same thing for my interlocutors. Similar to ethnography as a way of learning about people, my interlocutors invested time and effort to build social relations—pragmatic goals, favors, and gifts were a constitutive part of this effort.

Locating Efforts: Who You Are Depends on Who You Know

In his stories, the upholsterer Nikola used the word "world" (*svijet*) to indicate "people." For example, if a funeral, a wedding, or a humanitarian concert was attended by many people, he would describe it using the phrase *bilo je puno svijeta,* perhaps best translated as "the world and his or her friend was there." However, the notion of *svijet* does not only signify many people gathered in the same place. Rather, it marks the boundaries of a social world someone inhabits. When Nikola added, "A time comes when a man does not know the world [*svijet*], some have left, others have come. Time has to pass for a man to get to know the new ones," he suggested that knowledge about others is crucial to this *svijet.*

When Nikola was in Germany, this knowledge was shattered due to the BiH war, which became notorious for the large-scale ethnic cleansing of people of "other" nationalities from their places of residence. The forced, violent expulsion of people defined in nationalized terms as (Bosniak) Muslim and Croatian from the Town and the influx of displaced Serbs into the Town meant that the structure of Nikola's *svijet* was irrevocably changed over the course of the war. In order to find his place in the postwar world, time had to pass for him to get to know new people.

When meeting someone new in the Town, my interlocutors sought to ascertain who this new person was by learning *where* the new person was located in their own world of people (*svijet*). Just like the upholsterer Nikola, they would usually ask the new acquaintance about names, places of origin, neighborhoods, and workplaces in order to see whether they had a mutual friend and shared social contacts. I was present on numerous occasions when these locating efforts occurred, sometimes as a participant, sometimes as an observer. On one occasion, it happened during a meeting of the two focus/support groups for women experiencing menopause that I organized and led for a couple of months with the help of a local medical practitioner and a nongovernmental organization working with women with disabilities.[1] In each group, six to seven women got together every week to discuss their opinions, experiences, and practices relating to menopause.

My role was to facilitate their discussions, especially by introducing ethnographic examples of different ideas and practices relating to bodily changes after a certain age and by encouraging the participants to think through a variety of understandings of menopause that were present in BiH. The first group gathered women with disabilities together from a nongovernmental organization, while the second group was composed of women who were previously friends and acquaintances. Milena, who attended one of the two groups, joined the other group after a couple of weeks. It was not at the first but at our second joint meeting that the women tried to locate one another. Once it became apparent that Milena's *svijet* (world of people) intersected with the worlds of people of other women in the group, the atmosphere became more relaxed and open.

> *Milena:* I know that my mother had a cousin in Zagreb, he worked in the military. She used to go there every year for ten days to have tests done on her glands. She went to Belgrade too … to do tests at that time, whatever they [the doctors] knew about glands …
>
> *Čarna:* Did her cousin work in the hospital, or did he just live in Zagreb?
>
> *Milena:* He lived in Zagreb, and he knew those military doctors, it was easier for her that way …
>
> *Jana [interrupting Milena]:* And where are you from?
>
> *Milena:* From [a village in the Town's municipality]. And so, everything happened so fast that I cannot recall it all.
>
> *Jana:* You went to school, didn't you?
>
> *Milena:* Well yes, I went to school, I went about my own business actually.

The discussion concerning their mothers' experiences with menopause continued. Milena mentioned the year she was born, and Jana interrupted her once again, trying to find out who Milena was (that is, who Milena knew):

> *Bilja:* I am the oldest, born in '52. My sister was born in '53 and my brother in '55.

Milena: So was I.

Jana [asks Milena]: You were born in '55? Then you must have gone to school together with Slaviša.

Milena: Slaviša who?

Jana: Dragić.

Milena: At the elementary school?

Jana: Well yes.

Milena: He must have been in some other class …

Jana: There was Ivana Božić, they are the same generation, Marica Petrović? Pera Borić?

Bilja: You must know him, he is a vet.

Jana: Pera Borić, Rašo Popović—my brother who used to work in SUP.[2] Everybody went to this school. Slavica Rajić Božović.

Rosa: It was a grammar school, maybe she didn't go to the grammar school.

Milena: Yes, I did, I graduated from the grammar school, I am trying to remember, they weren't in my class, that's why I don't know them.

Jana: 4A.

Bilja: Angela was the teacher.

Milena: I think I was in C class, my class leader used to be … that … wife of the late Miro Perović.

Jana: Aha! Aunty Nevenka.

Bilja: Nevenka. She and my mum are cousins.

Jana: I was born in '57. I was in the grammar school too. When I was in the second grade, they were in the fourth.

Milena: Well, there you go, you are younger. The director used to be great, then, Budo.

Jana: Amalija was my class leader.

Milena: Well, Amalija was nice too, a bit sick—she took insulin—but really nice.

Jana interrupted the conversation about their mothers' experiences of menopause as soon as she recognized she had a chance of finding out who Milena "was." Once they realized that Aunty Nevenka was a point of intersection—a person they both knew—our group talk continued. Almost all of the women in the group participated in this locating effort; the only one who did not say a word was Marta, who moved to the Town after getting married. Her silence might be understood as an echo of differences between the "newcomers" and "old residents of the Town," articulated in the upholsterer's words quoted earlier.

Locating people within one's own *svijet* meant identifying them through a criterion that intersected and overlapped with sex/gender, ethnicity/nationality, age, and profession but that could not be fully subsumed under them. Personal histories of people—where they had lived; where they went to school; whether they moved out during the war and, if so, where to and how and with whose help; who their friends were—revealed important aspects of one's social position. In order to know who a person was, it was necessary to know who this person knew. For many people in the Town, personhood was shaped by interpersonal relations.

This is a point also made by Alexander in her study of statehood in eastern Turkey, where "social personhood is dependent upon engagement, or the possibility of engagement, with other actors" (2002: 20). The actors were other people—acquaintances, patrons, or friends—as well as the state in the multiple forms it took in people's narratives, fantasies, and everyday lives. Alexander suggests that connections constitutive of personhood may be directed at other people as well as at institutions, through the process of "extrapolating the images of concrete social relations into the more abstract sphere of relations between the person and the state" (ibid.: 22).

The act of investing similar amounts of attention, time, and effort in discussions of other people, their business, and their histories has occurred in many places besides BiH. Candea (2010) discusses the practice of "anonymous introductions" in Corsica, which entails becoming acquainted with other people without initially stating your name (or asking for another person's name) but instead searching for a possible mutual acquaintance. These anonymous introductions, Candea argues, "bracket the difference" between people, allowing them to make a connection before acknowledging the separation. To offer one's name at the beginning of a conversation would mean acknowledging the lack of an already existing relationship between the speakers. Therefore, in order to create such a relationship before acknowledging their separation, the speakers first locate a mutual acquaintance.

Avoiding saying one's own name to an unknown interlocutor enables both interlocutors to get to know each other's position within Corsica through talk about other people—friends, relatives, acquaintances—and thus to know "who" the other person is, or where she or he is within this particular network of relations. However, Candea found that this way of "doing personhood" (2010: 131) coexists with others, and he suggests that anonymous introductions allow "one way of 'doing' personhood to be bracketed in favour of another" (ibid.). This means that a way of doing personhood that is materialized through passports (exemplified by having a single, known name and permanent ID number) is bracketed in Corsica by anonymous introductions in favor of doing personhood in a way that constitutes a local way of knowing people, which "could effortlessly and silently stretch to include Continentals" (ibid.: 129).

The core difference here concerning efforts to locate others in the Town is that local Corsican knowledge about people does not stretch to include institutions (in the narrow sense of the word). This suggests that in Corsica there are multiple, but clearly separable, bracketed ways of doing personhood: the practice of personhood employed by the state is not enmeshed with the one employed through anonymous introductions. In the Town, on the other hand, local ways of knowing people affected people's engagements with state institutions and access to public services. Connections with public officials were constitutive of personhood as much as those with acquaintances, patrons, or friends. Personhood was shaped by negotiating connections both within and beyond local state institutions.

Accessing Public Resources, Making Connections

These half-obvious, sometimes effective, sometimes unimportant efforts to locate others were also a feature of encounters in healthcare and social protection. One of the most prominent topics of conversation among people who had recently undergone medical treatments was the doctors and nurses who had performed those treatments. People discussed diseases, procedures, and hospitals, but the most vivid and longest conversations were about persons. People always seemed to remember doctors' names, their overall attitudes toward patients, their educational histories, and sometimes even the names of their university professors. My interlocutors invested a lot of effort in finding out who the medical practitioners were—that is, how they were located with respect to my interlocutors and other people in the Town.

I learned about such efforts most often at the Sun, an organization working with children with developmental difficulties. There were fifteen to twenty parents (all women) who regularly brought their children to the Sun. The parents shared very few social positions. One had a law degree, one was a trained nurse, others had a high school education only. The majority of them perceived themselves as Serbs, but there were also women who perceived themselves as Bosnian Muslims/Bosniaks, and one perceived herself as a Croat. There were women who were in their late twenties and some who were approaching their fifties. Some of them had been victims of heavy family abuse, while others had harmonious families. Their children also had very different disabilities and some had more than one disability. Despite these differences, all parents shared the difficulties that came with the 2000s' policy reforms, which will be discussed in chapter three.

One of the women from the Sun was Sanja (pronounced Sanya), a woman in her forties who had a daughter with developmental challenges. She could not find a *veza/štela* connecting her with "the best psychiatrist" for her daughter: the head of the department in a local public hospital. Her attempts to reach him through the official hospital channels took weeks and included numerous phone calls and a lot of meandering through the hospital offices. When she finally managed to get the head of the psychiatry department to examine her daughter, she felt like all the effort had been in vain; she explained, "He did not do a single test; he simply prescribed her medication." Sanja had expected that "the town's best psychiatrist" would invest more visible professional effort. She expected him to ground his treatment in medically objective knowledge (rather than to base it on assumptions). Perhaps the medical history of Sanja's daughter was typical enough to not require any further tests or examinations. However, the problem was that without a *veza/štela* Sanja could not be completely sure.

Sanja shared her problem with the other women at the Sun. We sat in our coats and jackets in a poorly heated room filled with the smoke of our cigarettes. We listened to Sanja's story while drinking coffee and waiting for their children to finish a two-hour play and learning session with specialist teachers. What happened next was quite remarkable from my perspective. Over the course of the next hour and a half, this group of women laughed to express scorn for the opinion of the head of psychiatric care. They debated and rejected prescriptions he gave and offered Sanja several alternative courses of action. These included visiting two other psychiatrists, one in the Town and another who worked in Serbia, in a town less than an hour away right across the border. The parents were able to locate these two doctors through their own "worlds of people" and their own experiences. After a lengthy discussion and exchange of opinions, they reached a consensus on the best alternatives for Sanja's daughter.

There was something procedurally specific about this sort of support. The women did not try to improve themselves and their children or to actively rework their biologies (see Rose 2006; Rose and Novas 2007). Instead, they looked for the right social connections. Phillips (2011) suggests that mutual aid associations in postsocialist Ukraine often focus on empowering families through various psychological and physical forms of rehabilitation. There are also larger social activist NGOs that aim to intervene in the legislative frameworks and institutional setups of social issues and that establish connections to transnational funds and NGO networks more easily than mutual aid associations (Phillips 2008).[3] The meaning of "social" in such NGO-based social activism and mutual aid associations that work on psychosocial support is largely that of a sphere that extends outside of an individual. Such a vision was reflected in a Sarajevo brochure about the right to self-determination of people with developmental difficulties (SUMERO 2012).

According to the brochure, a person first has to take care of herself: she needs to be able to make individual decisions and choices about herself and her own life as well as to develop the skills required to communicate, to solve problems, and to represent herself. Only once she develops such individual skills will she be able to connect to others who are in a similar position so that they can jointly advocate for their mutual rights in their community and country of residence. Here, responsibility for one's well-being is largely placed on the individualized subject: people have to achieve their full psychosocial capacities to be able to connect with others in a similar position, so they can exert activist pressure on the community and the state to respect their human rights.

This conceptualization of the "social" as extending beyond an individual has widely circulated throughout international and local organizations in BiH in connection with developmental efforts to restructure welfare, alongside peace building and strengthening civil society. Many NGOs and citizens' associations across the country have focused on empowerment through psychosocial services and on changing legislature and institutional frameworks for various social issues through the concerted actions of empowered individuals (Hart and Colo 2014; Stubbs 2001).

In some instances, these efforts appeared to be effective and to produce new forms of knowing, being, and acting. For example, the president of the Sun seemingly wholeheartedly adopted this philosophy and promoted it in her attempts to teach the mothers to be more proactive citizens through professional psychological workshops and various activist projects (see chapter four). However, at other moments, this concept of the social could not encapsulate the everyday connections and relationships that people established and the effects of this on their sense of self.

The idea of the social as extending beyond the person is different from the idea of a "social personhood" that is shaped by interpersonal relations. I do not refer here to Taylor's concept of a "porous self"—an enchanted world in which spirits, demons, and cosmic forces merge with humans—or to his concept of a "buffered self"—of disenchanted Western modernity in which "I can see the boundary as a buffer, such that the things beyond don't need to 'get to me,' to use the contemporary expression" (2007: 38). Instead, I would like to suggest that women from the Sun—and many other people in BiH—practiced a kind of "social personhood," as summarized in the saying "Who you are with—is who you are" (*s kim si takav si*), or more idiomatically in English "Tell me who your friends are and I will tell you who you are."

Since personhood could not be neatly distinguished from the social worlds one inhabited, the attempts to expand connections and/or relations with others in order to achieve a particular, personal goal were often interpreted as corrupt, irregular, or simply wrong from the perspective of "an individual" conceived as separate from "the social." The informal work and support that parents invested in one another at the Sun was mostly relational: they helped one another to locate people outside of the organization. They provided the social dimension to psychosocial support, but in a manner that was not prescribed in the abovementioned brochure. The reasoning and practices of these parents suggest that people preferred to receive medical treatment from someone they were able to locate within their own world of people (*svijet*). Although no money was exchanged, Sanja's pursuit of medical treatment for her daughter may seem backward or corrupt from a perspective in which boundaries between an individual, society, and the state are imagined as clear-cut.

From a different perspective, such a pursuit made sense for at least two reasons. First, a personal relationship with the doctor increased people's trust that doctors did their best. They thought that a doctor who cares is a doctor who makes a professional effort to consider all possibilities, conducts tests on these possibilities, and thus objectively ascertains the most effective course of action. They believed that a doctor who was a part of Sanja's *svijet*—and who could thus personally relate to her—would provide her daughter with such a treatment.

The parents did not clearly differentiate between whether doctors doing their best meant them following the prescribed procedure or meant being engaged in their work. From a legal point of view, this difference is important. If a doctor does not follow a prescribed procedure without a *veza/štela,* that presents a legal offense. However, there is no legal offense if a doctor does follow the prescribed procedure for all the patients but is engaged and goes the extra mile for the patients with a *veza/štela.*

I have no way of knowing whether there was a better treatment for Sanja's daughter than the medications prescribed by the head of the department—I cannot tell whether it made sense, from a medical point of view, to look for another doctor and another prescription. But the desire for more tests, a different treatment, and a different doctor are important on their own. Jansen (2015) argues that people across BiH yearn for "normal lives," or, more specifically, for the certainty and predictability of everyday life that can be provided only by following established, institutionalized procedures. Parents at the Sun regularly expressed the same yearnings, and Sanja's desire for standardized medical tests was a direct reflection of this.

Second, pursuing a different doctor made sense also because the discussion at the Sun reiterated who Sanja was as a person. She was not a "nobody" (*niko*), an irrelevant person to be sent away after five minutes by a doctor who invested no visible medical effort. Although she was unemployed and had a very low income, she was a "somebody" (*neko*): she had her *svijet* to turn to. In Sanja's case, her attempt to find a *veza/štela* was not an instrumental strategy designed to obtain the treatment in the context of scarce resources—because her daughter had been prescribed *a* treatment. Rather, being able to locate doctors and thus to establish a personalized relationship with them was a means of conducting two tasks at once: generating the trust that you have received the best possible public service and confirming where you were socially located (and so able to reproduce your own personhood) in the Town. The instrumental and the social dimension of such pursuits were indivisible.

Knowing by Sight

Another mode of expanding one's own *svijet*—and thus the pool of potential *veze/štele*—was "knowing someone by sight" (*znati nekog iz viđenja*). The phrase is much used throughout BiH and the other former Yugoslav states; I have used it for as long as I can remember. Since personalized knowledge about other people turned out to be of great importance for my research, I started paying attention to when the phrase was used and began to ask questions about what it meant. In short, knowing someone by sight meant being familiar with stories told about someone and being able to contact her or him, rather than actually having been introduced to this person, or even knowing what she or he looked like. Often, people had actually seen people they knew by sight on at least one occasion—in a café, on a street, in a photo, and so on. People claimed they knew someone by sight if she went to their school but was not in the same class; if he had lived in the same refugee settlement as you but wasn't close to you; if you had worked at the same place but on different shifts; and so on.

Nevertheless, the act of having seen someone was not necessary. Rather, in order to know someone by sight you had to be connected to him or her through a person, or a group of people, who would tell your stories to one another and who could also introduce you to one another if needed. You did not have to be of the same nationality, age group, or gender—even though some of these vectors of power would increase your chances of knowing someone. In order to know a person by sight, it was enough to have an acquaintance who, for example, had gone to school with you, who had perhaps lived in the same refugee settlement as that other person, and who had told you her stories.

Knowing by sight was also important for getting favors done. For instance, Marko and Ana Ilić were parents of a baby born with premature retinopathy. During my fieldwork, they organized a *humanitarna akcija* (humanitarian action) in order for their baby to be medically examined at a specialist clinic in Moscow, with the possibility of undergoing surgery. The Ilićs started raising money, largely through favors, from various public and private actors. Chapter six will discuss the course of such humanitarian actions for medical treatments abroad in more detail. Here, I wish to consider in more detail a situation in which Marko asked a woman he knew by sight for a favor.

Marko and Ana decided to open a humanitarian telephone number as a part of their humanitarian action. In order to do so, they had to find a legal entity that would register the number for them. Marko remembered that he knew by sight the president of the local religious charity Holy Mother, Ratka. Both Marko and Ratka had lived in Sarajevo before 1992 and, after having moved to different places during the war, had both settled in the Town afterward. Over the course of the years and their shared "refuchess" experience (or "the strategic deployment and movement of nationalised persons across nationalised places," Jansen 2011: 140), Marko had heard stories about Ratka helping others through her charitable activities.

He went to the monastery in the center of the Town, walking inside its shop, where the worker gave him Ratka's phone number. Marko told me he would be eternally grateful to her. Ratka said, "Wait, don't move; I'll be there in a minute." She came to meet with him right away and opened a humanitarian number for the Ilićs. Through the humanitarian number they raised approximately 6,800 KM (EUR 3,400) for the trip to Moscow. Similar to certain forms of public sociality in post-Soviet contexts, *svijet* transformed people "from individuals defined by state-based subject positions, such as citizen and migrant, into fellow travellers across lines of power" (Dzenovska 2014: 272).

I myself got to know several people by sight through the Sun. During our regular meetings at the organization, I learned not only about the marital statuses, education, and workplaces of the parents of children with disabilities who regularly came to the Sun but also about Dragana's complicated abortion; Milica's strange taste in men; Selma's problems with her mother-in-law; Ivana's medical history, colorful clothes, and choice of thong underwear, and so on. I never met Dragana, Milica, Selma, Ivana, or many of the other people mentioned in these conversations, but after some time, I felt as if I knew them. I learned bits and pieces of their personal histories and I had a way of getting in touch with them if I needed to—through women who regularly came to the Sun.

In addition, these stories traveled in both directions. After a couple of encounters outside of the Sun, I realized that at least some of these women, whom I had never met, must have heard bits and pieces of my own personal history and that they had a way of contacting me if needed. Knowing someone by sight did not therefore have to mean actually meeting someone, but rather meant being involved in sharing stories about them and knowing how to contact them. Relations sustained by sight were mediated through others, generated and reproduced through storytelling. People who one knew by sight constituted a part of one's own *svijet*.

Sociality with a Purpose: The Politics of Local Knowledge

Veze and *štele* seem to have had a long history in BiH. While I am not aware of any works outlining the historical specificities of *veze* and *štele,* my assumption is that *veze* and *štele* in socialist and post-socialist BiH are closely related, but distinct practices. Here, I follow Ledeneva's (1998) argument that *blat* in Russia today has strong roots in the Soviet experience but should be considered a contemporary phenomenon. The ways in which *veze/štele* were intertwined with the public administration of the Yugoslav system of socialist self-management may significantly differ from the "intrusion" of *veze/štele* into the redistribution of resources in the contemporary BiH neoliberalizing and supervised democracy. The case in point is the postwar and postsocialist practice of humanitarian actions (*humanitarne akcije*) in BiH that utilizes *veze/štele* in a way that was not possible during the Socialist Federative Republic of Yugoslavia (SFRY), not least because the Yugoslav healthcare system provided access to practically all forms of healthcare abroad.

As we will see in chapter six, the conceptual possibility and the very need for humanitarian actions could not have existed during the socialist period—it was a result of the postsocialist transformation. Whatever *veze/štele* enabled during the socialist Yugoslav era, this changed with the fall of the SFRY. Similar to *guanxi* before and after the introduction of a capitalist economy in China, *veze/štele* in BiH since the fall of Yugoslav socialism may have "declined in some areas of life but found new breeding grounds in others" (Yang 2002: 463).

Historical and ethnographic works indicate that various forms of sociality with a purpose have been used in former Yugoslavia over time. These include godparenthood (*kumstvo*), neighborhood (*komšiluk* or *susjedstvo*), and, more recently, *raja* (pronounced *raya*). Hammel (1968) suggests that *kumstvo,* as a form of ritual kinship, was established in the rural areas of prewar, socialist Yugoslavia with a person of higher status and prestige, who had to fulfill a number of financial and material obligations. The *kum* (godfather) or *kuma* (godmother) could be replaced by another person if they could not meet the expectation of helping the family in a crucial moment.

Raja is a framework for sociality that has recently started to gain analytical attention, mostly through the work of Nebojša Šavija-Valha (2013), a philosopher and anthropologist from BiH. In emic terms, *raja* is a group of friends, as well as a subaltern "cultural milieu," a "niche," or a "moral code" in Sarajevo that links certain people together via reciprocity into a seemingly apolitical relationship that requires its participants to leave aside their mutual ethnic, national, religious, class, and many other social differences in order to relate to one another on egalitarian grounds.

Despite *raja*'s insistence on mutual equality of participants, social, political, and economic differences between *raja* participants do not disappear—the differences that are excluded from *raja* are relocated to the parts of everyday life that cannot operate on the basis of participants' direct, total, and ultimate reciprocity (this includes practically any segment of life in which people do not share the same knowledge, such as schools, workplaces, healthcare institutions, and so forth). Furthermore, *raja* performs no function aside from helping people socialize in a particular way: "*Raja* is not a productive community, it is just a community, as well as a template, a code of specific socialization of subjects, finally a subject socialized in a specific way" (Šavija Valha 2010: 77). In line with this emphasis on nonproductivity, for Sarajevans, the opposite of *raja* is a *papak,* or a person who leaves the chain of reciprocal help, pays attention to socioeconomic differences between people, and establishes relations with others on the basis of self-interest.

Despite *raja's* proclaimed anti-ideological character, Šavija-Valha argues that relationships among *raja* participants are not as egalitarian and apolitical as they may initially seem, for they depend on gender differences:

> If *raja* strictly applies the principle of displacement of all excesses of significations—ethnic, religious, class, professional, and so on—*raja* should also displace gender significations ... [However] only women are expected to exclude their excess of female significations and to appropriate the excess of male significations ... It is exactly in relation to gender differences where the ideological construction of *raja* becomes apparent. (2016: 176)

In contrast to *raja,* people who constituted one another's *svijet* did not attempt to discard mutual social differences, although they focused largely on mutually shared social positions and experiences. Furthermore, *svijet* as a framework for sociality that helped people to "get things done" involved relations of reciprocity as well as those of inequality and hierarchy. As a matter of fact, under certain conditions, the management of ambiguities in *svijet* brought power. In chapter five, I will demonstrate that people who skillfully provided favors to others across multiple public and private arenas managed to generate a form of rogue power that was personalized but worked through institutions.

Since in *svijet* there was no active attempt to displace social differences and hierarchies, it perhaps bears more resemblance to *komšiluk* as a framework for sociality. Prewar *komšiluk* in BiH predominantly included people living nearby, who were:

> often considered as closer than the closest relatives. Who else would lend us a bowl, a plate, a coffee grinder, a cup of sugar to help us avoid embar-

rassment (*da bi se spasio obraz*) in front of an unexpected guest? Who else should first try homemade cookies or cabbage rolls, but the closest neighbors? It is easier to ask them for a small loan until a salary or pension gets paid, than the closest relatives. They will watch the children when needed. They will look after the apartment during the annual vacation. They will be called to help fix damage in the home. They are the first port of call for help when illness strikes as well. (Mujačić 1973: 41)

In anthropological, ethnological, and historical studies of BiH, the notion of *komšiluk* as a small-scale and intimate, yet political, framework for sociality has occupied a prominent position (see Bringa 1995; Hann 2003; Roth 2006). In academic and political circles, one of the dominant interpretations is that the concept of neighborhood presents a mechanism for the regulation of interethnic and interreligious relations by creating reciprocal obligations among people who live in proximity to one another while belonging to different ethnonational groups (Bugarel 2004; Hayden 2002; see also Baskar 2012). Criticizing such an interpretation of neighborhood through the lens of ethnonational and religious differences, Sorabji noticed that, during the 1990s, the notion of *komšiluk* became a "handmaiden to the political debate" (2007: 97), because it was used partly by war leaders as a rhetorical device and partly by international actors who saw *komšiluk* as a mechanism that could have prevented the war and that had the power to rebuild a multiethnic, multicultural BiH. In her reading, *komšiluk* is a form of social relatedness that creates morally and religiously imbued duties toward people living in one's proximity, irrespective of their ethnonational and religious belonging. Similarly, Henig (2012) has found that in Bosnian villages nowadays *komšiluk* regulates social relations, moral obligations, and personhood among people who identify with the same ethnonational and religious categories.

Before the war, physical proximity was very important for establishing the close-knit relations of *komšiluk,* although other factors played a role in shaping neighborly relations as well. On the basis of his 1970s sociological research in Derventa, a town in BiH, Mujačić (1973) mentions that approximately 20 percent of people said that they cultivated neighborly relations because of a shared workplace or childhood memories, irrespective of their physical proximity. Mujačić also found that people who developed *komšiluk* relations very often had an ethnonational identity, profession, and/or workplace in common, as well as having a similar income and material status. In 2009 and 2010, *komšiluk*—as a physically distinctive part of the

Town—was of little importance for most of my interlocutors in the Town.

Although they did exchange coffee, gifts, and stories with some of their neighbors, there was no sense of shared togetherness within the whole *komšiluk* for many people in the Town. This sense was likely lacking because the structure of the Town's population had drastically changed in the past twenty years. According to the census data, the national numbers in the Town in 1991 were as follows: Serbs 59 percent, Muslims 34 percent, Croats less than 1 percent, Yugoslavs less than 5 percent, others less than 5 percent. In 2013, the national numbers were Serbs 85 percent, Bosniaks 12 percent, Croats less than 1 percent.[4] The population of the Town also increased, which means that some of its neighborhoods and infrastructure were built anew.

In such a context, many communal and personal issues in the Town were regulated through a nexus of storytelling, combining a sense of responsibility for others' well-being, with the shared obligation to help—both of which are important elements of sociality in the *komšiluk*, despite the contemporary lack of importance of the *komšiluk* as a physical unit (Helms 2010). This nexus formed the grounds of *svijet* as a framework for the regulation of communal and personal issues.

There are at least three similarities between the forms of sociality usually relegated to the framework of *komšiluk* and those performed by my interlocutors in the Town in their own world of people (*svijet*). One such similarity includes making an effort to find out the identity of a new person by locating people you have in common with her or him. Yet another similarity refers to knowledge by sight—the habit of getting to know (about) people through stories shared about them. A third similarity consists in people's trepidation concerning "what others might think about them," which was a powerful way of regulating behavior in the Town (cf. Venkatesan 2009). Attaching importance to the opinion of others is a relational category that affected one's sense of self and thus how often parents would take their child with developmental difficulties for a walk and in what part of the Town. It affected how many lovers young people would decide to have, how older people dealt with the bodily changes that accompany aging, and so forth (Brković 2010). Both *svijet* and *komšiluk* modes of relating include these three characteristics, up to a certain point. Thus, although the physical neighborhood was not a particularly useful point of reference in the everyday life in the Town, the mechanisms of sociality usually present in *komšiluk* were.

Although none of these mechanisms of sociality in the Town worked exclusively among conationals (or exclusively among people of different nationalities), they had political effects. They did more than regulate ethnonational relations, for *svijet* was an important framework for reproducing one's gendered, aging, sexual sense of self as well as a sense of responsibility for others' survival and well-being. The politics of local knowledge about *svijet* also shaped engagements with civic and state institutions, because it helped to gather knowledge about how things worked. When applying for healthcare and welfare programs and services, people often collected information regarding the necessary documentation and procedures not by calling the relevant institutions or visiting their websites but through other people: they would call someone from their own *svijet* who had already undergone the same procedure and submitted the same application in order to learn how the process works and, sometimes, which public official was in charge of it.

As we have seen in Sanja's case, this did not necessarily happen for just instrumental reasons. Caldwell suggests that in getting things done through informal connections in Russia, knowledge is a crucial resource that works as "a socializing force that brings people together" (2004: 74). In the Town, generating knowledge about public welfare services informally, through local social worlds, also connected people and reinstated who one was as a social person. In most cases described in this book, local knowledge was not first and foremost a pragmatic endeavor whose purpose was expanding a pool of potential *veze/štele*—because this knowledge also recreated people's sense of self and their mutual social obligations.

However, we should also not ignore the fact that such knowledge about others was often used as a means of gaining access to various things, including public healthcare and welfare. The weaving of a *svijet* permitted people to draw on possible connections to different possible futures, in a context where they might be needed at some point. This inseparability of the instrumental and the social might be more easily recognizable if we compare it with ethnography as a way of learning about other people.

Not unlike ethnography, *svijet* includes a certain kind of sociality with a purpose. In a similar fashion to my interlocutors, I tracked people who knew other people in order to access something or someone I needed: a piece of information, an interview, an opinion, an opportunity to do participant observation, and so forth. At some points, I also tried to understand who people were by finding out who they knew and in what capacity. My aim, as an ethnographer, was to develop interpersonal relations with various people in the Town and to become a participant in their everyday practices in order to be able to conduct research—in other words, I cultivated social relations with a certain purpose.

However, I do not think this means that my ethnographic research was an ironic engagement. Neither I nor many of my interlocutors behaved *as if* we participated in a particular kind of sociality, while knowing full well that we were *actually* after something else: information, access, data, and so forth. Being an ethnographer often depends on cultivating "shared concerns" (Jansen 2015: 1–29) with the interlocutors and on being able to participate in social relations with more or less skill as a neighbor, collaborator, or friend. The same impossibility of being able to clearly distinguish the purposeful, pragmatic dimension from the emotional and social investments characterize many relations within *svijet* and ethnography as a way of learning. With this in mind, let us take a closer look at how *veze* and *štele* created personhoods as well as material benefits.

Notes

1. For a more detailed account of these focus/support groups, see Brković 2010.
2. The local administrative and police unit in the SFRY.
3. For a critique of civil society as a normative ideal during postsocialist transformations, see also Hann and Dunn 1996; Bilić 2012; Stubbs 2007.
4. Agency for Statistics of Bosnia and Herzegovina 2016.

Chapter 2

Favors Reproduce Social Personhood

"I don't think that *štela* is something to be proud of, or that a person should think that getting a job via a *štela* is a normal thing to do." Marina, a student, said this to me one day while we were sitting on a bench in front of a local language school she attended. Marina recounted a story about her cousin, who entered the local hospital during his wife's delivery with a gun. This family could not find a *štela* to the gynecology department, so the man went armed into the hospital to make sure that the doctors would do their best to protect his spouse. As violent and scary as this story sounds, it reflects a strong aversion to *veze* and *štele*. In Marina's eyes, in "normal" countries people are not driven to the verge of madness for not having a strong *štela*. Most of my interlocutors did not prefer getting things done through favors, but they kept pursuing them nonetheless. They usually criticized the state for making work, welfare, and healthcare unpredictable and uncertain and other people for "doing everything" via *veze* and *štele*.

People repeatedly asserted that *ne možeš naći posao bez veze* (you can't find work without a connection), *ne možeš se liječiti bez veza* (you can't get treatment without a connection), *kod nas sve može i ništa ne može* (here, "everything is possible and nothing is possible"), *u ovoj državi ništa ne radi* (nothing works in this state), and so forth. However, although my interlocutors criticized favors as a general characteristic of BiH society, they would describe those who personally helped them to get something via a *štela* through idioms of morality and friendship—the "patrons" were "good," "moral," and "caring" persons who help "more than a sibling would." This chapter explores how people in BiH relied on favors to get things done, using idioms of morality and friendship, even if they did not appreciate the need to do so.

With respect to Eastern Europe, interpretations of favors may be grouped into three broad perspectives. I will refer to them as "culturalist," "systemic," and "moral" arguments and offer a brief overview of each in this chapter. The culturalist perspective explains away favors as a part of Bosnian culture or mentality, ascribing timeless, essentialized qualities to BiH and its citizens. The systemic interpretation was developed as a critique of culturalist arguments. It presents favors as a sensible and rational response to transforming postsocialist systems marked by incomplete, dysfunctional, or partly functional markets and democracies. In doing so, the systemic interpretation of favors also does something potentially dangerous: it reproduces a particular idea of how "proper" polities, markets, and democracies are organized.

Drawing from the repertoire of concepts concerning development, this interpretation implies that if Eastern European countries were to consistently model themselves on the political and economic systems present in Western Europe, there would be no need for favors. However, interpreting favors as local responses to failing statehood and dysfunctional institutions perpetuates the hegemonic story about the inevitable direction of progress and modernization, thus impoverishing the political imagination. By taking the political, economic, and social systems in BiH as the most relevant frame of reference, the systemic explanation of favors does not take into account that favors may shape personhoods. It also fails to demonstrate how favors become entangled with transnational processes.

Critical toward the systemic perspective, some ethnographic studies of Eastern Europe focus on the morality of favors. A moral perspective suggests that Eastern Europeans want to obtain things in a veering way, because favors provide the means of carving oneself into a particular moral person (Humphrey 2012). Grounded in Laidlaw's framing of ethics as "the possibility of choosing the kind of self one wishes to be" (2002: 324), this interpretation of favors points to the importance of sociohistorically conditioned choice. While it may provide a useful lens for thinking about some instances of favors, most of my interlocutors did not quite prefer getting things done through favors. They tried to personalize the state through *veze* and *štele* even when it seemed there was no instrumental reason to do so, while condemning the whole thing.

This chapter suggests that *veze* and *štele* persist in BiH because they shape people's social personhoods—and in so doing, have implications for the reproduction of power. In terms of Edmund Leach (1993), *veze* and *štele* are metaphorical, rather than metonymic, relations. *Veze* and *štele* are tools for translating the language of citizenship rights into the language of care and personal relations and vice versa. They provide a historically meaningful way of locating oneself at the "intersections," rather than the "interstices," of networks linking the state to society (Alexander 2002: 150; see also Vetters 2014).

Deeply rooted in historic legacies of BiH, they helped my interlocutors to reproduce their unequal sociopolitical positions, to make the state work for them, and to remind the state officials that they have certain responsibilities to others both as citizens and as socially located persons. As we will see throughout the following chapters, the need to be both a citizen and a socially located person, when accessing public welfare resources, is not a specifically Bosnian and Herzegovinian, or a Balkan, or an Eastern European peculiarity. Rather, this need has been emphasized by global redefinitions of responsibilities for others away from welfare state–based models, toward something else. The significance of *veze* and *štele* in BiH sheds some light on how global changes in state–citizen relations have been undertaken and to what effects.

Samra: Finding a Wheelchair for Her Son

Samra was a fortysomething Bosniak woman living in a rusty, one-bedroom house with her mother and two sons. One of Samra's sons had severe and multiple developmental difficulties, including paraplegia. Samra's family lived off the meager social welfare help the state provided and Samra's occasional work as a fortune-teller. A certain number of (mostly, but not only) women from the Town regularly visited Samra to have their fortune read using a technique, popular in the region, in which one's fortune is read from a freshly drunk empty coffee cup (described below in more detail). Others visited her for dream interpretations or a fortune-telling based on Samra's visions. I regularly visited Samra in her home. There was no need to let her know I was planning to visit in advance, for it seemed as if guests were always in the living room.

Over a number of shared coffees and beers, I found out that Samra had been married to a Serbian man. She had stayed in the Town throughout the war, following the common pattern of women staying in, or moving to the territories held by the national group to which their husband belonged during the war. However, when their son with developmental difficulties was born in the early postwar years, Samra's husband left, never to return. Samra frequently referred to herself as a "cabbage woman" or a "cabbage girl" (*kupu-sarka*). Since the area around the Town was known for producing delicious cabbage, this was a way of inscribing herself into a place she felt to be her home and to claim her sense of belonging to the Town beyond the ethnonational categories of Bosniaks, Bosnian Serbs, and Bosnian Croats.

At the same time, Samra was convinced that her son's developmental difficulties were caused by a national hatred that the Bosnian Serb medical staff in the Town's hospital had expressed during the baby's delivery. Recounting to me a number of nationalist insults they had directed at her as a Muslim (Bosniak) over the course of the delivery, she said she was convinced that the doctors did not do all they could to help her and her baby and, instead, treated her complicated delivery unprofessionally. She was also convinced that with a strong *veza/štela* within the hospital, none of this would have happened. This suggests that Samra believed that *veze/štele* could trump nationalist hatred, even in the early postwar years. However, since neither she nor her husband had power or influence in the Town, Samra was left to herself.

After her husband left, Samra had to rely on social protection provisions, having no other options and having no one else with whom she could leave her developmentally challenged son for eight working hours. Samra's mother was around, but at her age she was in need of care herself and certainly was not in a position to provide it. One way of supplementing their income, consisting of the welfare aid and her mother's pension, was to intensify her fortune-telling activities. In 2009 and 2010, women who came to Samra's home to have their fortunes read brought coffee and sweets and left five to twenty convertible marks (approximately two and a half to ten euros) after the session was over.

One day, while we were having coffee with her neighbor Ismeta, Samra recounted the story of how her son got the wheelchair. Dragana, a woman who ran a nongovernmental organization (NGO) working with people with paraplegia, obtained—as a humanitarian aid for Samra's son—two custom-made wheelchairs from Banja Luka, the capital of the BiH entity Republika Srpska. Samra knew Dragana "by sight" (*iz viđenja*). The first time Dragana came to Samra's house to talk about the wheelchair, they shared a coffee. After finishing their drinks, Samra read Dragana's future from the leftover coffee sediment. Dragana took Samra's son's measures, which were required for constructing the wheelchairs. A couple of weeks later, Samra received the two custom-made wheelchairs. Importantly,

Samra recounted to me how she sometimes read coffee for social workers who, as a part of their official duties, visited her house from time to time. Some social workers refused this personalization of their expert-user relationship, while others welcomed it.

As in many other places across the Balkans, coffee was made in the Town by adding ground coffee to boiling water and then waiting for the mixture to boil once again. Sugar and sometimes milk were added after the second time the coffee was brought to the boil, according to taste. The coffee grains were large enough to leave sediment in the cup. After drinking the coffee, the cup would be turned upside down and the sediment would start sliding down the internal walls of the cup. After five to ten minutes, a coffee reader would turn the cup back over and start reading from the Rorschach-like shapes left by the sliding sediment on the cup's walls. Different marks, numbers, and letters had different meanings. There were "his-and-hers" sides of the cup as well as a side that concerned the past and a side that offered a glimpse into the future.

The anthropologist Elissa Helms suggests that the coffee-drinking relationship among BiH women is crucial for thinking about postwar reconciliation, because it was a "marker of normal(ized) relationships, implying a level of communication if not trust" (2010: 24; see also Stefansson 2010). Coffee drinking was a practice embedded "in wider patterns of neighborly relations and mutual aid, those relationships most violently and physically disrupted by ethnic cleansing" (Helms 2010: 24). In other words, those with whom you would share a cup of coffee at your house were those with whom you wanted to establish and maintain some degree of cooperation, mutual care, and help.

For Samra, sharing coffee was a means of embroiling social workers and NGO representatives in a kind of relationship that resonated with the meanings attached to neighborly relations (*komšiluk*). In this case, the wheelchair was not the result of a *veza:* it was the result of a humanitarian donation. Dragana contacted Samra first, and Samra's son would have probably received the chair with or without coffee readings. However, Dragana might not have remembered Samra as a potential recipient of the wheelchair if she had not already known her by sight. Samra's attempts to personalize her relationship with NGO and social workers is telling, conveying dominant ideas about welfare support and "how things get done" in the Town.

By presenting herself as a fortune-teller (*gatara*), Samra tried to stay on the radar of social and humanitarian workers by inscribing herself into their social worlds. She did not have a great deal of *veze* and *štele* linking her with influential people in the Town. Instead, she tried to personalize relationships and cultivate potential *veze* and *štele* by providing something like a countergift for public welfare support, in line with her resources and abilities.

Samra thought that simply being a citizen was not enough to obtain enough welfare support. Without a *veza*, without someone to take care of her in a personalized manner, her delivery turned into a terrible experience, during which she was insulted and shamed on nationalist grounds while her baby ended up severely disabled. In order to gain the best welfare support possible, Samra performed her gendered and religious self so that she could personalize her relationship with providers of welfare support, evoking the solidarity and sociality of *komšiluk* (neighborhood).

This tells us a lot about Samra's perceptions of the state. It is also indicative of how people often got things done in practice. I believe this was a smart move, because, as we shall see in chapters three and four, without having some kind of personal relationship with social workers, the users of social services could not predict whether and when they would be informed about new social provisions that they had a right to obtain. Instead of citizens' rights, this enactment of public welfare support was grounded in ideas about duty and care, practiced in and through personal relationships. But before we focus on how *veze* and *štele* affected citizenship practices in the second part of the book, let us examine how favors in Eastern Europe have been interpreted in popular and academic discourses.

Mentality Rooted in Biology and History: Culturalist Explanations

> *Štela, veza*—that's just part of our mentality.
> —Milena, a forty-something woman

> The internationals do not just use *štela*, buuuuuuuuuuuuut … i.e., perhaps there would be no *štela* if only foreigners worked there, but Bosnian mentality in the form of nepotism has sneaked into all spheres in which international organizations operate—it is startling to hear how many friends and family and husbands get pushed into mysterious new jobs, ahhh! And our people form the majority of the staff in all international organizations, so it's completely obvious. I, for instance, never got a job via *štela*—

since I am not from here and I didn't know anyone "important," but I know of many different cases.
— An anonymous internet forum user

In numerous everyday and popular accounts, the need to get things
done through favors is often interpreted by making references to
"mentality." Understood as rooted in culture and history, and sometimes in biology, mentality frequently serves as a justification for
the need to pursue favors in BiH. My interlocutors in the Town often described *veze* and *štele* as largely inescapable, as if they spread
throughout all of society and the state. As the quotations above illustrate, people talked about *veze* and *štele* as part of "our mentality" —
as something one pursued to get things done, whether or not they
liked this way of doing things.

The idea that *veze* and *štele* result from a specific mentality is popular in former Yugoslav countries. The notion of mentality refers to
a set of psychological and cultural characteristics presumably shared
by all conationals (or all inhabitants of a particular region). As one
"of the most abused mythologemes in journalistic and, generally, in
popular discourse" (Todorova 2004: 5), "Balkan mentality" was often used by my interlocutors to explain why people pursued favors
even when there was no apparent need to do so.

Yet they did not always take the Balkans as their frame of reference. As the two quotations above indicate, people often referred
to "our mentality," or switched between "Bosnian" and "our" mentality when discussing *veze* and *štele.* Depending on their personal
political viewpoints, people in the Town evoked Bosnian or Serbian
mentality and, perhaps most frequently, "our mentality" (*naš men-
talitet*). This reflects a popular narrative strategy in former Yugoslav
countries: referring to the language, culture, or political situation as
"ours" allows users to talk about all kinds of thing without making
political statements about nationality (Jansen 2005a).

The vagueness sometimes inscribed into the pronouns "we" (*mi*)
and "our" (*naš*) offers people a means of discussing a variety of topics — south Slavic language varieties, former Yugoslav nationalities, or
regions — without making them fit within strict national categories.
In other words, saying "our language" (instead of Bosnian, Croatian, Montenegrin, or Serbian) allows one to avoid the question of
defining who is a speaker of what language or a member of which
nationality (if any) while simultaneously being concise and clear.
Therefore, claiming that "our mentality" explained the persistence
of *veze* and *štele* enabled my interlocutors to express their point of

view, while who "we" were, as defined in precise national terms, remained ambiguous.

Bosnians were not the only group who made use of mentality as an interpretative framework. The international humanitarian and developmental workers in BiH explained many of their everyday problems in a similar manner—by invoking the concepts of "socialist mentality" and "Bosnian mentality." Coles notes:

> Although internationals blamed the prior socialist government and mentality for a variety of ills, such as dependency, low tolerance of risk, and market obstacles, this rationale was deemphasized in daily life. Rather, Bosnians' negative qualities, which were perceived as hampering their progress into the modern capitalist arena, were often naturalized and taken out of their historical context. (2007: 81)

Along similar lines, Bose suggests that many in the international community in BiH would undoubtedly reply affirmatively to the question of whether "ordinary Bosnians have a herd-mentality with no conception of where their 'real' interests lie, that they do not appreciate the international community's enormous investment in rebuilding Bosnia from rubble, and that they are intent on actively sabotaging their own future" (2002: 9).

As a set of psychological and cultural characteristics wired into our brains, mentality is sometimes understood as being conditioned by nature. On other occasions, mentality is assumed to be the result of BiH historical legacies: socialist rule, the experience of Ottoman and/or Austro-Hungarian rule, and so forth. Irrespective of whether this explanatory mode assumes that *veze* and *štele* persist because of biology or because of history, it enacts a Balkanist discourse through which people, places, and practices in the Balkans appear to be eternally ambiguous and stubbornly nonmodern (Todorova 2009; see also Bakić-Hayden 1995; Čolović 2013; Njaradi 2012; Obad 2014).

Culturalist explanations rely on what Wright (1998) calls an "old" anthropological understanding of culture as a homogeneous and small-scale system of meanings evenly shared by all members of one discrete group. Such a conception of culture has received extensive criticism in social anthropology because its analytical and explanatory potential is very limited and because it is politically problematic (Kuper 1999). The idea that *veze* and *štele* persist because of Bosnian culture or mentality contributes to the process of essentializing and othering Bosnians as somehow nonmodern and non-European.

Early postsocialist studies criticized culturalist ideas about favors precisely on these grounds, developing a different line of interpretation in response that focuses on characteristics of nationally defined economic and political systems.

The Systemic Perspective

Ledeneva's (1998) argument that the pursuit of favors in Russia constitutes a specific kind of economy—an economy of favors—has inspired numerous studies of the intersections between favors and economic practices. The systemic perspective suggests that the responsibility for perpetuating the need for favors lies in the transitioning political and economic systems of particular countries. From such a perspective, favors were a strategy employed to deal with the shortages and other problems of socialist economic systems, and they persist today because postsocialist economies are still flawed, although in a different way.

The systemic perspective was developed as a criticism of the idea that *blat* (a concept that refers to various informal practices in Russia) remained important after the fall of socialism because it is somehow ingrained in the "Russian soul." Ledeneva historicizes *blat* by pointing out that it has served different needs in different historical moments. During socialism, *blat* developed "together with the regime and reflected its changes"; at first it provided "the basic necessities such as food, jobs, and living space," and later on "the more sophisticated needs of late socialism associated with education, mobility and consumerism" (2009: 260). In the postsocialist period, new types of shortages appeared, and *blat* today fulfils the very different needs of a flawed market economy: "Access to money, making a living, and getting a well-paid job become the 'new power' of personal networks" (ibid.: 264). Ledeneva explicitly suggests that postsocialist informalities present a way of compensating for the defects of the market economy:

> In the same way that the planned economy was not really a planned economy and was actually run with [the] help of *tolkachi* ("pushers" for the plan completion in industry), *blat* (use of personal networks for getting things done), *pripiski* (false reporting) and other informal practices, the market economy today is not really a market economy. This is due primarily to the key role that unwritten rules still play in the system. The state is partly responsible. (2011: 723)

Thus, the systemic perspective suggests that "it's not the people, it's the system" that pushes people to rely on informality.

The market economy is still not *really* a market economy; the young democracy and the new public administrations are still maturing. The system is full of flaws and inconsistencies—and therein lies the need to pursue favors. The informal way of getting things done presents a rational and sensible strategy for living in and dealing with (post)socialist ambiguous legal, political, and economic environments. By taking the nation–state—that is, the national economy and national politics—as the main unit of reference, the systemic perspective reproduces the Westphalian political imaginary. It perpetuates the image of postsocialist countries as not quite properly modern and as not having fully caught up with the West. It also reflects a specific politics of knowledge in which studies of concepts such as "the market" and "democracy" in non-Western contexts may be utilized "only as sources of the local and particular knowledge required for constructing the universal knowledge of the discipline" (Mitchell 2004: 101). As Morris and Polese argue:

> These and similar conceptualizations of informality as one of a number of barriers to post-socialist societies' "normal" development towards market capitalism and democratic governance are part of a continuing "transitological" approach to studying post-socialist countries … variously rehashed as developmental and modernization theory, but always having a normative framework and hinging on a teleological view of "transition" towards "democratization" and an Anglo-American vision of post-Fordist market institutions. (2014: 6)

Importantly, in the systemic perspective, the "system" that is in transformation is imagined as a (nation–)state: people in Russia obtain things through *blat* because the Russian market economy is still not really a market economy. Bosnians get things done through *veze* and *štele* because the BiH state is underdeveloped.[1] Informal networks in which favors were exchanged "have helped develop the postcommunist or postsocialist (as anthropologists refer to it) academic field" (Ledeneva 2009: 266). These informal networks of exchanging favors may also help us understand how global shifts in ideas about responsibility for survival and well-being were translated to Eastern European contexts.

The systemic perspective does not appear to translate too well into ethnographic arguments. A focus on fallacies pertaining to economic and political systems cannot explain in what way *štela* sneaked into the international organizations, which presumably had good resources and financial support, as the second quotation above illustrates. Neither can it help us understand how, sometimes, people in the Town pursued *veze* although the official system seemed to be in order. Most of my interlocutors did need a *veza* and *štela* to obtain something that otherwise they could not reach. And then there were occasional examples of people like Samra and Sanja (see chapter one) who personalized institutional relationships and pursued favors even when there was no clear systemic obstacle standing in their way. These "unnecessary" efforts suggest that *veze* and *štele* were not just strategic tools people used to overcome weaknesses of the BiH economy and politics.

As a matter of fact, my interlocutors did not discuss the BiH state as weak but as removed from their everyday needs and struggles. They claimed that the BiH state allowed some people to do and to have everything, while others could not obtain anything. The problem was the unpredictable selectiveness of welfare state institutions, more than their weakness. People throughout BiH used *veze* and *štele* to make the selectively (dis)interested state work for them—to ensure that they would not fall through the growing gaps of welfare programs and services. Pursuits of favors included locating people and thus achieving a particular form of ordering in which local, personal knowledge about people overlapped with institutional knowledge.

I Prefer *Veze:* Moral Arguments

Some anthropological criticisms of a systemic perspective focus on the moralities attached to favors. A number of anthropologists have demonstrated that informal engagements in Eastern Europe affect how people see themselves as moral beings. For instance, Pine criticizes developmental discourses on corruption and criminality in Poland by suggesting that the gray economy "has its own kind of morality that links it to the family and household, relations of trust, and extended sociality" (2015: 25). Despite their pervasiveness, not all gray activities are subsumed under the "positive morality of a domestic ethos" (ibid.: 31). Only the gray activities that are intimate and interpersonal are valued as moral. Gray activities in public arenas, including top-level politics, and organized business are perceived as immoral or amoral by Pine's interlocutors.

Similarly, Humphrey criticizes systemic explanations of favors because of their insistence on economic rationality. She suggests that favors in Mongolia and Russia are more than ways of compensating for Soviet shortages or for flaws of postsocialist systems. In her reading, favors persist because they affect people's sense of self and confer a sense of self-worth: "Favors choose people and make them feel special" (2012: 36). Getting things done in a "veering" way in Russia and Mongolia confirms personal ingenuity and social standing in the eyes of others. Humphrey also suggests that, because of this moral aesthetic, people *prefer* favors to following official procedures:

> Many people prefer the "favor mode"—in other words, they will do things this way even if it is perfectly feasible to adopt the official route. Performing an action as a favor adds a "gratuitous" extra to any practical function it might have and turns the act into something that is incalculable. (2012: 23)

This point reflects Laidlaw's (2002) argument that moral practices differ from social ones because morality requires an element of personal choice. Unraveling Durkheim's conflation of social and moral facts, Laidlaw suggests that morality is founded upon a (socially and historically grounded) possibility of choosing what kind of a person one wants to be and of carving oneself into that particular personhood.

If personhood is socially shaped, morality entails the freedom to decide which particular personhood to pursue. This understanding of freedom does not imply that one can be whatever one wants to be. It is more an acknowledgement of the fact that society is not a discrete homogeneous whole with a singular morality and that people actively engage on a day-to-day basis with particular socially and historically grounded selfhoods. In Foucault's (1978, 1984, 1990) terms, freedom implies the ability to choose which of the available "technologies of self" one will pursue. Thus, ethnographic arguments that focus on the specific moralities of favors are based on an assumption that people willfully make personal choices about whether to get things done in a veering way. Carving oneself into what Humphrey (2012) calls a "normal hero" means *choosing* to get things done through favors; every pursuit of a favor is, then, an instance in which one reproduces oneself as a clever, resourceful person, valued in the eyes of others.

When people do not prefer or willingly choose to do things via favors, then we are talking about social, rather than moral, entanglements between favors and personhoods. This is the case with *veze* and *štele*. Although favors in socialist and postsocialist contexts may offer a persuasive language of friendship and morality for voicing political and everyday claims (Buck 2006), they should not necessarily be regarded as cultural values to be respected.

Ong's work indicates that in China using kinship and friendship relations, called *guanxi*, for professional purposes should not be analytically regarded as a value of Chinese culture, because it is a deeply unfair, contextually specific practice that operates as "basically a structure of limits and inequality for the many" and provides opportunities only for the few (Ong 1999: 117; see also Danielsson 2014). I suggest that people did not see *veze* and *štele* in the Town as a particularly moral endeavor because structural links between favors and power and inequality (discussed in Part Three) were often perfectly clear to them.

As the second quotation above illustrates, many people claimed that "everybody else" relied on favors, but not them ("I, for instance, never got a job via *štela*—since I am not from here and I didn't know anyone 'important,' but I know of many different cases"). When my interlocutors did describe their own pursuits of favors, they did not quite express a sense of self-worth as a "normal hero." They expressed gratefulness to the favor providers, but their stories sounded more like a confession. For instance, one day I was having a coffee with a young employee of the municipal government named Petra. Petra and I first met several months before, during a humanitarian event she helped to organize. Afterward, we met regularly for coffee in a local café whose walls were covered in mirrors, and she assisted me in obtaining information from others in the municipal government.

This day, Petra described how she managed to secure a permanent position through *veze* in her political party with a mixture of entitlement, resignation, and defensiveness. In a low voice, she recounted how her parents and a parents' friend got involved, pulled the strings among the higher party officials, and managed to get Petra permanent employment. In Petra's view, with a university degree and excellent grades, she had the right to a decent job. Petra said that if it took a *veza* to access something she had a right to, so be it. The mixture of gratefulness and resignation and the confessional tone with which my interlocutors commonly discussed *veze* and *štele* indicate that they did not enjoy pursuing them. If people found some value in doing things in a veering way in the Town during my research, it was a tainted value—not something to brag about.

However, I think it is important to remember that people do not have to like particular forms of relating to others for these forms to be socially effective. We do not need to appreciate the strings—categories, practices, relationships—that shape us in order to be shaped by them. In other words, although many people in BiH seemed to dislike the veering way of doing things, *veze* and *štele* did help produce particular kinds of personhood. The kinds of *veze* one could pursue reestablished who one was as a social being relative to other people. In different ways for different people, *veze* and *štele* reproduced people's gendered, aging, nationalized, professional, and many other kinds of a sense of self as well as new and ambiguous forms of power. If in Soviet Poland, informal activities "often evoked in their protagonists both pride and shame—pride in having ingeniously gamed the system, shame in having lowered oneself to do so" (Wedel 2009: 53), in postwar, postsocialist BiH, there was no clear system to be gamed.

However, there were things people thought they had a right to. The sense of entitlement Petra articulated was an important aspect of talk about *veze* and *štele*. Drawing upon the socialist heritage or personal experiences of life in socialist Yugoslavia, many of my interlocutors felt they had a right to free, quality healthcare, a well-paid job, social welfare provision if they were unable to work, stable housing, a decent pension, and having a family. As mentioned earlier, my interlocutors often expressed what Jansen (2015) calls "yearnings for 'normal lives.'" This was wonderfully summarized in Zoran's statement when he said, "Even though my state does not need me, I need it" (*Ako mene moja država ne treba, meni ona treba*). This yearning presented a criticism of life as mere survival (*preživljavanje*) and articulated hopes for the kind of life that is protected through predictable and stable welfare structures.

Even Though My State Does Not Need Me, I Need It

Zoran, the man who called for an ambulance to come for his father (see the Introduction), told me a story one day about a young man who had graduated with honors from the Faculty of Medicine a couple of years earlier. Allegedly this man could not find a job, so he made a press release that stated, "If my state does not need me, I don't need it" and announced that he would leave the country. He got a job a day later. Zoran joked and said he would do the same, only he would say, "Even though my state does not need me, I need it."

The story suggests that Zoran yearned for a state that would guarantee greater predictability and certainty in everyday life. Zoran was looking for a job when he told me the story and, in order to connect himself to the state, he looked for a *štela*. His job search did not involve following websites or newspapers for job posts. There was only one library in the Town and Zoran had several options: he could either find a connection (*veza/štela*) that would enable him to get a job there, move to another town where he would also need to find a *veza/štela* for a library job, or change professions and do something else.

He got his B.A. in library studies from the University of Belgrade in December 2009. Zoran was thirty-two years old and, as was the case for most unmarried people of his age, he lived with his parents in an apartment in the center of the Town. He was in a long-term relationship and both he and his partner were looking for jobs so they could move in together. Zoran's family had been living in the Town before the war. His mother identified as a Muslim (Bosniak), while his father considered himself to be an Orthodox Serb. Zoran, on the other hand, claimed he was not interested in people's nationalities and was a follower of several strands of New Age philosophies. His interest in religion was significant and he frequently quoted various religious thinkers in his everyday talk, regardless of whether they were linked with Confucianism, Islam, Orthodox or Catholic Christianity, or Judaism.

Zoran's invocation of the state was not just confined to anecdotes and stories. He went to the director of the main town library to talk with him. The director told him to be patient, stating that while he was willing to employ him, he could not at that time. Zoran hoped he would get the job for at least one year under a state-run program of youth probationary employment. Under the program, young people worked on a trial basis in public institutions and the government paid their (very low) salaries. The procedure to apply for the program involved several steps. When the government announces a new round of the program, the public institutions tell the government which job posts they need the most and the government decides the actual number of jobs they will fund. Once this number is known, institutions announce a call for applications, young people apply directly to the institutions, and the institutions select employees from these applicants.

In order to get a job, Zoran did not issue a press release. Instead, he chased up his connections (*veze/štele*) to convince the director of the library to ask the government for a new job post. He went to various public institutions to talk with people there, hoping to find a *veza/štela* to the library director. He returned repeatedly to the library and befriended several library employees. Zoran did not know exactly who the "right people" were, so he invested a lot of effort into finding this out. Once, Zoran and I went together to the library and ended up talking with the newest employee for an hour. Standing in the poorly lit corridor, we learned about the informal hierarchies and personal traits of the library managers from this young woman. She also told Zoran who the members of the board of governors of the library were so that he could see whether he might find a *veza/ štela* connecting him with one of them.

She advised him to find someone who would convince the director to ask for more job posts from the government. At one moment, she said, "Ask Ratka to push it. If anyone can, she can." Ratka was a woman with many functions in the Town whose ability to help others in their pursuit of favors was well known. I got to know many people who she helped and I heard many more stories about Ratka providing favors for others. As we will see in chapter five, Ratka seamlessly moved across and translated between different orders of knowledge and practice. Her political influence in the Town was largely the result of her helping others to pursue *veze* and *štele* within public and private welfare arenas—merging the duties and obligations of the state with humanitarian and personalized care, both in narrative and in practice.

Ratka's daughter was the best friend of Zoran's partner and also Zoran's friend. Zoran asked his partner to help him contact Ratka and his partner spoke with Ratka's daughter. She then told Ratka, her mother, about Zoran's job hunt. Ratka decided to help Zoran get the job. The government announced a new round of openings in the program, the library advertised for new employees, and Zoran got the job. He got it as a part of the program but also thanks to Ratka: "*Ratka je to sredila*" (Ratka sorted it out), he said.

Performing Social Personhood

By now it is clear that the terms *veze* and *štele* were used in the Town to mark very different kinds of relations, some of which were imbued with gendered or religious meanings, others with age-related or kinship-based meanings, and so forth. The concrete pursuits of *veze* and *štele*—on the part of Zoran, Samra, and Sanja as well as hundreds of others—do not point to an abstract, formal consistency. Instead, in my experience, they did something different each time, depending on the person involved in the act and the people with whom she could get in touch.

For instance, Zoran's *veza* to a job was an "extended" relationship, since it involved at least five people. It reflected love, friendship, and kinship relations between Zoran, his partner, her best friend, and the best friend's mother, Ratka. On the other hand, Samra's attempt to personalize relationships with NGO and social workers was dyadic and marked by gendered meanings of neighborly help. Zoran's pursuit of favors was quite different from Samra's. Since they were different people, they drew from different repertoires of claims and evoked the responsibility of others in different ways.

As *blat* does in Russia, what one *veza/štela* entails, another *veza/ štela* may not (see Ledeneva 1998).[2] It *could* involve sexist expectations but does not necessarily (Brković 2015a). It could imply a nationalist bond—whereby a Bosnian Serb would especially help another Bosnian Serb, but not a Bosniak; but again, it does not have to. And so forth. People's social positioning influenced the directions in which they could pursue favors and also how much choice they had in this. Success (or failure) in finding someone to do a favor for you was partly a consequence of people's differing social positions. At the same time, the kinds of favors that people were *able* to pursue shaped their social positions.

Dunn (2004) suggests that the system of favors in Poland, called *znajomości*, offers a way of interpreting personhood as a composite of social relations. When Polish people engage in *znajomości* to obtain goods or to negotiate jobs and services, they reproduce their personhoods as entities embedded in and constituted from multiple links with other human beings. Therefore, *znajomości* refers to the important work of constituting oneself as a social person through one's relationships with others. Similarly in Turkey, as mentioned in chapter one, social personhoods—those that are made via favors—are not fixed within one sociopolitical network but "inhabit a whole variety of networks of different types, complexity, and, often, conflicting demands" (Alexander 2002: 19).

In her discussion of the personalization of the state in Turkey, Alexander asserts that looking into how people make connections with one another, to push forward or block administrative objectives, entails "a parallel exploration of personhood" (2002: 22). This is because personhood, as a sociohistorically situated sense of self, is shaped by a variety of mutually intersecting relations—including national, gendered, racialized, sexualized, and class-based ones (see McCall 2005). In a similar manner, both Zoran and Samra reproduced their respective social positions and performed their personhoods. Favors, thus, persist not just because the official "system" does not work but because they shape who people are socially. Social personhood is a relational entity and the pursuit of relations (*veze/štele*) was constitutive of it.

In his study of clientelism among impoverished people in Argentina, Auyero criticizes the idea of "much of the academic discourse … [that] interest is the driving force behind much of the support that political patrons and brokers obtain from their 'clients'" (2001: 13). He suggests that clientelist informal problem-solving networks do two things at the same time: they ensure material survival and reproduce shared cultural representations and identities. Webs of social relations that brokers cultivate with their clients and an array of common cultural idioms may be of greater importance for those involved than the goods and benefits they acquire in this way. In Argentina, political clientelism merged with rational self-interest and sociocultural investments, providing impoverished people a means to survive in both a material and a social sense.

However, there is an important difference between Auyero's ethnographic study and my interlocutors in BiH. In Argentina, clientelism was related to a clear political identity of being a Peronist. Clientelist practices contributed to the reproduction of the shared political identity of Peronists and vice versa: their shared sense of belonging to a group of Peronists fostered clientelist forms of dependence. In BiH, on the other hand, there was no overarching social or political framework that subsumed different pursuits of favors. *Veze* and *štele* flourished both within and outside of the political parties and they were different for different people. The exact meaning of each *veza* or *štela* depended on both the person who made the pursuit and the people she pursued. In brief, my interlocutors reproduced various kinds of identities and different elements of their social personhoods when pursuing favors.

When *veze*—which literally translates as "relations"—are approached as relations that reproduce particular social personhoods, both Samra's and Zoran's efforts make sense. From such a perspective, Samra's decision to transform an official administrative relationship into a personal one is not so surprising: *veze* and *štele* were not just a mechanism used to gain access to a scarce resource or to overcome an administrative obstacle on the way to a resource. They were also a way to reiterate who Samra was as a social being and her position of being a fortune-teller (*gatara*) in the world of people (*svijet*) that she inhabited within the Town. *Veze* and *štele* enabled people to perform their personhoods, while obtaining access to various public and private resources.

Zoran, on the other hand, did face an obstacle: he had to pursue *veze/štele* if he wanted the job in the library. Still, his pursuit of *veze* and *štele* meant cultivating relations and his social personhood along the way. He returned repeatedly to the library, befriended people who worked there, and worked on becoming a part of their everyday routines. By asking his girlfriend to ask her best friend and her mother Ratka for help, Zoran reinstated himself as a partner and as a friend. He had to be a part of the "world of people" (*svijet*) of the library employees, as well as a part of Ratka's *svijet,* to get the job. The product of his pursuit of favors was thus not just the job but a particular sense of self, others, and the unequal relations between them. Most often, when people pursued *veze* and *štele,* they reproduced hierarchically ordered social networks they could access and their position within these networks.

The kinds of *veze* and *štele* people could access depended on—and reproduced—what kind of and how powerful a social person they were. This is why people would say, "*Everything is possible and nothing is possible*"—what mattered at one point for one person did not have to matter at another point for a different person.

Metaphoric Links

Despite the experiential heterogeneity of *veze* and *štele,* all of these relations shared something: they had to be actively pursued and they allowed people to translate across different social languages. The explanation for why my interlocutors perceived such diverse pursuits of *veze* and *štele* as more or less the same thing—why they recognized and discussed various ways of making a link to others as a *veza* or a *štela*—may lie in the characteristics of these relations in translating expectations across social orders. Through them, people merged expectations of friendships and administrations, personalized care and public social welfare, socially grounded personhoods and citizenship. If *veze/štele* cannot be understood as one discrete entity, it is because they enabled people to make links between different orders of knowledge and experience and to navigate different expectations. The work of Edmund Leach is useful for thinking about this, because it focuses on the different forms a relationship can take.

Leach (1993) made a distinction between metonymical and metaphorical relations. In his terminology, a "*metonymical link*" between entity A and entity B exists when A and B belong to the same "code," or the same "order": in other words, they are metonymically linked when they can be read in the same way, as a part of the same chain of signs. For example, the link between written musical notes is metonymical, since they belong to the same code of the musical alphabet. The link between letters B and C is also metonymical, since they belong to the same code of the English alphabet. On the other hand, a *"metaphorical link"* between entity A and entity B exists when A and B do not belong to the same code, or the same order. The relationship between musical notes written on a piece of paper and the finger movements of a musician is metaphorical, since notes and finger movements do not belong to the same code—one is the code of musical notes; the other is the code of finger movements.

Metaphorical links cannot be read in the same way but require the translation of one code (notes) into another (finger movements). In Leach's terms, *veze* and *štele* are metaphorical relations: people used *veze* and *štele* to translate the bureaucratic and public language of citizenship into the language of personalized relations and vice versa. They presented a way of displaying the rational as the compassionate distribution of public resources and vice versa. Zoran was required to make an official application for a government-funded program of youth probationary employment to get a job for one year—but this was not enough on its own. In order to induce willingness in the library director to ask the government to fund a temporary job post, he had to make himself visible and knowable as a particular social person through a chain of people.

Similarly, in order to learn about new welfare provisions, Samra always followed the official protocols *and* made herself visible and knowable as a particular kind of a social person to the social and NGO workers. Dissatisfied with the prescriptions she received for her daughter, Sanja turned to her informal parental support group to help her find a personal link to another doctor, convinced that without such a personal link, medical practitioners would not invest enough care and effort in the treatment (see chapter one). In this way, over the course of my fieldwork, people constantly made metaphorical links when accessing welfare; they presented themselves as both citizens and socially located persons—daughters, friends, boyfriends, sons, kin, fortune-tellers, and so forth—and negotiated different codes in their pursuit of welfare.

Thus, although experientially different—because they worked among persons socially situated in particular ways—*veze* and *štele* had systemic effects. When the numerous individual pursuits of favors to access public and private resources in BiH are taken together, their effect on the relationship between the state and society becomes apparent. Citizens experience BiH as a state differently after the end of the war for at least four reasons, favors being one of them.

First, people's experiences of the state depended on how skillful they were in cultivating bonds with "the right people" and evoking their compassion, alongside the language of citizens' rights. Second, experiences of the state depended on where one lived, since each entity, canton, and the Brčko district had its own welfare laws (Maglajlić-Holiček and Rašidagić 2007). Third, people experienced the state differently depending on what sense of national belonging they claimed in their place of residence—on whether they belonged to the local ethnonational majority or minority (Human Rights Watch 2000). Fourth, all of this was affected by whether the dominant emphasis of building BiH statehood at that moment was placed on postwar reconstruction and reconciliation, the postsocialist transformation of property relations, and/or EU membership. As we will see in the following chapters, EU member state building and the redefinition of public and private duties and obligations made the pursuit of *veze* and *štele* particularly relevant, in a new way.

Conclusion

In this chapter, I took something from systemic and moral arguments, and left something aside, in order to make sense of the gap between people's dissatisfaction with favors and their persistent pursuit of favors. From moral arguments, I take the idea that *veze* and *štele* reproduce personhood. What gets left aside is the assumption that Bosnians prefer *veze* and *štele* because of this: they did not choose the veering way of doing things as a means of carving themselves into moral persons.

What I take from the systemic perspective is its emphasis on a system. However, instead of understanding this system as a more or less discrete and bounded unit with nation–state borders, I take a transnational perspective: I suggest that we need to focus on how transnational and global processes affect the need to obtain resources through personal connections, compassion, and humanitarianism in particular countries and in particular fields (such as social protection) in these countries.

Ethnographic analyses of postsocialist countries criticize the concept of a straightforward transition to a well-known destination (advanced democracy and a neoliberal economy), pointing out that Eastern European countries are going through a complex process of transformation toward something not quite defined (Lampland 2002; Hann 2002). They explore the imaginaries and materialities of old socialist and new neoliberal statehood (Dunn 2008; Mikuš 2016); gendered regimes of care and social security (Haukanes and Pine 2005); disappointments stemming from new democratic practices (Greenberg 2014); the inescapability of nation–state myths and cosmologies (Verdery 1999); and so forth.

With respect to favors, ethnographic studies have often used the language of ambiguities, tensions, and negotiations. The pursuit of favors across postsocialist countries challenges various foundational concepts in Western social sciences: relations between people linked through favors in postsocialist Europe are often neither purely instrumental nor just friendships (Verdery 1996; Thelen 2011); objects exchanged through favors are neither commodities nor gifts, but rather both (Stan 2012); favors are ambivalently positioned between "corruption" and "moral forms of exchange" (Rivkin-Fish 2005; Wanner 2005).

Taking a cue from such studies, I suggest that *veze* and *štele* are so overwhelmingly present in BiH because they are implicated in the reproduction of social personhoods and, through that, power and inequality. In this chapter, I addressed the question of how *veze* and *štele* work—metaphorically, rather than metonymically, linking different state and social orders of knowledge and experience. I have also engaged with the question of why *veze* and *štele* are persistently present in everyday life in BiH, but I have only partly answered this question, focusing on their social and affective dimensions.

I will put more emphasis on the second part of the answer to the *why* question in the following chapters. When *veze* and *štele* shape who accesses public welfare and how they do it, it means that the "state" and "that which is not the state" (Gupta 1995: 393) are intertwined, instead of being consistently separate. This intertwining of society and the state was the result not just of a complicated and troubled process of state building but also of the ways in which transforming the BiH state into an EU candidate country and a potential EU member state was conceived of and undertaken in 2009 and 2010.

Notes

1. Patronage and clientelism throughout Mediterranean Europe are often interpreted in a similar functionalist manner as "a fitting and rational strategy employed to remedy the State's failure or shortcomings …

simply a rational choice within the context of a permanent failing statehood" (Giordano 2012: 23).

2. Ledeneva suggests that Wittgenstein's concept of "family resemblance" or "family likeness" is useful for understanding a similar lack of formal consistency in *blat* relations in Russia. There is not one element distinguishing *blat* relations from all other types of relations. Instead, *blat* contains "a complicated network of similarities and relationships overlapping and criss-crossing" (Ledeneva 1998: 38).

Part II

Citizenship

Chapter 3

Local Community and Ethical Citizenship
Neoliberal Reconfigurations of Social Protection

> It seems to me that there is no distinct system and model;
> it is rather a case of "sort it out by yourself."
> *Chair of a seminar on social protection*

This is how the chair of an educational seminar on social protection described social policy reforms from the mid-2000s. New social policies framed "local community" as the primary framework for meeting citizens' social protection needs and introduced almost no procedures or legal obligations. Most forms of support—such as a daycare center for children with disabilities, subsidized transportation, or educational and leisure activities—were relegated to the local communities. They were supposed to be organized and financed by the civil and the private sector, or through a public–private partnership. As a result, the users could not know what sort of support they would get; this depended on the financial abilities and moral inclinations of their local communities. This policy change created an environment that my interlocutors perceived as fairly confusing. People had to "sort it out by themselves," because there seemed to be no distinct system or model to follow.

This chapter argues that ambiguity became a constitutive element of a mode of governance created through the translation of internationally supervised and neoliberally infused social policies. The new policies created an environment with no "distinct system and model," in which ambiguities proliferated. Admittedly, local state institutions were assigned a certain role: in the Republic of Srpska, most social protection provisions were organized and financed through municipal budgets.[1] However, this was far from enough to survive: the municipally provided basic provision was almost twenty times less than the average salary, while the average salary was insufficient to cover basic living expenses. Local communities were supposed to step in and help to finance and organize social protection. In order to motivate their local communities to help, people mobilized whatever relationships were at their disposal—including *veze/štele*. This was not simply an unintended consequence of policy transfer. Neither should it be infantilized as an unfortunate stepping stone to a fully working and developed state and society. Instead, it reveals ambiguities that are a constitutive part of globally circulating ideas about ethical citizenship.

Following visions of post welfarist statehood, the BiH state that was being built over the past two decades was not imagined as a welfare state whose administration would provide equal access to public resources for all BiH citizens on the basis of agreed-upon criteria. Rather, some sort of a "partial" citizenship was emerging, both in the sense of citizenship being to some degree curtailed (not whole) and of being personalized (not impartial). Partial citizenship simply means that, across BiH, users of social protection experienced welfare support in different ways. The location of claimants made a difference—both in the sense of their place of residence and the social worlds they inhabited. Partiality was due to several reasons.

First, placing responsibility on the local communities introduced ambiguity over the status of social protection: sometimes it was framed as a humanitarian gift, sometimes as a civic right, while on other occasions it was a matter of luck and chance. In the midst of this ambiguity, social personhoods (who people knew and in what capacity) affected the sort of protection one could get. Second, local elites kept the labyrinthine administrative structure of BiH alive and well.[2] This was particularly the case with Bosnian Serb and Bosnian Croat ethnonationalist politicians who strived for separation and the creation of mononational states. With thirteen ministries of social protection operating across the BiH's territory, the support people would get in two different towns differed greatly. Third, a perplexing web of international actors often operated through projects focused on particular places within the country, rather than the country as a whole. The project-based reforms created different experiences with social protection in different locations and further contributed to fragmentation of BiH statehood.

Partial citizenship—or the fact that welfare redistribution was ambiguously linked to citizenship—was a result of these combined strivings to redefine the relationship between citizens and the state. In order to develop this point, I will first describe the effects of translating the visions of a local community from social protection policy documents into everyday life. I will then offer a brief account of various actors who contributed to the fragmentation of state sovereignty while simultaneously building the BiH state.

Sort It Out by Yourself

One warm autumn day in 2009 I went with Jole, the president of the Town's Red Cross and Red Crescent office, to an educational seminar. The seminar Partnership and Community Services was organized by the Banja Luka Center for Social Work (Banja Luka is a BiH town). It was held in the public library, which was the main venue for educational and cultural events. Jole and I sat in the back rows of a large conference room. He exchanged greetings with local nongovernmental organization (NGO) activists and employees of state institutions, such as the local Center for Social Work and the Public Fund for the Protection of Children.

The chair introduced the seminar as an opportunity to learn about the benefits of public–private partnerships and about integrating the "whole community" into the protection of socially vulnerable groups. He said with some resignation that no one from the private sector had shown up, although actors from the public, civil, and private sector had all been invited. The lecturer was the director of the Center for Social Work (CSW) in another Bosnian town. She claimed, "The way to do things today" involves the formal cooperation of the state and the civil and the private sectors, signed contracts, and a clear division of responsibilities.

Her talk suggested that engaging the civil and the private sectors opens up market mechanisms in social protection, thereby consolidating resources and leading to the dissipation of a one-sector monopoly. This comment referred to the dissipation of the presumed monopoly of the state over social protection—although social protection during the Socialist Federative Republic of Yugoslavia (SFRY) was decentered to a significant extent, as we will see later. The lecturer also spent a considerable amount of time discussing the personal traits of a "good manager," because, she claimed, good managerial skills were crucial for the successful running of state and civil sector organizations working in the field of social protection.

The question and answer session indicated that the model presented by the lecturer contrasted sharply with the everyday experiences of people in the audience. The difference between how things *ought* to be done and how they *are* actually done became one of the topics of discussion in the room. A woman from the audience raised her hand and said that the model the lecturer proposed "looked fine in theory" but was inapplicable to everyday practices.

They actually already cooperated with different sectors, she said, but not in the form of formalized public–private partnerships. The lecturer responded by admitting that transforming personalized co-operation into a formal relationship with written contracts is a big challenge that nevertheless "has to be undertaken in today's world."

To this, an older social worker in a leather jacket sitting near me ironically murmured, "I [give] to you, you [give] to me" (*ja tebi, ti meni*). Noticing that I was paying attention to his words, he continued, "Who else could try to sell us wisdom (*prodati nam pamet*) but Banja Luka? This is just verbiage, milled and then remilled (*prazna slama, pomlaćena pa mlaćena*). If there isn't enough money, you can't do anything." Lack of money was a frequent criticism of social protection. During my fieldwork, the basic social protection provision for children with special needs, decided upon and funded by the municipality of the Town, was KM 41, or EUR 20.5 (Džumhur, Jukić, and Sandić 2010: 45).[3] It was impossible to survive solely on this sum. For comparison, the average net salary in the Town in 2009 and 2010 was around KM 770, or EUR 385 (Republički zavod za statistiku Republike Srpske 2011: 437–38), while the monthly basket of consumer goods[4] was around EUR 800.[5]

Besides the lack of finances, another frequent criticism of social protection in this context was the lack of care. When the lecturer talked about the need for private business owners to contribute to social protection, the man in the leather jacket said, "They are not interested in those who need social welfare help, for fuck's sake (*Ne interesuje njih socijala, jebo te bog*). They act as if they were members of parliament."

Such moralizing criticism of the lack of care was frequently expressed by my interlocutors and it went in different directions. Social workers usually talked about private actors as uninterested in others' well-being and focused solely on increasing personal profits or gaining political power. They also occasionally claimed that users of social protection are only interested in financial provisions, rather than in wider initiatives aimed at improving their social position, but that had no immediate financial benefit. Then again, many users of social protection talked about social workers and other state officials using the phrase *upala mu/joj je kašika u med* (literally: "her or his spoon landed in the honey," meaning "she or he won the jackpot"). Jobs in state institutions meant regular salaries, a large number of vacation days, and various opportunities to travel or earn honoraria. In a country rife with high unemployment, working in the state apparatus was often seen as a way to take care of oneself, while nominally taking care of public issues.

This seminar illuminated a discrepancy between the EU-recommended principles of social protection and their practical, everyday organization in the Town. It also brought two important issues to the fore. First, the discussion crystallized the widespread sense that social protection was a random undertaking, succinctly summarized by the chair as a case of "sort it out by yourself." The randomness of social protection in the Town was clearly visible to all interested parties, and *veze* and *štele* often helped one navigate one's way through this. Examples of cooperation between state, civic, and private actors were usually forged ad hoc, with the aim of utilizing whatever resources were available among people who knew one another and who had shared personal and professional interests. This is where *veze* and *štele* have found their place.

Second, the ironic remarks of the man in the leather jacket illustrate that "good" and "caring" persons were imagined as the backbone of the social protection system. In his view, private actors did not show up at the seminar because they did not care. When public and private actors did form partnerships, it was because of personal benefits (I give you, you give me). Many others similarly interpreted lack of money for social protection as the result of there being too few good and caring persons. Such moralizing criticism was fostered by the reform of social policies that offered a new kind of imaginary of state–citizen relations.

Imagining Ethical Citizenship in Social Policy

The early postwar years in BiH were marked by the efforts of international NGOs to provide direct relief to people in urgent need, which effectively reduced social policy to humanitarian assistance (Stubbs 2002: 325). The focus shifted in the 2000s to developing programs, strategies, and policies with more lasting effects. The internationally supervised change of welfare policies from the mid-2000s was reflected in a document called the Medium Term Development Strategy (MTDS 2004–2007) for BiH.[6]

The MTDS envisions social protection as a field regulated by voluntary work, the cooperation of the state with NGOs, and corporate social responsibility motivated by tax benefits.[7] Maglajlić-Holiček and Rašidagić (2007: 162) point out that, while the MTDS "aims to implement market principles in social welfare and to promote the development of alternative forms of social care," the document "does not include a clear elaboration of these declarative concepts." As a matter of fact:

> The Action Plan, which represented the key component of the MTDS, spelt out which ministry was in charge of preparation and implementation of each policy, but did not elaborate further. Within these ministries, no clear idea existed on how the task was to be implemented, nor were any instructions prepared by the government(s) on how to proceed with it ... For example, within a proposed measure to transform the financial and operational structure of Centers for Social Work towards a project-based funding framework, a time frame of only half a year was proposed, with responsibility outlined only as belonging to the relevant entity ministries in charge of social welfare. (Maglajlić-Holiček and Rašidagić 2007: 162)

Changing welfare frameworks without sufficient (or any) procedural guidance about which organization or actor should be responsible for what element of social protection reform most likely resulted in a sense that you had to "sort it out on your own," as expressed by the chair of the seminar. Instead of clear procedures and named organizations, the MTDS offered the "local community" as one of two key institutions responsible for social protection:

> The institutions in charge of social protection in RS are the RS Government and the local community. The RS is responsible for regulating and defining relations, rights, responsibilities, authorities and the contents of social protection. The local community is the framework for meeting the majority of personal and joint needs of citizens, including social protection.[8]

Presenting the local community as an "institution" in charge of social protection in the entity crystallizes the ambiguities of social policy documents. First, local community was not a legal concept, but a category of practice. It could be understood as an institution only in the sense of stable, valued, recurring patterns of behavior (Huntington 1965). Yet, the primary aim of the MTDS was to redefine existing patterns of behavior on new grounds: the MTDS was intended to transform certain stable, valued, and recurring patterns of behavior into new (presumably better) stable and valued patterns of behavior.

Therefore, a local community was simultaneously an institution that had yet to be built *and* given a large share of responsibility for social protection.

Second, referring to a local community (*lokalna zajednica*), rather than to local self-government (*lokalna samouprava*), presents one of the key changes in comparison to the former SFRY socialist framework. Social protection during the SFRY was decentralized and funded by municipality-based forms of self-government.[9] Local self-government existed also in the 2000s, as a legally and procedurally clear political framework for regulating life in the municipalities:

> Local self-government is the right of citizens to directly participate in realizing shared interests through their democratically chosen representatives, as well as the right and the ability of the bodies of local self-governance to regulate and manage, within legal limits, public issues under their jurisdiction, and which are of interest to the local population. Local self-government is realized in municipalities and cities, and is undertaken by citizens and bodies of units of self-government. (Article 2, Law on Local Self-Government)[10]

Referring to the "local self-government" as the institution in charge of social protection would have meant placing primary responsibility for survival and well-being on the municipal governments, and thus the state. In order to open up room for non–state actors, the MTDS offers an internally coherent vision: if social protection users motivate individuals to volunteer, NGOs to cooperate with the state institutions, and private companies to offer social responsibility programs, their needs will be met. In other words, if all elements of the local community provided a portion of support, the parents of children with disabilities could get the help they needed. However, this created legal and procedural uncertainties over who should be responsible for what, on what grounds, and in what way. In the mid-2000s, social protection was redefined from being a right guaranteed on the basis of citizenship status to context-specific support provided by various moral and compassionate actors alongside the state.

In the MTDS, as in numerous contemporary welfare policies, local community presents a space where legal rights and ethic/moral duties merge together. Rose writes that the language of community in UK and US politics "is used to identify a territory between the authority of the state, the free and amoral exchange of the market, and the liberty of the autonomous, rights-bearing individual" (2000: 1400).

It is part of a politics of behavior in which human beings are understood as ethical creatures—rather than as citizens, rational actors, or psychologically motivated beings. This "ethopolitics" is nowadays evoked in different countries and transnational contexts:

> The stake has to be generated in the community-based ethic that shapes the values that guide each individual. This is to be accomplished through building a new relation between ethical citizenship and responsible community fostered, but not administered by the state ... The person whose conduct is to be governed is believed to desire personal autonomy as a right, but autonomy does not imply that individuals live their lives as atomized isolates. They are understood as citizens, not of societies as national collectives, but of neighborhoods, associations, regions, networks, subcultures, age groups, ethnicities, and lifestyle sectors—in short, communities. (Rose 2000: 1398)

This understanding of a community can be seen in different documents in the Town. For instance, the Sun, the aforementioned NGO for children with disabilities, published a parental guide based on the relevant legislature. The guide includes a table (see Table 3.1 below) that indicates that in the contemporary, "social model," meeting the needs of a child with a disability is the shared responsibility of parents, public agencies, education, and governmental and civic

Table 3.1. *Social Model versus Medical Model of Social Protection,* *"Parental Guide"*

Current Condition— Medical Model	Future Condition—Social Model
Committee for examining developmentally disabled children (Committee for Classification)	Committee for assessing needs and directing developmentally disabled children
Child is approaching "normal" functioning, individual feelings of guilt because they are different	There is no guilt attached to individuals, instead the environment is adjusted to meet the needs and abilities of the individual
Failure to consider individual needs, assigning all children to a category (for instance, care rendered by other persons, special school)	Considering the individual needs of a child in the environment in which they live

Current Condition— Medical Model	Future Condition—Social Model
Parents as passive observers, only responding to questions asked	Parent as active, his [*sic!*] opinion is also appreciated
No assessment of needs, but of deviation from "normality"	Assessment of needs, as well as of the capacities of the parents and local community to meet those needs
Special needs refer to a medical deviation from "normality," and education in a special school	Special needs refer to the supplementary or special support that could exist as concerns a child's communication and interaction, cognitive abilities to learn, the emotional and social functions and behaviors of a child, or the bodily and sensory abilities of a child
Committee consists only of healthcare employees	Interagency work of the Committee (healthcare, social protection, education, governmental and the NGO sector)
Committee reaches its opinion on the basis of a single examination	The work of the Committee is a much more dynamic process in which the present needs of a child are regularly and repeatedly assessed, following a planned dynamic, in accordance with the effects of the presented interventions and changing situation
Child's position is passive	Child's opinion is appreciated
Non standardized intelligence tests, which are not adjusted to the conditions of our country	Standardized intelligence tests that differentiate intellectual inefficacy on the basis of social, cultural, and educational neglect
Suggested interventions, the first course of action: state protection (care rendered by other persons, special school, boarding-type institutions)	Suggested interventions, the first course of action—possibilities offered by the local community
Legally unclear monitoring of the Committee's work	Clearly determined monitoring and impact on the quality of the Committee's work

sectors—in short, of society and the local community. The guide also suggests that in the earlier, socialist, "medical model," the primary responsibility belonged to the state, which placed parents and children in a passive position.

Notice that the "medical model" in the guide includes three named, specific forms of intervention provided by the state: care rendered by other persons, a special school, and boarding-type institutions. The social model, on the other hand, does not specify any particular intervention. This is because the forms of intervention offered by the local community depend on the compassion, interests, and abilities of the local community in question. This means that the support offered in the Town would not be the same as that offered in Sarajevo or Banja Luka. It also means that as a parent of a child with a disability, one cannot really know in advance what one's citizenship entitlements are, because they depend on the local context and the goodwill of various actors in one's community.

Ethical Citizenship and Local Community in Everyday Life

If the local community "looked fine in theory" as the framework for providing social protection, as the audience member during the seminar said, it contrasted sharply with everyday experiences. This is because policy is not a coherent body of knowledge and practice that can be straightforwardly transferred in a horizontal direction, across countries, or vertically, from policy makers to policy implementers and only then be slightly altered to accommodate the flavor of the local context, if needed. Instead, as Lendvai and Stubbs (2009) argue, different elements of policy move in different directions, and not always simultaneously. As policy moves, it becomes "revised, inflected, appropriated and bent in encounters of different kinds" (Clarke et al. 2015: 15). This does not mean that each move of policy produces unforeseen effects but that it always has the potential to do so. Approaching policy as a form of translation takes into account that "when policy moves, it is always *translated*, that is, it is made to mean something in its new context" (ibid.: 9).

One change that took place in the translation of welfare policies across and within BiH was the practices of *veze* and *štele* finding their place in the protection of survival and well-being. Users of social protection were more likely to access what they needed if they managed to connect with the "right" people in their community, the "right" NGO representatives, volunteers, or private donors willing to help them. *Veze* and *štele* provided people with a meaningful way to establish such links. Let us take a brief look at this now, before discussing it in more detail in chapter four.

One of the biggest problems concerning social protection for children with disabilities in BiH was obtaining information about available services (Džumhur, Jukić, and Sandić 2010: 48). In the Town, the responsibility for finding information was primarily relegated to users. The local CSW had no procedure in place to inform all of its users at the same time about changes being made to social protection services and provisions—and there was no plan to implement such a procedure. It was largely up to the users to make the effort. The center offered information during the infrequent regular social workers' visits to the families or when those users visited their offices before the deadline—if the social worker they stumbled on remembered to share the information. Those who were eligible, but did not acquire this information on time, had to apply again in the future. Consequently, information—as an important resource—was not distributed evenly among all citizens and face-to-face interactions took on a great significance.

To give one example, Mina was a tall, university educated, single mother who quit her job after giving birth to a boy with developmental disabilities. At the Sun, she often described social protection as "mysterious" (*misteriozna*). When I asked why, she recounted how she found out that she had a right to apply for additional financial support almost by accident. A couple of years before my fieldwork began, she went to the CSW to ask them to stop paying her the basic social protection provision, because, she said, such a small amount of money did not make any difference in her life. Ivona (the director of the Sun and an employee of the center) refused Mina's plea, looked at her case file, and advised her to apply for a different financial welfare provision for which she was eligible. Mina was granted the additional provision. She started to occasionally visit the Sun from that point on in order to learn about different forms of support.

Frequent visits to the Sun provided parents with a way of cultivating personal relations with the social workers and thus of making sure that they would access new information on time. If citizenship in this context was a partial relationship, the Sun was a place where the parents could make sure they would get the most out of this partiality. This was particularly visible on the day when Ivona dropped by our regular, twice a week session, with information about newly introduced social welfare provisions for which some of the mothers from the organization were eligible.

The Sun sessions were held at an old, rusty house located at the back of the CSW. A paper scotch-taped on the front door of the house indicated that this was a location of "an association for helping mentally underdeveloped persons" (*udruženje za pomoć mentalno zaostalim licima*). Between fifteen and twenty parents, all mothers, took their children to the Sun regularly. While the children were working with the special teachers in one room, I sat with the parents in a separate room, where we boiled coffee on a small kitchen stove, chain-smoked, and chatted. The room, despite its aged and stained furniture, was enlivened with many colorful toys scattered around, children's drawings hanging on the walls, and bright curtains on the windows.

The house had one more room and a small bathroom, mostly used by the children. Ivona arrived about half an hour after the session had started. When she entered the room, the atmosphere became very cheerful, filled with loud greetings and personal questions about children and family life. Ivona explained the conditions for the new provision, instructing the parents on where to obtain the relevant documents and informing them of the deadline for submission. When she left, the women praised her professionalism as well as her compassionate and kind personality.

Ivona's role at the organization condenses partialities of citizenship in this context. When she came to the Sun, she was a representative of the state; she was a source of information about future decisions that the center and the municipality would make. Simultaneously, she was a civil society representative; she was the director of the Sun, who secured regular finances from the center and occasionally submitted project applications to other funding bodies. In this way, Ivona was the parents' direct *veza/štela* to both the state and the civic thread of social protection. The parents needed Ivona to keep the Sun going, to learn what they were entitled to and how to obtain it, to put in a good word about them when working on their personal case files, to call them if a document was missing before rejecting the application, and so forth.

Her visits to the Sun were irregular and infrequent. The parents sometimes complained that Ivona and others from the center did not care about them. On other occasions, they expressed gratitude and complimented Ivona, as they did during the visit described above. The parents understood the Sun partly as something they were entitled to have by law and partly as something that was given to them through the goodness of Ivona's heart. Since the Sun would not have existed without the CSW, it was a state-led initiative. At the same time, the Sun would not have existed without the compassion of so-cial workers and, as such, it was their personal humanitarian initiative.

At a later date, I asked Ivona why the information about new ser-vices was not distributed evenly among all those who are potentially eligible. She said that this was a problem and she criticized the ar-bitrariness of public programs. However, she also transferred this responsibility to the parents. She suggested that those interested in improving their situation come to the Sun or the center at least once in a while and maintain relations with the social workers and other parents. Ultimately, it was up to the users, not the center, to "sort it out" on their own. Thus, what the users described as an "accident," as a "mystery," and/or "luck," the social workers sometimes inter-preted as "self-responsibility" and "self-motivation."

This narrative did not transform the parents into "self-responsible" citizens. Instead, it strengthened the partiality of citizenship, that is, the importance of social personhood for pursuing citizenship rights. The center expected the users to proactively pursue information—not through websites, email lists, mobile phone messaging services, or newspapers but by maintaining personal relationships with the so-cial workers and other parents. Those who maintained good relations were "rewarded" by learning new information and obtaining provi-sions. Although each user might have been legally entitled to social protection, the relationality of favors was still one of the constitutive elements surrounding access to provisions and services.

The parents engaged in "sociality with a purpose" in order to en-sure that they could access provisions and programs they were fully legally entitled to as citizens. They paid attention to being close to the social workers and having good personal relationships with them. They also worked on expanding the pool of people they knew per-sonally through locating efforts and knowledge by sight, the knowl-edge practices described in chapter one. The Sun was the place where most of this happened. It was the place where they accessed infor-mation about social protection with relative ease; where they learned stories about other people in the Town, their personalities and his-tories; where they shared experiences and opinions about particular social workers or healthcare practitioners; and so forth. The women engaged in relational labor in order to get the most out of the social protection that depended on their local community.

That the everyday enactments of a local community involved *veze* and *štele* may appear to be unexpected, or even paradoxical. As men-tioned earlier, approaching policy as a form of translation incorpo-rates contradictions and paradoxes as an integral part of the way in which policy moves and works in different contexts. Policy translation is not a simple substitution of one term by its equivalent in another language. Rather, "translation is a selective and active process in which meanings are interpreted and reinterpreted to make them fit their new context" (Clarke et al. 2015: 35). In social anthropology, the translation of concepts, cosmologies, relations, and practices generally "rests on a kind of 'controlled equivocation'" (Hanks and Severi 2014), whereby usually only one actor—the ethnographer—bears responsibility for losing certain features from the "original" and adding supplementary ones to facilitate readers' understanding of how other people live.

The translation of social policies across BiH was more of an uncontrolled attempt to reach such an equivocation, whose aim was to change the material conditions of life. This was an "uncontrolled" equivocation due to virtually innumerable and often mutually incompatible international and local agencies engaged in translating social protection policies into the BiH context, resulting in a "highly fragmented, unstable and crowded space of governance" (Stubbs 2014: 9). The variety of international and local actors who worked on developing the country for various purposes turned BiH into a kind of "laboratory of citizenship" (Štiks 2013) and a site of "complex social and political engineering" (Lendvai and Stubbs 2009: 681). They also deepened what Stubbs (2015: 87) calls the "paradox of the semiperiphery," whereby in southeastern Europe "all manner of project interventions are possible in a flexible 'open space' but these rarely achieve what they set out to, precisely because of the same lack of 'thick' structures in which they can be implemented."

This makes it relatively easy to experiment with various forms of intervention and simultaneously prevents any systematic change. Let us take a closer look at how local nationalist political elites and the international developmental agents worked on creating different, but similarly partial, forms of statehood and society.

Building while Fragmenting the State

Political and ethnographic analyses, in addition to the everyday experiences of my interlocutors, suggest that the simultaneous fragmentation and building of Bosnian statehood took place along two main axes. The first is the axis of ethnonationalism, inscribed on the BiH constitution and most loudly promoted by the Serbian, Croat, and Bosniak nationalist politicians. The second is the axis of the international community, with its conflicting aims and heterogeneous projects often directed at a particular locale in BiH, rather than across the whole country. There is a vast body of literature in political science, sociology, gender, nationalism, and peace studies that explores the effects of these two axes of life in BiH.

The following discussion does not in any way attempt to provide a review of this literature or a comprehensive overview of the related topics. Instead, it offers a quick glimpse into how ethnic nationalism and the international community contributed to the fragmentation of state sovereignty while simultaneously building the state, a glimpse necessary for following the discussion and arguments in the later chapters of this book.

The Fragmentation of Sovereignty: Ethnic Nationalism

The fragmentation of sovereignty is clearly visible in the labyrinthine administrative structure, which persists largely because ethnonationalist political elites disagree over the future of the country. Ethnonationalist Bosnian Serbian politicians invest a lot of effort in keeping the two existing entities strictly administratively divided, with the aspiration of making the Republic of Srpska independent one day. The Bosnian Serb ethnonationalist elites frequently rhetorically evoke the possibility of a referendum on independence for the Republic of Srpska as a "just" cause and represent the entity as a state in various places (Tuathail 2013), thus reflecting "a penchant for the Bosnian Serb wartime goal of creating a Serb national state out of the remnants of Bosnia-Herzegovina" (Kostovicova 2004: 276).

As a result of their secessionist ambitions, many politicians in the Republic of Srpska strongly oppose any initiative that could, potentially, contribute to dismantling the entity's boundaries, including administrative separations of healthcare and social protection systems (Tuathail and Dahlman 2006). Croat ethnonationalist politicians exert a similar opposition to any reform that could, potentially, create centralized state institutions in the Federation of Bosnia and Herzegovina or across the whole of BiH (Grandits 2007; Vetters 2007). While Croat ethnonationalist politicians attempt to keep the cantonal divisions of the federation in place, Bosniak ethnonationalist political elites strive to promote the increased centralization of the country.

As a result of the labyrinthine administrative divisions, none of the welfare responsibilities—including social protection, health, pensions, and employment—are assigned to the country-level institutions. Instead, each entity is responsible for planning, financing, and delivering welfare in its territory. Furthermore, the federation has ten different ministries for healthcare and social protection in its ten cantons, and the Brčko district has its own welfare institutions, with their own legal and procedural rules. Thus, "country-level social policy reform requires an engagement with 13 ministries responsible for decision-making and legislation" (Maglajlić-Holiček and Rašidagić 2007: 151). This has the following consequences:

> The services one receives still largely depend on where one lives. In one of the poorer cantons in the Federation of Bosnia and Herzegovina, a war-disabled veteran with a head injury and mental health problems may only receive from his local Centre for Social Work KM12 (approximately EUR6) per month to support his family of four, while in the richer cantons … the amount is approximately ten times as large. (Maglajlić-Holiček and Rašidagić 2007: 163)

Contemporary conflicting ethnonationalist visions of BiH's future were first articulated during the 1990 BiH elections, when the vote was split between nationalist parties claiming to represent the three majority ethnonational groups (Hayden 1993, 1999).[11] It should be noted that communitarian divisions of BiH are not a contemporary phenomenon. Bougarel (1996: 87) suggests that, historically, "the principle which has given structure to the Bosnian political order has not been citizenship, but rather communitarian identity." Throughout the nineteenth and twentieth centuries, ethnonational communities had great importance in the redistribution of political and economic power in the country. Mutually incompatible regimes that ruled the country—the Ottoman Empire (1463–1878), the Austro-Hungarian Empire (1878–1918), and socialist Yugoslavia (1945–90)—all used the communitarian principle to organize political, social, and at times economic relationships in BiH, although in quite different ways. The roles and responsibilities of ethnonational communities in BiH changed once again in the 1990s.

The ongoing relevance of the ethnonational principle for the political and social organization of the country is apparent in their constitutional grounding. The 1995 BiH constitution prescribes ethnonational identity as being the basis of political subjectivity. The preamble of the BiH constitution states, "Bosniacs, Croats, and Serbs, as constituent peoples (along with Others), and citizens of Bosnia and Herzegovina hereby determine that the Constitution of Bosnia and Herzegovina is as follows."[12] This ethnonationalist definition of the political subjects of the country (as Bosniaks, Croats, Serbs, and others) effectively means that the "others" have the same citizenship rights as members of the three constituent peoples, *except* when it comes to a range of issues, including voting and elections (Sarajlić 2012; Shaw and Štiks 2012).

For instance, constitutionally defined "others" could not be elected to one of the three places in the state presidency or the House of People of the BiH Parliamentary Assembly (the European Court of Human Rights judged this to be unlawful in 2009, but the constitution has not yet been changed).[13] These "others" may be people who identify as members of Roma and Jewish groups native to BiH, as Bosnians (i.e., as nationals of the whole country of BiH), as citizens with no sense of ethnonational belonging, as citizens with multiple senses of ethnonational belonging, and so forth. Importantly—the constitution does not acknowledge any non national principle of organizing political life.

There have been numerous political actors, processes, initiatives, and even political parties founded upon non ethnic and non nationalist logics in the past two decades. However, their strength has been challenged on various accounts, not least by the BiH constitution which promulgates ethnonational identity as the only viable political subjectivity and as the most important part of a person.[14] With such a constitution, BiH can be understood as an "ethnopolis," or "democracy of ethnic oligarchies rather than a democracy of citizens" (Mujkić 2007: 113). The ethnonational politics, inscribed in the constitution and propagated by the BiH political elites, is one of the factors that prevent building state administrations that treat people in a "blind" way, first and foremost as Bosnian citizens and then (if at all) as persons socially located as Bosniaks, Croats, Serbs, women, men, or something else.

The Fragmentation of Sovereignty:
The International Community

Another, equally important, axis of fragmentation of sovereignty of the BiH state is the international community. The term "international community" marks a loose network of international humanitarian, peace-building, and developmental organizations, embassies, and agencies that have been present in BiH since the 1992–95 war. The international community played a constitutive role in the war dynamic, war landscapes, and peace negotiations (Bugarel 2004). After the war, various international actors started supporting the reconstruction of the country and shattered relations among people living in it, attempting to reverse the wartime ethnic cleansing as much as possible (Dahlman and Tuathail 2005; Jansen 2006). Their activities of peace building, the transformation of socialist institutional structures, and later EU member state building were directed at establishing a workable multiethnic state with a pluralist democracy, a functioning civil society, and liberal market economy (Bougarel et al. 2007).

Critical studies of the international work in BiH suggest that state building, peace reconciliation, and democratization in this context could be interpreted "as external impositions that fail to resonate with local worldviews, lack fundamental legitimacy, and in one assessment even threaten to mirror a 'European Raj'" (Baker 2012: 850; see also Gilbert 2012; Hayden 2005; Knaus and Martin 2003). In 2009 and 2010, the agents of large-scale societal transformations in BiH included numerous international organizations, such as the European Union, the World Bank, the International Monetary Fund, the United Nations Development Programme, UNICEF (United Nations Children's Fund), the Regional Co-operation Council, the Office of the High Representative, and many international and local NGOs and think tanks. The sheer number of these different actors who employed various aims, intentions, principles, and mechanisms created an "intermestic sphere" (see Stubbs 2005), an amalgam of international and domestic actors, characterized by "a fundamental lack of clarity about where government and authority reside" (Deacon and Stubbs 1998: 100).

This lack of clarity concerning government and authority was productive for exchanges based on favors. Supporting the peace building and postconflict reconstruction of the BiH polity, the international community nominally opposed political clientelism and the "veering" way of doing things common among BiH nationalist politicians of all three major ethnonational groups. And yet, there are cases that suggest that neoliberal restructuring of policy *encouraged* clientelist ways of relating and that the international actors turned a blind eye to the administrative irregularities created in this way.

For instance, a team of international auditors found a number of illegalities during the privatization of the giant Mostar aluminum plant in the early postwar years (in the Federation of Bosnia and Herzegovina) but "for political and practical reasons" recommended that ownership should stay as it was at the moment (Pugh 2005: 451). Pugh argues that the reason for this was certain coinciding interests between the international and local elites to capture and sell public goods for private profit. The international community aimed to squeeze "public economic space as a key to developing the liberal peace" (Pugh 2005: 452), while local ethnonationalist political elites aimed to gain as much profit as possible from privatization.

The example of the Mostar aluminum plant indicates that international actors did not always necessarily care about the clarity and regularity of procedures through which the privatization of former publicly owned institutions occurred, while the local nationalist elites used their own clientelist social networks and "worlds of people" to profit from this. If we take into account the fact that neoliberal political economy has been imprinted in many peace-building initiatives throughout the world since the late 1980s (Pugh, Cooper, and Turner 2008), the following does not come as a surprise:

> The clientist and neoliberal mechanisms for managing investment, shares, and profits [in BiH] are dissimilar. But the normative assumptions of the external actors and the interests of domestic elites coincide in extracting profit from public goods and in fostering opportunities from privatization and discrimination against social ownership. In this there is common ground between international and domestic parties as well as friction and resistance. (Pugh 2002: 467)

Therefore, partial citizenship—or different forms of state support that different people can get—is at least partly the result of international efforts to build a state that will serve to supervise competition among market-oriented actors, whose sovereignty is not crucial, for it will presumably be transferred "to the post-nation state Union" once BiH joins the EU (Venneri 2010: 154). Reforms of social protection were one step taken in building such a state.

Conclusion

In many ways, BiH seems to be on the same track as countries that have moved somewhat away from the ideal of indifferent public administration over the past few decades. The values of the Weberian ideal of bureaucracy include rule-bound hierarchy, expertise, neutrality, and a clear division of authority and responsibility. Such values are represented as old-fashioned, unenterprising, and anachronistic in numerous political, academic, and managerial discourses of the West. In Anglo-Saxon contexts, the idea of a "new public management" has been introduced, which includes the fragmentation and decentralization of a large state-run bureaucracy into smaller, mutually competing, market-oriented, and flexible public agencies (Du Gay 2005). Du Gay (2008) argues that this change in the direction of governance includes sidelining traditional bureaucratic indifference in favor of an "ethic of care for the other," which means encouraging officials to conduct their administrative duties with a sense of compassion.

In the new theories of management, employees have to demonstrate that they are personally invested in their work—engaged, participative, and empowered (such expectations are seen in public as well as private institutions; for an account of participative management strategies in a Russian–US factory; see Cohen 2015). In the United Kingdom, even the welfare claimants have to demonstrate that they are "engaged," albeit in a very specific manner, by recording their job-seeking activities online and meeting a defined hour quota (Foster 2017). New theories of management point out that the administrations following the Weberian model usually fail to fulfill their promises: Weberian bureaucracy is selective, exclusionary, and alienating, rather than blind. However, I think we should remember that it is selective, exclusionary, and alienating toward groups defined according to specific criteria, for instance, persons living with disabilities, immigrants, refugees, the Roma, prisoners, LGBT (lesbian, gay, bisexual, and transgender) people, and so forth.

The partiality of contemporary BiH administrations is of a very different kind, because there seem to be no clear criteria of exclusion. Accessing social protection in the Town largely depends on the ability to navigate one's social world, in other words, on participation and engagement enacted in a particular manner.

During the seminar *Partnership and Community Services*, the lecturer focused on the formalization of cooperation and signed contracts, rather than on the ways in which equal social rights could be given to all citizens. Her discussion of ideas concerning personal managerial skills, public–private partnerships, and the local community displaced definitions of institutional responsibilities and procedures of social protection. While the recommended social protection model, discussed during the seminar and introduced in the policy documents, provided the means to formalize arbitrariness, it did nothing to introduce impartiality, certainty, and predictability in reforms of social protection provisions.

Parents from the Sun found themselves having to cultivate good interpersonal relations and to pursue favors in order to learn about and to access forms of support they were entitled to as citizens. Favors, as practices that affected the production of personhood through one's relations with others, had their place in the delivery of social protection. In a context in which statehood was being redefined as it was being built, *veze* and *štele* provided a historically grounded way of relating to others in a local community.

Notes

1. Municipalities also decided on the amount of the obligatory provisions and the number of recipients of obligatory provision. Municipal governments had a legal right to introduce, or to deny introduction of, special provisions and to decide about the amount of the special provisions and the number of recipients of special provisions.
2. As mentioned earlier, BiH has thirteen governments (two entity governments, the Brčko district with its own government, and ten cantons with their respective ten governments in the federation entity). There is also the Office of the High Representative (OHR), which has governmental functions and a wide network of international organizations working on planning and implementing projects focused on state building, peace building, democratization, the privatization of formerly public companies, the marketization of formerly public services, and so forth.
3. Some users received additional provisions, including a one-off allowance (*jednokratna pomoć*), special allowance (*izuzetna novčana pomoć*), or an entitlement to an additional allowance for assistance and care rendered by other persons (*pravo na dodatak za pomoć i njegu od strane drugih lica*, or *tuđa njega i pomoć*). Still, many relied on just the basic social protection provision (*stalna novčana pomoć*, literally: "permanent financial support").
4. The basket of consumer goods, or market basket, refers to a list of commonly bought food and household items. It is used to track changes in the prices of the items on the list from one month to the next, and so there are overall changes in the trends of prices. In the entity, the basket of consumer goods is calculated by the Confederation of Trade Unions of the Republika Srpska (Republika Srpska Trade Union).
5. The average net salary in the entity of the Federation of BiH for the same timeframe is in the same range (Republički zavod za statistiku Republike Srpske 2011: 119).
6. Maglajlić-Holiček and Rašidagić write, "This MTDS was adopted by the BiH Council of Ministers together with the entity governments in February 2004, initially as the Poverty Reduction Strategy Paper, or PRSP. In accordance with the BiH Constitution, its implementation was accepted by the Parliamentary Assembly of BiH in March of the same year ... but also by the respective entity parliaments" (2007: 162). They

also point out that the reform was planned to be funded by supranational organizations, such as the World Bank.

7. The Medium Term Development Strategy is available online (European Commission).

8. "The Medium Term Development Strategy" (European Commission: 167).

9. From the mid-1950s until the 1970s, the main form of self-government was the municipal government. Later, the so-called self-managed communities of interest (*samoupravne interesne zajednice,* or SIZs) governed social protection, healthcare, accommodation, infrastructural works, and so on (Geršković 1974: 4; see also Leskošek 2009).

10. The Law on Local Self-Government (Zakon o lokalnoj samoupravi) of 2004 also specifies that the "municipality is the basic territorial unit of local self-government, formed for a single part of an inhabited area, for one inhabited area, or for more than one inhabited areas" (Službeni glasnik Republike Srpske 2004, article 7).

11. The elections in 1990 became (in)famous because three nationalistic parties won the majority of votes in almost all BiH municipalities: SDS (*Srpska demokratska stranka,* or Serbian Democratic Party) as the Serbian representative; SDA (*Stranka demokratske akcije,* or Party of Democratic Action) as the Bosniak/Muslim representative; and HDZ BiH (*Hrvatska demokratska zajednica BiH,* or Croatian Democratic Union BiH) as the Croat representative.

12. The Constitution of Bosnia and Herzegovina 1995.

13. Dervo Sejdić and Jakob Finci, identified as Bosnian Roma and Bosnian Jewish, could not stand for election to the top state bodies because they were constitutionally defined as "others." They submitted a lawsuit to the European Court of Human Rights, which, in 2009, found that the ineligibility of "others" to stand for election to the House of Peoples and to the Presidency in BiH violates the European Convention on Human Rights. In 2011, the Parliamentary Assembly of BiH set in motion a constitutional reform aiming to amend this human rights violation. However, the implementation of the constitutional reform is, in early 2017, still pending.

14. For a similar legal "freezing" of an ethnonational definition of culture in the 2007 Serbian constitution, see Brković 2008; Milenković 2008; also Vasiljević 2011.

Chapter 4

Pursuing Favors
within a Local Community

Moral Citizens, Active Citizens

"A parent's biggest desire is for her child to die a day before her. What will happen to our children after we are gone?" Magdalena said this one day at the Sun. Other parents present at the meeting agreed with her. One of them added, "Yes … who will take care of them after we are gone?" Such poignant comments illuminate the profound lack of certainty over the future that the parents faced. The conditions under which it became possible to articulate a desire for one's child to die a bit before one were created after the 1992–95 war, with the closure of many social protection boarding-type institutions from the Yugoslav era. A daycare center for children with disabilities was supposed to replace some of their services.[1] One of the problems for the mothers from the Sun was that construction of a daycare center was repeatedly postponed.

This chapter discusses agentive positions that were available to the mothers from the Sun, who were expected to proactively lobby for the improvement of social protection. Neoliberal reconfigurations of welfare often reposition "poor single mothers" as an "embodiment of the non-neoliberal subject, the nonenterprising, the non-self-sufficient" (Kingfisher 2016: 9). Understood as "dependent on the state … they travel as a negative image" of an ideal, self-reliant, and flexible subject (ibid.). There are many different ideas on how to transform poor single mothers into ideal neoliberal welfare subjects. As we saw in chapter three, the translation of social policies in BiH stressed the need to develop personal managerial skills. Making the local community responsible for social protection in the Town forced mothers from the Sun to envision previously nonexistent paths toward the improvement of social protection—including navigating social relations. As one developmental expert pointed out, welfare actors had to be managers who created associates and alliances where none had existed before.

The ideal of a self-sufficient welfare subject is at the background of many contemporary reforms. For instance, it was present in South Korea, where the government of a "neoliberal welfare society" (Song 2009: xi) did not just prioritize "particular populations (the homeless and the unemployed youth) in order to control labor and sociopolitical insecurity, but also promoted governable subjects within these prioritized populations," by creating distinctions between the "deserving" and the "undeserving" citizens. In former Yugoslav countries, the fall of socialism brought about profound changes in welfare arrangements. The Socialist Federative Republic of Yugoslavia (SFRY) had "rejected the soviet model of governance and, as a result, created a welfare system, inspired by the European traditions" (Stambolieva 2015: 382).

After the violent dissolution, former Yugoslav republics developed different approaches to organizing welfare—combining neocorporatist, paternalistic, and neoliberal visions in various ways.[2] While I do not think that BiH was a neoliberal welfare society similar to South Korea (Song 2009), social protection workers did promote a particular neoliberal vision of a self-sufficient welfare subject.

This chapter looks at how a group of mothers in the Town responded to such visions: how they acted when it mattered and how they did not act when they did not think it mattered. The chapter explores what constituted a meaningful political and civic act for the parents and how they negotiated their position in relation to demands of being self-sufficient, proactive, and flexible. The parents did not wholeheartedly embrace such new requirements. They were often purposefully ignorant and stubborn. However, there were certain moments when they "started moving" (*kada su se pokrenuli*) and when they "became active" (*kada su se aktivirali*).

These moments, which both the parents and the social workers recognized as movement and activity, illuminate how the politics of survival and well-being were organized in everyday life. When they *were* proactive and flexible, they pursued *veze* and *štele* to negotiate the improvement of social protection. Favors provided people with a flexible path to state services and resources. Acting by seeking *veze* and *štele* was not the result of a "flawed" and "incomplete" democratization and marketization of BiH but a context-specific way of performing the new requirements of social protection to be proactive and flexible. *Veze* and *štele* in the Town in 2009 and 2010 presented the sociohistorically grounded enactment of the postwar developmental expectations placed upon BiH citizens.

The parents also often ignored the opportunities to "take things into their own hands." Being passive, yet stubborn in their expectation of public support, the mothers from the Sun spent most of their time at the organization cultivating relations with social workers and waiting for the state to finally "do its job." For this reason, social workers largely perceived the parents as ignorant and incapable. The presumed parental ignorance and stubbornness articulated a yearning for a welfare system in which social protection would be framed as a citizenship right. Ignorance and stubbornness can be understood as quiet criticism of the current framework in which social protection was shaped by personal moral inclinations as much as by the legislature. This was one of major differences from the organization of social protection during the SFRY.

In the SFRY social policy imaginaries, responsibility for social protection was assigned to the local level: it was decentralized, organized, and delivered within municipalities and financed through local self-governing units. With the postsocialist, developmental reforms, social protection was also decentralized. However, its status was much more ambiguous: it was the responsibility of a local community and, therefore, simultaneously a civic right and the product of the compassion, moral duty, and goodwill of the public, private, and civil society actors. As a result of the labyrinthine BiH administrations and this ambiguity concerning its status, social protection was different for different citizens. Let us take a closer look at how social protection was organized during the SFRY.

Between Rights and Moral Duties

One day I joined the parents from the Sun for a roundtable discussion organized to mark the end of the working group's planning the construction of the daycare center. The president of the working group was Ratka, the same person who ran the Holy Mother and whose position of power will be discussed in chapter five. The speakers invited to the roundtable included the municipal representatives, representatives of state-run institutions for social protection, and a nongovernmental organization (NGO) activist from another Bosnian town who was also the father of a child with developmental disabilities. This parent activist talked about the successful construction of a daycare center in his town as an example of good practice. He also explained the role that he and his association, consisting of parents of children with disabilities, had had in the project, suggesting that the users had to be proactive in order to obtain a daycare center. Since no certain entitlements exist, people do not know what sort of support they may get, and they have to ask for it themselves, said the father activist:

> This is no longer the system which had maybe existed before the war, [in which] I know what I am entitled to, the lottery and so forth. An association is like a company, you write projects, you look for money yourself. No one will give it to you unless you ask for it yourself.

Someone from the audience responded to this by saying, "You did a good deed." This comment reproduced ambiguity over whether a daycare center is a public service or a favor and, if a favor, whose. The same person continued praising the parent activist, his association, and all the people involved in the construction of the daycare center in that town on moral grounds.

After the roundtable discussion I visited the Sun with the parents. Ivona, the president of the Sun and a social worker, was also there and repeatedly talked about the father activist. The mothers at the Sun could take him to be a role model, she said, because this man was "educated," "cultured," and "persistent." She added that he was also lucky, because "all the pieces fell into place for him" (*sve kockice su mu se složile*): the director of the Center for Social Work in his town was the spouse of the municipal mayor in that town. Thus, with the support of both the center and the municipality, this man had easily found investors for the construction of the daycare center.

Responding to this, the parents from the Sun said that they would be persistent until they were lucky. "Luck" was thus not just a matter of chance but something that could be gained or cultivated over time. Being lucky—having "the pieces fall into place"—meant that people found a way of making the ambiguity concerning social protection work for them. Such an intrusion of moral sentiments and luck into social protection was not necessarily the goal of the policy reforms. New social policies were supposed to introduce market principles in social protection and so help to dissipate the presumed state monopoly in this field. Yet, when one looks at how social protection was organized during the socialist Yugoslavia, things get more complicated.

In many socialist Eastern European countries, social work was abolished as a professional discipline, because other public institutions were supposed to meet all the welfare needs of the population (Hering 2009). SFRY officials, on the other hand, organized social work as a professional discipline, assuming this was a temporary necessity after World War II to meet the needs of children without parents, families of fallen partisan soldiers, and persons disabled by the war (Leskošek 2009; Švenda Radeljak 2006).

Yugoslav social protection was organized through a network of public institutions established across the country, such as the Centers for Social Work, which first opened in 1956.[3] There were also many specialized, boarding-type institutions for children without parents, youth, the elderly, people with disabilities, and so forth.[4] These institutions were made responsible for ensuring their survival and well-being: throughout the 1960s, the SFRY ratified laws on social protection that explicitly stated that the municipal Centers for Social Work had responsibility for all segments of social protection (Ajduković and Branica 2009: 255).

Social protection was decentralized to the municipal level, and it had the double role of providing support and serving as a tool of state control over the population. The Council for the Social Protection of the (Yugoslav) Federal Republic of Bosnia and Herzegovina defined the profile of a social worker in 1956 as a public servant "whose basic task lies in securing the rights of a citizen on the basis of the existing legislature," by "advising those who need this and who ask for this support" as well as those in need who the social worker discovers (Papo 1971: 3, qtd. in Miković 2006: 448). Overall, social workers simultaneously helped and controlled people who lived under their jurisdiction (Bašić 2013: 130; Leskošek 2009; Zaviršek 2006). By gathering knowledge, advising on what sort of support to (not) provide, and influencing the actions of state bodies (such as police searches for spouses who did not pay alimony), social workers were a biopolitical tool within the framework of Yugoslav socialist modernism (see Collier 2011).

During the 1970s, social protection was further decentralized. This was achieved by establishing self-managing communities of interest (*samoupravne interesne zajednice*, or SIZs). According to the 1974 constitution, the resources for social and infrastructural needs were to be collected and redistributed by the SIZs on the basis of a self-managed contract (rather than collected via taxes and redistributed through municipalities and other "state and para-state institutions"; GZršković 1974: 5). The SIZs were designed to manage healthcare, social protection, infrastructural works, and housing, or all those fields,

> where it is socially necessary to have the users organized on the principles of reciprocity and solidarity, since they have the resources and the rights over those resources, in order to meet their social needs and general contemporary conditions of life, and in which the market cannot be a regulator of social needs. (Geršković 1974: 4)

This means that, instead of the municipal officials, committees "consisting of activists from local communities were involved in making decisions on people's rights" (Leskošek 2009: 242). The result of this change was a very complex administrative system that produced many ambiguities. Yet, histories of social work in the SFRY do not indicate that there were ambiguities over the sort or the status of support people could get. As the parent activist indicated, in the SFRY system, "which had maybe existed before the war, I know what I am entitled to." People were entitled to social protection as citizens in need. They did not have to be self-motivated, lucky, proactive, flexible persons who successfully evoked the compassion and morality of others. Under such conditions, a desire for one's child to die a day before one could not be articulated: parents knew full well what would happen to their children if they died.[5] Yearnings for a "normal life"—the life of predictability and certainty—became possible under the post-Dayton conditions.

Stubborn Yearnings

Yearning for a normal life in post-Dayton BiH, the parents occasionally refused to act as self-sufficient welfare subjects. On one such occasion, they quietly ignored a project involving sewing handbags to raise money for the Sun. During a regular meeting, Ivona, the director of the Sun and a social worker, entered and announced that the organization would receive the support necessary to buy the material for the parents to make handbags. The handbags would be sold, and the money raised this way would be used to fund the organization's activities. I came to the meeting the following week excited about this change of dynamics in the organization.

However, the parents did not seem to share my excitement. When everybody gathered at the office, we started making coffee, smoking, and gossiping as usual. After a couple of minutes, I got up, went outside, and brought the materials from another room. I said that, perhaps, we should start sewing the bags, as it would take a lot of time to make them. Magdalena, who was the informal leader of the group, said, "Definitely, we will start working on that soon." I sat down and joined the ongoing conversation, and the sewing was not mentioned again. The bags were never made, and unraveling why things happened this way—or rather, why the bag making *didn't* happen—points to the structure of entitlement and expectations that this group of women had as citizens.

A couple of weeks later, I was sitting in Ivona's office, located at the shabby wooden barracks of the local Center for Social Work. By that point it was clear that the bags would not be made, and Ivona said, "These mothers are uninterested, passive; they do not want to move, to work, to be engaged. Although, it is difficult for them, it is not easy to be a parent, let alone to be a parent of such a child." She could not believe that the mothers had not made any handbags, given that she had arranged for a donation to buy the materials and created a simple plan that the mothers should have followed in order to raise some small funds for the Sun. In utter disbelief, she continued for some time talking about how mothers need to be active and to start moving if they want to help themselves. She even added that the mothers are not "the most capable people, intellectually, and we need to find other parents who can make things happen."

From the perspective of the organization's leaders and volunteers, the parents seemed to be far from flexible agents who would be willing and able to managerially take things into their own hands and negotiate better social protection in various public and private arenas. However, toward the end of her outburst over the mothers' inability and passivity, Ivona said something quite different: "They are not realistic. They do not understand that everyone in the state is in a difficult situation, and they refuse to see that. They behave as if they are the only ones with a problem." The person who was realistic, in Ivona's opinion, was an adult man with developmental challenges who occasionally visited the Sun and who had said that they should not expect the municipal government to help them if they cannot help themselves. Ivona's irritation was caused by the passivity of the parents as well as by their refusal to "realistically" not expect too much from the municipal government.

Drawing on her experience, Ivona was well aware that the women were perfectly capable of organizing themselves and acting when they thought it mattered and was meaningful. A year earlier, Ivona had witnessed a situation in which the same mothers managed to convince the Town's mayor to push the municipal parliament to introduce a new social protection provision. She also knew that the parents were willing and able to impose their own views regarding the distribution of money within the organization. After a humanitarian exhibition organized by the Sun with the help of volunteers a year earlier, the parents decided to split the (meager) earnings among themselves, instead of investing it in the organization. Ivona and other people from the organization were not too pleased by the parents' decision. Another (not quite welcome) instance when parents raised their voice took place during the previously mentioned roundtable, which presented the results of the working group on a daycare center for children with disabilities. Some of the mothers from the Sun strongly criticized the plan presented. One of them said:

> Thank you so much for this, but I can tell you right away that such a daycare center won't be good and that it will not be built. Why? Because there were no parents in the working group. I do not want to criticize anyone or to question anyone's expertise, but the parents are those who have to be with the children every day and they have to be included in things that are of their concern.

With these words, the woman tried to include the parents from the Sun in every step of the construction of a daycare center, including the working group. There were at least two reasons for this. First, the parents saw themselves as people with a different form of expertise: the kind that comes out of everyday lived experience and intimate investment in the well-being of children with developmental disabilities. Second, as they later commented, having a parent in the working group would have allowed some of them to become even closer to Ratka and other influential actors, such as the mayor.

The working group's plan, which they discussed that day, made clear that the daycare center would have to be the result of a public–private partnership, but it did not state any specific public or private organizations that would take part in its construction. Later conversations indicated that Ratka and her organization the Holy Mother were on everybody's mind. Ratka's very presence in the working group—let alone the fact that she was the group's president—reinstated the ambiguity in public and private roles and responsibilities. Ratka embodied a particular mode of power stemming from the skill of managing ambiguity, which will be discussed in chapter five. A parent close to Ratka would have become a direct *veza/štela* (connection) to the decision makers, for herself as well as for the other parents. This was not just a matter of imagination and belief: such intersections between the personal and the professional can be traced in the "examples of good practice" that the parent activist presented during the roundtable.

It was episodes like this—making financial decisions, convincing the mayor to introduce a new provision, claiming a different kind of expertise, and having a position in the working group—that challenged the idea of parents as incapable. In such moments, it was apparent that the passivity of the parents was not a result of their "pathological dependency" on the state or their inability to recognize the need to be proactive. Instead, it stemmed from their disappointment with the current social and political framework and a yearning for a different one.

Jansen suggests that "yearning for normal lives" is a particularly apt description of the simultaneous desire for hope and the lack of it present among many people in BiH. Yearning in this sense denotes a persistent longing for an object that is absent from the present moment. It is a political affect that can be oriented both toward the past and toward the future (unlike nostalgia, which is directed to the past, or hope, which is directed to the future), which makes it analytically productive for understanding the possibilities of agency in BiH (Jansen 2015: 54–57).

Throughout the former Yugoslavia, normal lives present a widely used emic concept that can be understood in terms of living standards, predictability, stability, social welfare, and having "a place in the world" (Greenberg 2011; Jansen 2009a). For many people, including the parents from the Sun, most of this seemed to be lost with the dissolution of the SFRY. Therefore, parental stubbornness and ignorance can be understood as an expression of nostalgia for a socialist statehood, for "that system which maybe had existed before the war, [in which] I know what I am entitled to, the lottery and so forth," as the parent activist said during the roundtable. Yet, it was more than this.

The parents from the Sun also often discussed "normality" in relationship to the social welfare system in Scandinavia and other Northern European countries. When they talked about what normality looked like, they sometimes discussed documentaries about daycare centers in Finland and Norway, stories they heard from their relatives who lived in diaspora about the healthcare system in Sweden, and so forth. Thus, the parents yearned for normal lives that they thought took place in some other time (SFRY) and in some other place (Northern Europe), but *not in the here and now*. Their decision not to make or sell the bags makes sense when understood in relationship to this. Most of them were single parents and they had no intention of giving up their short intervals of free time at the Sun for an activity that promised to result, at best, in a one-off, small, non-systematic form of financial support.

The parents ignored the opportunity to generate a small profit for the organization because they stubbornly yearned for normal lives in which welfare would be framed as an unambiguous citizenship right—rather than as a prize for being a proactive, self-sufficient welfare subject. The exact political and economic contours of a welfare framework as a right were less important to them. The more important thing for the parents was that—however it may appear—such a framework was absent from their everyday experiences.

In this way, references to the normality of earlier socialist times, or of faraway Northern Europe, offered a way of criticizing the conditions they lived in. Under these conditions, being a citizen did not necessarily mean one would gain access to the required welfare support: if everybody in the local community was responsible for social protection, then really no one was responsible. The fact that the parents willingly chose when and how to "start moving"—which sometimes surprised and sometimes annoyed those around them—suggests that their yearning also contained hope (or perhaps, in Jansen's words, a "longing for hope," 2015: 54) that normal lives may become accessible in the future. With this in mind, let us take a look at how parents navigated their way to the mayor.

Citizens/Heroic Mothers Go to the Municipal Government

During a regular meeting at the Sun in the summer of 2010, one of the parents said, "There is a real wall [*bedem*] on the way to the mayor." From the parents' perspective, he seemed to be the only person able to increase social protection provisions and, at the same time, was almost unreachable. The parents did briefly navigate a way around this "wall" by asking others for a favor. A year earlier, they had arranged a meeting with the mayor, also thanks to a *veza/štela*.

The purpose of the previous year's meeting was to convince the mayor to introduce a new social protection provision. The women recounted to me numerous times that, while they had waited for the mayor to come to the meeting, he entered the room and simply said to one of his assistants, "Tell me how much this would be on a yearly level" (i.e., how much money it would take from the municipal budget). When he heard an estimate, he nodded and said, "Alright, let's vote on it today." The parents claimed that the municipal parliament decided to introduce the new provision the same day. They were certain that the new provision would not have been introduced if they had not asked for it themselves and if they had not had a strong *veza/ štela*. In other words, the social support would not have been slightly improved if they had not been proactive, as well as socially located, beings.

A few days later, Magdalena called me and asked me to go with the parents to the municipality government the following week. During our regular Monday meeting, we discussed which issues to raise at the municipality and we talked extensively about the process of scheduling the meeting. On Saturday, Marija's husband had called Mr. Vuković, his acquaintance and the vice-president of the municipal parliament, to set up a meeting with him on Tuesday. Even though we wanted to discuss problems concerning social protection, we were going to meet with someone who had never worked in a "social sector" of the municipality. Magdalena said that Vuković was a "very strong man" (*vrlo jak čovjek*), which meant that he was politically influential. She also explained to me that without Marija's husband, or some other kind of a connection, they would not have been able to schedule a meeting.

Although the parents often loudly criticized those who used *veze* and *štele* to obtain things, they did not hesitate to use whatever connections they had at their disposal in this situation. A meeting scheduled without a *veza/štela* would have been with "someone unimportant, someone who does not make decisions about anything," said Magdalena with some resignation. The head of the municipal social sector was such a person. An officially scheduled appointment with him seemed like a waste of time to these women. Officially running a sector of municipal governance and being perceived as a person with any actual influence over it were not necessarily the same things.

On Tuesday morning, the six of us met in front of the municipality building at 8:45 and waited for Magdalena, who was late. Vuković's assistant telephoned us at 8:55 to ask where we were. Marija verbally expressed fear as well as excitement. Selma was angry because Magdalena was late, and she said, "What are we to him? It would be awful to miss this opportunity." Once Magdalena arrived, at 9:05, we went to Vuković's office. What first attracted my attention in the office were images of Orthodox saints on the walls and a yearly calendar with a picture of Jesus' face on the top of a black shelf.

We did not introduce ourselves, and the conversation started with Vuković's question: "How are you doing?" This opened a subtle negotiation process between the parents and Vuković. Magdalena replied, "As one has to be. We do not want to complain, but it could be better. It could be much better." Vuković continued talking in the same between-the-lines manner: "Fine, that's good, one shouldn't complain, but have faith and optimism. Problems seem to be much more difficult when one complains. When one has hope and faith, problems diminish." To this, the women responded with a brief description of some of their everyday problems and continued with a detailed account of things that could be improved in the legal and practical organization of the municipality's social protection services. In other words, they came prepared with excerpts from the existing legal acts and with proposals concerning how to harmonize the municipality's legal and practical regulations with those laws.

By the end of the meeting, every one of those women in the room had said at least once that they were not asking for charity but for things they were *legally* entitled to. This repeated attempt to frame social protection as a citizenship right, and therefore as clearly distinct from moral duties, lost some of its strength when Vuković addressed the women as heroes, because of all the troubles they had to deal with every day. The meeting lasted for one hour, throughout which Vuković kept reassuring us that the mayor knew of all their problems. He concluded by saying, "Well, now I am here. I work here and I am familiar with how things work around here—the mayor is God. He has many things to solve, but this is one of his problems as well."

Since Vuković was not familiar with social protection issues, he promised to set up a meeting for us with the mayor. However, a week later, Marija came to the association with bad news: Vuković had informed her husband (note: not her) that the mayor had refused to meet with us. This failed attempt at navigating the municipal government confirmed the position of the mayor as an almost unreachable person—but the only one able to help. Even though the women entered the municipality offices to meet with the vice-president of the municipal parliament, this did not change anything. They had to meet with the mayor.

The parents decided to pursue another route into the municipality government, that is, another *veza/štela*. Mina decided to call Ratka, who she knew by sight (see chapter one). Ratka met with Mina a couple of days later and the meeting with "God" was scheduled. Ratka claimed that the mayor had never been asked about the meeting with us, because he would never have said no. This information provoked a lot of discussion among the parents. They developed several assumptions and possible explanations for why the meeting was not scheduled the first time around: both Vuković and the mayor, and perhaps even Marija's husband, could have lied. However, after some time, they agreed that Vuković was the only person responsible.

This meeting was scheduled for Tuesday, three weeks after our first meeting. This time three of the women who went to the meeting with Vuković could not come, but two others joined us. We met on time, entered the building, and were escorted to a meeting room. The mayor's assistant told us where to sit, because, surprisingly for us, the media were going to be present at the beginning of the meeting. After nervously waiting for fifteen minutes, Magdalena started making sexual jokes, and they asked me to take photographs of them in the mayor's chair. The tension waned and, ten minutes later, the mayor and a woman working in the social sector of the municipality entered the room. Television crews came as well, shooting some footage before leaving.

The first issue that arose was a disagreement over figures: Ivona had previously told us that the municipality's 2010 budget for social protection was effectively 4 percent; the official budget guidelines on the municipality's website listed 8 percent, while the mayor claimed it was between 11 and 12 percent. After we disagreed with this percentage, he admitted that these numbers depended on "the way one calculates." He said that *socijala* (an almost derogatory term for the users of social protection)[6] always occupies the worst position and that he had to listen to the differing needs of various poor people. By this, he expressed his understanding of the women's position, while simultaneously asking for them to understand his position. Such an evocation of understanding reinforced the ambiguity between the mayor's personal and institutional responsibilities.

The mayor was keen to talk about the daycare center, and we insisted on the almost equal importance of the construction of a daycare center *and* of the increase of social provisions. The meeting ended with his promise to see how much they—the people in the municipality—could do for next year's budget and to speed up the planning and construction of a daycare center. After the meeting, the mayor invited Ratka, who happened to be around, and one of the parents to give statements for the press.

Navigating Favors

Favors seem to be particularly important in contexts in which people need to be "lucky": when there are no clear procedural scripts for how things should be organized and no certainty about who is responsible for what. In the world of the international organizations in BiH, in which employment was often a matter of chance and luck, a similar use of sociality with a purpose took place—in the form of networking. The practice of networking for employment opportunities implies presenting oneself as a particular kind of a person and establishing links in all possible directions in order for you to get yourself "on the radar" of potential employers, and of staying there. Among the international employees, networking was framed as a valuable personal skill, while *veze* and *štele* were detested as a form of corruption.

However, in these same organizations, "it was a matter of tacit understanding among the Bosnian employees, that the language of 'professionalism' with which the 'internationals' coded their use of private networks for gaining or maintaining employment at the Mission, was no different from the local practice of *štela*" (Koutkova 2016: 120). The parents used *veze* and *štele* to generate alliances and paths to the improvement of social protection.

Favors offered a logical way of seeking out new associates, navigating different actors, and invoking ideas of duty and responsibility for socially located persons (rather than citizens' rights in relation to the state) as the grounds of social protection. As the ethnographic vignette about the meeting at the municipality reveals, the parents had to change and adapt their social positions in order to negotiate the best possible social protection support for their children; sometimes they were seen as citizens, sometimes as heroic mothers, and sometimes, on yet other occasions, as passive and needy *socijala*. The parents occupied these and similar positions with more or less ease, or at least did not loudly oppose any of them.

Their negotiation of these different social positions did not quite look like what Gershon (2011) describes as "the neoliberal notion of agency." Gershon writes that this conception of agency presupposes "a self that is a flexible bundle of skills that reflexively manages oneself as though the self was a business" (ibid.: 537; see also Martin 2005). This means approaching people as businesses who tend to their own qualities and traits as owned assets and who use market rationality to reflect on social relationships and social strategies. The neoliberal notion of self also involves a distance from which "one is always faced with one's self as a project that must be consciously steered through various possible alliances and obstacles" (Gershon 2011: 539).

The activities of the parents from the Sun did not mirror such ideas. The parents did not discuss themselves as anything remotely similar to businesses, and they did not see their qualities and traits as owned assets that could be turned into something financially valuable. Also, they did not talk about themselves in ethnoreligious or nationalized terms. Rather, they stressed their citizenship status and their gendered roles. The parents often talked about themselves as troubled citizens left alone by both the state and society, as good mothers who would do anything for their children, and as fighters who had to struggle with indifference and prejudice on a daily base.

However, the parents *did* spend a lot of time reflecting on their social relationships and strategies, and they consciously steered around different obstacles and possibilities. Although the parents did not see their personhood in businesslike terms, their procedures of negotiating better social protection were flexible. Their navigation around the wall separating them from the mayor was a flexible movement during which they fulfilled the requirements of being both citizens and socially located persons (a mother, hero, *socijala*, spouse, friend, acquaintance) when needed. Furthermore, parental ignorance and stubbornness were part and parcel of their flexible adaptation, since flexibility includes an element of active selection from a cornucopia of possibilities (Martin 1994: 37).

It does not require a continuous adaptation to all possible options, but a repeated effort to meet those requirements that provide the best opportunities. This was what the parents did: when it mattered from their perspective, they engaged in relational labor, adapted to the needs of the moment, met the politicians, gave statements for the media, and so forth. When the parents did not think that a particular route to improvement mattered, such as the making and selling of bags, they were ignorant and simply let things slip past them. Behaving in a proactive and flexible way in this context meant pursuing favors, rather than engaging in other kinds of activities.

Notes

1. A daycare center is a social protection institution where parents can leave their children to receive professional care and education for eight hours every working day.
2. For a detailed comparative analysis of welfare regimes in Croatia, Macedonia, Serbia, and Slovenia, see Stambolieva 2016. Stambolieva (2015) also suggests that the analysis of welfare transformation in BiH has proven to be especially difficult due to the administrative fragmentation

of the state apparatus, limited sovereignty, and the ensuing complexities of governance.

3. Although social work was initially supposed to be a temporary solution, its professionalization and the new social issues generated by socialist modernization created the need for more social workers. The Schools for Social Work, which offered two-year education programs, were established across the SFRY (Croatia in 1952, Slovenia in 1955, Macedonia in 1957, BiH and Serbia in 1958; see Zaviršek 2008). The social workers found jobs in Centers for Social Work as well as in institutions for healthcare, education, disability insurance, larger companies, or employment offices. In BiH, professional social work was organized in the early 1950s, initially with only ten social workers who had just graduated from schools for social work in other Yugoslav republics (Miković 2006: 448).

4. Leskošek writes that there were also some voluntary organizations in the country, but "they were not independent, because they were founded and financed by the state" (2009: 240).

5. Children with special developmental needs and with no immediate family members were placed in a specialized boarding institution.

6. *Socijala* is a term that more narrowly refers to the users of social protection (i.e., those who have to rely on public support in order to survive). In a wider sense, *socijala* evokes images of poverty, hardship, or charity. For instance, on a popular website from Serbia, Vukajlija (http://vuka jlija.com/socijala?strana=1), where visitors write their own definitions of various words, under the entry *socijala* are the following descriptions:

   1. Any room that has a specific, below-the-average social atmosphere. Sometimes it can even have a particular odor which is easy to recognize … The walls definitely remind one of the working class, yellow-stained walls are painted up to one meter from the floor with an oily paint which usually has an undefined green color, so that dirt sticks as little as possible on the wall. The walls are yellow because of the cigarette smoke, because in such rooms no one respects the no-smoking sign … Tables and chairs were made in 1954. The tables do not even look so old, because they are covered by the torn out and creased blue or plaid table cloths … The chairs look as if they once used to be state-of-the-art of designer creativity, back in their time. Now they do not know how many bottoms they have hosted.

   2. A very good thing if you live in a "normal" country! Literally, social help in all such countries is almost twice as high as our average salary [this is followed by an example; as in many "real" dictionaries, *Vukajlija* users often give examples of a particular definition]:

      I hear you live in Switzerland! How is it there?
      Well, let me tell you, I don't do a thing.
      How come? How do you make a living?

Well, brother, I get *socijala* and *prst u uvo*! [literally, a finger to an ear; this presumably means that the second interlocutor does not have to worry about anything because of the social support they get in Switzerland]

4. *Socijala* is when you switch from Winston to another cigarette brand, because the price of Winston increased.
5. It's when you get into a cab, ask if they offer a discount on trips ordered by phone, and if they do, you go out, phone the cab company, and get the discount.

Part III
Power

Chapter 5

Managing Ambiguity in Social Protection

Inequalities Concerning Favors: The "Goddess" of Welfare

After the meeting with the municipal mayor described in the previous chapter, a group of parents from the Sun met Ratka in the municipal hallway. This was not unexpected: if you needed to access welfare support in the Town, the chances were that you would stumble upon Ratka at some point. Ratka had many functions: she was a member of the local municipal parliament, a close associate of the mayor of the Town, and a member of his right-wing nationalist party, the SDS (Serbian Democratic Party), which played a leading role in the 1992–95 war. Ratka was also the director of an influential local Orthodox Christian charity and the head of the municipal Coordinating Committee for Social Protection. Finally, she ran municipal welfare work groups and was a language teacher in a public school. Such a diversity of roles meant that Ratka was a busy woman who provided favors in various public and private arenas. Her ability to help others was well known in the Town, and people often claimed she was "wonderful," "caring," or even a "goddess."

Since I was with the parents that day, I saw that the mayor and one of the parents from the Sun had moved over to where the TV crews were standing to give press statements. The mayor invited Ratka to give a press statement too, although she had not been present at the meeting. This event demonstrates that people in the Town perceived *veze/štele* as fairly important: Ratka was the person who did the parents a favor by scheduling the meeting with the mayor. As a direct link between the parents and the mayor, Ratka was considered to constitute an important enough part of the meeting itself. Later that afternoon, I watched the TV report about the meeting. It was not clear in what capacity Ratka gave the press statement: as a member of the municipal parliament, as the president of the religious charity, as a member of the mayor's political party, as the head of the municipal committee for social protection, as a concerned citizen, or as someone else.

Her words did not reveal whether she was present at the meeting or what her role was regarding this particular issue (social support for people living with disabilities). Such ambiguities about Ratka's roles and responsibilities appeared to be the rule, rather than the exception; in many cases, it was unclear whether Ratka helped others because she had a public responsibility to do so or because she experienced an "impulse of philanthropy" (Bornstein 2009)—that is, a personal drive to help—or some combination of both.

This chapter explores the form of power gained by the successful management of ambiguity in social protection. It ethnographically focuses on the social position of Ratka in order to shed light on how favors reproduced unequal power relations. The chapter argues that people who successfully managed ambiguities concerning responsibilities in social protection accumulated power. People who were able to help others access a resource via *veze/štele* in several public and private arenas occupied the position of a person able to manage ambiguity. Assuming many different roles allowed one to manage ambiguity, while giving away public and private resources. This was a position of simultaneous official and unofficial influence created by intentionally keeping the boundaries between the public and the private ambiguous.

That ambiguity and power were firmly related and embodied in a single person is not a Bosnian, or a Balkan, peculiarity—patrons and brokers gain power by successfully managing ambiguity throughout the Mediterranean and Eastern European contexts—as, indeed, people have done in different times and places (Schmidt et al. 1977; Eisenstadt and Roniger 1984; Li Causi 1975). However, such links are often discussed as characteristics of "dysfunctional" states and societies (see chapter two). My argument criticizes the assumption that ambiguity can be related to power only due to the specificities of developing contexts.

Gathering power by managing ambiguity became possible in a new way with the neoliberal dispersion of responsibility for welfare, exercised by both international and local actors who worked in the country. The widespread importance of *veze/štele* in welfare was not a peculiarity of Bosnian, or Balkan, cultures or a sensible response to the systemic deficiencies of a developing country. Instead, the significance of *veze/štele* was a reflection of ambiguity about public and personal responsibilities introduced by the internationally supervised welfare reforms. In order to unpack this argument, we first need to rethink ambiguity as a constitutive element of hegemonic discourses and modes of governance.

Hegemonic Ambiguity

Ambiguity in anthropology is approached from different vantage points. Most often, ambiguity has been understood to contain potential for a world ordered otherwise (see Augé 1998; Herzfeld 2005). Ambiguity has the potential to challenge the stability of identity categories, thus posing conceptual and practical difficulties for the modernist ways of thinking and acting. However, it does not always necessarily do so. The hegemonic view of the Balkans, for instance, turns ambiguity on its head:

> Far from an apparent stability and fixity that the analyst must unpick to reveal the fluidity and indeterminacy upon which it is based, the hegemonic discourse on the Balkans insists that the region is fluidity and indeterminacy personified, right on the surface, a completely explicit fog, as it were. (Green 2005: 12)

In other words, although "most (modern) hegemonic assertions … are aimed at avoiding or concealing ambiguity, not asserting that ambiguity is the point of something" (Green 2005: 10–11), the lack of clear-cut boundaries between categories does not inherently have the potential for a world ordered otherwise. Indeed, ambiguous and hybrid identities can be claimed as an essentialist possession. A case in point is an understanding of Istria, Croatia, as a region where cultural and linguistic hybridity is "rooted in the soil," due to the different states, borders, and people that came and went through the region throughout the twentieth century (Ballinger 2002). Such an understanding of hybridity does not subvert essentialist frameworks but instead reproduces them, serving as a demarcation point between the presumed Europeanness of Istria and the Balkanness of the rest of the former Yugoslavia (Ballinger 2004; see also Brunnbauer and Grandits 2013; Reeves 2013).

Furthermore, Green argues, hegemonic discourse on the Balkans as a place of ambiguity is a "fantasy with teeth," in the sense that it shapes not just how things seem but how they are (2005: 158). Understanding the Balkans as an impossibly ambiguous place may be "an ideologically mediated invention," but it also "affects how things are, whether or not people believe the invention" (ibid.). Similarly, in BiH's welfare assemblages, ambiguity had "teeth." Whether or not people thought that social protection should be, or is, ambiguous, its ambiguities were actively generated, intensified, or transformed into clarity (very often via *veze/štele*).

However, not everybody could do this. People who were able to manage ambiguity of welfare were those with more power; their power stemmed from and further reproduced ambiguities of social protection. Wedel uses the term "flexians" to describe actors who generate power by managing ambiguity in contemporary international politics, consultancy, and development: "These players live symbiotically within the system, quietly evading and stretching its rules as they help mediate its transformation. The new system they help fashion blurs the boundaries between the state and private sectors, bureaucratic and market practices, and legal and illegal standing" (2009: 15).

Working for others is an important feature of flexians—they occupy public roles that are supposed to serve the greater good of the community (Stubbs 2013). Yet, the way in which they do so depends on—and reproduces—ambiguities between public and private roles and responsibilities, enabling the further production of flexible power: "Flexians thrive on ambiguous identities, appearances, loyalties, and borders of practically all kinds" (Wedel 2009: 45). Ratka's practices of establishing, calibrating, and translating relations between public and private arenas could easily be understood as a case of flexianism. Providing favors to others—*and* occupying multiple public and private roles at the same time—produced power through the management of ambiguity.

This was a sort of "lawless and prerogatory power, a 'rogue' power par excellence" (Butler 2004: 56). Butler offers the figure of a petty sovereign as a tool to think about the organization of power in contexts where the institutional and legal frameworks of a state are bracketed, for instance in camps such as Guantanamo Bay. These figures "are beholden to nothing and to no one except the performative power of their own decisions," (ibid.: 65) and, although they are not "true sovereigns," they are "constituted, within the constraints of governmentality, as those who will and do decide on who will be detained, and who will not, who may see life outside the prison again and who may not, and this constitutes an enormously consequential delegation and seizure of power" (ibid.: 62).

A similar form of petty sovereignty, a personal power that works through institutions and that reflects resurrected sovereignty within the field of governmentality, was possible in the Town not because institutional and legal frameworks that protected survival and well-being were bracketed, or placed on hold, but because they were made ambiguous.

Postsocialist Neoliberalism

I argued earlier that neoliberal reconfigurations of welfare in BiH produced an environment in which the status of social protection was profoundly ambiguous, while its procedures were often left open to personal imagination and skill (see chapters three and four). In this book, neoliberalism is understood not as a consistent set of policies or a coherent body of knowledge and practice that travels globally but as a term that marks a period of experimentation and transformation of relations between society and the state, going away from the welfare state models to something else in various directions and with different intensities on a global scale.

While the contours of this something else are not yet clear, some of the basic ideas underpinning neoliberal restructurings are that the market relations should be allowed to regulate any sphere of life and that the state should reduce its role in the economy and protection of its citizens, particularly the vulnerable ones. In one shape or another, these ideas can be found in "mobile calculative techniques of governing that can be decontextualized from their original sources and recontextualized in constellations of mutually constitutive and contingent relations" (Ong 2006: 13). Although these techniques of governing may have spread across the globe, they do not automatically form "the dominant or organizing principle for the places and sites where they appear" (Clarke 2008: 138). In BiH, for instance, neoliberal restructuring of social protection created ambiguities that were managed through favors.

Neoliberalism was articulated as a contingent response to particular, historically shaped problems of the welfare state during Cold War discussions about how best to organize the relationship between the state, society, and economy (Collier 2011: 136).[1] Arguing against the idea that neoliberal policies spread across the world through a network of right-wing associations, think tanks, foundations, and university departments that "packaged the neoliberal ideas of academic economists as a clear and concise course of action and had the resources to promote this package worldwide," Bockman suggests, "The origins of neoliberalism were not in hegemony but in liminality" (2007: 343).

Focusing on the work of an Italian think tank called CESES (the Center for the Study of Economic and Social Problems), Bockman asserts that neoliberalism emerged from conversations led at liminal places that were established during the Cold War between "Soviet socialism and Western capitalism."[2] These conversations allowed the right-wing and the left-wing economists and scholars from both the East and the West to learn about capitalist and socialist experiments, thus contributing to different goals. For instance:

> To members of the Mont Pelerin Society, socialism became a laboratory for economic knowledge, knowledge that they could then use for battles about capitalism back in their home countries … This knowledge was not only utopian or ideological; it also allowed economists and economic elites to understand capitalism through knowledge about socialism and thus shaped the neoliberal political project itself. Furthermore, this knowledge also allowed those on the left in the East and the West to understand actually existing socialism and what socialism could become. This detailed knowledge about the other—Western capitalism or Soviet socialism—could not be obtained directly, but rather had to travel through liminal spaces. (Bockman 2007: 347)

Similarly, Collier suggests that neoliberalism does not present a coherent ideology, but rather "a form of critical reflection on governmental practice distinguished by an attempt to reanimate the principles of classical liberalism in light of new circumstances—most centrally, for my purposes, the rise of the social state" (2011: 2). He asserts that neoliberalism cannot be reduced to policies such as shock programs, privatization, or budgetary austerity, because these policies were articulated under the specific historical conditions of the late twentieth century and new problems and new responses have appeared since (ibid.: 136). Criticizing the idea that neoliberalism means the end of public welfare support, and particularly of social protection, Collier writes that neoliberalism emerged as a contextually specific response to the problems of the welfare state. In post-Soviet Russia, it included attempts to reprogram the state by appropriating elements of Soviet state infrastructure into new, flexible, and quickly transforming modes of governing:

> I did not find that neoliberal thinkers were blind to the need for social protection. I did not find in neoliberal reforms a total program of mar-

ketization or government through calculative choice that wiped away the existing forms of Soviet social welfare. In the domains I studied, neoliberal reforms propose to *selectively* reconfigure inherited material structures, demographic patterns, and social norms. They suggest new ways of programming government through the state that retain the social welfare norms established by Soviet socialism. (Collier 2011: 3, emphasis added)

I think this selectivity is of key importance in understanding the shape that the process of neoliberalization took in BiH. Neoliberalization gave rise to risks and problems as well as to chances and opportunities for various groups of people throughout the world (Montoya 2014; Hodges 2014). Hickel suggests that neoliberalism presents

> a *selective* use of free market principles in favor of powerful economic actors. For instance, US policymakers gladly embrace market freedom if it allows corporations to exploit cheap labor abroad and undermine domestic unions. But on the other hand they refuse to heed the WTO's [World Trade Organization's] demands that they abolish their massive agricultural subsidies (which distort the competitive advantage of third world countries), because that would run against the interests of a powerful corporate lobby.[3]

Across Eastern Europe, postsocialist states did not simply withdraw from welfare; instead, "neoliberal reforms reconfigured preexisting divisions between public and private" (Read and Thelen 2007: 4). A reconfiguration of the relationship between "state" and "society" and between "public" and "private" means that various postsocialist state actors continue to shape welfare, but their responsibilities and procedures have changed in unprecedented ways (Petryna 2002; Stan 2012). The neoliberalization of social policies in former Yugoslav countries was a contested and unfinished process during which the labor market was thoroughly liberalized, but there was resistance to the privatization of pensions and only partial marketization of some health services (Deacon, Lendvai, and Stubbs 2007). The status of social protection in BiH was also changed, whereby responsibility for social protection was spread throughout the local community among state, civic, and private actors, as we saw in chapters three and four.

The selective reconfiguration of different aspects of social protection has led to the proliferation of ambiguities. In the Town, (ridiculously small) financial provisions are paid from the state budgets, while providing a daycare center and similar institutional services are presented as an ambiguous, both moral and civic, duty of interested public, private, and civic actors simultaneously. Furthermore, as a result of the selective reprogramming of the state, new forms of sociality have become relevant (Collier and Way 2004; Matza 2012; Read 2007; Stan 2012).

The case in point in BiH is humanitarian actions (*humanitarne akcije*), which will be discussed in chapter six. In humanitarian actions, public funds were often redistributed on the basis of compassion and the personal connections of a family in need—and the same thing happened in programs such as committees for one-off support and the mayor's discretionary financial help to individuals in urgent need. Welfare assemblages in postsocialist countries often contain such gray zones in which ambiguities are normalized (Harboe 2014; Harboe and Frederiksen 2015). Muehlebach's (2011, 2012) work suggests that these sorts of shifts are not a strange by-product of postsocialist transformations but a more general direction taken by contemporary neoliberalizing logics of governance. Muehlebach demonstrates that the Italian state in the region of Lombardy has withdrawn social service programs for the elderly and the unemployed over the past few years.

At the same time, the state has initiated highly moralized discourses according to which citizens should be compassionate and kind toward those who need help, which has led to a phenomenal rise in voluntarism. In this way, the protection of the elderly and the unemployed in Lombardy ceased to be a citizen's right. Instead, it has become the responsibility of "loving citizens" and "ethical citizens": those who work in charitable or religious organizations. Similar experiments across Europe have moved the responsibility for welfare from the state to the wider social community, encouraging new forms of uncertainty as well as new, voluntary and humanitarian, ways of understanding and practicing citizenship. Morality is a constitutive element of the delivery of social protection in BiH as well, which has opened up a space to get things done via *veze/štele*, often with the help of persons such as Ratka.

Spending Oneself through Favors

My interlocutors from the Sun sometimes called Ratka "a goddess" (*boginja*). By doing so, they followed the common practice in post-Yugoslav countries of using superlatives to refer to a person who does something extraordinary; people would use the terms "king" (*kralj*) or "empress" (*carica*) to indicate their admiration of someone's abilities or to mock someone's stupidity instead of evoking royal or imperial polities. Similarly, the term "goddess" did not resonate with particular religious meanings but expressed adulation and praise of Ratka's extraordinariness.

Parents from the Sun also often said that Ratka puts her heart into helping others, that she "spends herself" (*troši se*) for the sake of others, and that everything she does will "eat her up" (*poješće je*), unless she is careful and takes care of herself. The terms they used indicate that with every bit of help, Ratka gave a part of herself to others: every favor Ratka conducted contained a part of her own personality. She could "spend" herself and "be eaten up" by doing things for others because favors were more than practical tools to overcome the deficiencies of the BiH economic and political systems: favors reproduced people's identities and senses of self (see chapter two). *Veze/štele* bore the inerasable marks of people's personalities.

I met Ratka most often at humanitarian events organized in the Town. I also volunteered at her religious charity, the Holy Mother, for five months. Although I often talked with her, Ratka's position and influence became apparent to me through listening to how other people talked about her. Stories concerning Ratka's help were numerous and recounted to me by many different people in the Town. We learned some of those stories in earlier chapters—Ratka helped people register a humanitarian telephone number (chapter one), receive medical treatment (chapter two), get a job (chapter two), meet with public officials (chapter four), and so forth. Let us take a closer look at more such stories.

Public Resources

As we saw in chapter two, Ratka helped Zoran to get a job at the local library. Formally, Zoran did not need Ratka's help to get the job. He had all the credentials necessary for it, and the library was in need of new workers. Ratka's favor in this case meant inducing a personal willingness in the director of the library to open a call for a new job post and to give the job to Zoran. Even though formally the application procedure was followed by the book, Zoran could not get the job without Ratka as a *veza*.

Ratka also helped Sanja, a parent from the Sun, to arrange an appointment with a medical practitioner for Sanja's child. This particular practitioner was very busy, so he put Sanja on a waiting list. Since Sanja had to see him as soon as possible, she got in touch with Ratka.

Ratka called the practitioner and asked him to agree to Sanja jumping the queue, which he did. Sanja met with him a couple of days after Ratka's phone call.

Private Resources

Accounts of Ratka helping people to access public services were closely intertwined with stories about how she helped through the Orthodox religious charity called the Holy Mother. One of those stories was about a phone call Ratka received from a family who did not have the money required to pay an electricity bill. This was especially disturbing since the medicine for their child had to be kept in the refrigerator. Ratka immediately called the accountant of the Holy Mother and made sure that the bill was paid a day later.

I heard another such story from Magdalena, another parent from the Sun. As mentioned in the Introduction, Magdalena had to send her son's medical test results to Norway and Sweden for special analyses. She needed money to mail the results, so she called Ratka to ask for help. Magdalena remembered that Ratka's response was "Stand right there and wait for me." Ratka came soon with KM 200 (EUR 100). The immediacy of her response was one of the most frequently commented on aspects in these stories.[4] After hearing Magdalena's account, another parent at the meeting approvingly said that Ratka was "the only person in the municipal government fighting for our children." Public roles in the municipal government did not seem too different from private charitable activities.

Public–Private Partnerships

A rumor going around in 2009 and 2010 was that the daycare center for children with disabilities would be opened in a partnership between the municipality and the Holy Mother, whereby the Holy Mother would raise donations and the center would be run with its help. An obvious problem with this plan was the conflation of a public service with religiously motivated charitable work—in a country where two decades ago religious and ethnonational divisions between (Muslim) Bosniaks, (Catholic) Croats, and (Orthodox) Serbs were one of the key elements of the war (Bougarel et al. 2007).

A less visible problem with this plan was that it reinforced existing ambiguities of power arrangements in the Town. Ratka was not only the director of the Holy Mother but also the head of the municipal bodies working on planning the daycare and coordinating social protection. Upon hearing that she could be responsible for opening and running the daycare center, the parents from the Sun seemed to be even more in awe of her than before. The possibility for a much needed service to be provided in cooperation with her charity weakened any potential criticism of the conflation of religious motivations with a sense of public entitlement.

Furthermore, the notion of "public–private partnerships" offered a new framework to interpret the already existing practices of informal cooperation. During our interview, Ratka said to me:

> I used it [her role as a politician] a lot, I can say freely, because we received the greatest amount of help from the municipality—official help, directed to organizations and projects, and help from individuals. For example, the largest donations came from the mayor—from his personal resources. He once gave us KM 4500 [EUR 2250] of his yearly travel allowances, another time he gave us 10 percent of his salary. Then on another occasion he gave us KM 2,000 [EUR 1,000], which was 10 percent of his salary for six months, I think … and all of the officials on the level of the municipality [gave donations].

This quotation illustrates well how Ratka rhetorically conflated public responsibility for welfare with the mayor's personal goodwill. She briefly mentions "official help" to the Holy Mother, that is, the financial support coming from the municipal budget. She then jumps straight to the mayor, conflating the mayor's gifts with the municipal budget. Her words make it hard to distinguish the line between the public obligation of the mayor and the personal donations he gave, which suggests that the responsibilities of public officials were easily understood as officials' personal gifts.

Keeping-while-Giving

While we sat in the ornamented dining area of the local Orthodox church, which also served as the offices of the Holy Mother charity, Ratka was explaining to me how she "spent" herself for the sake of others. She said, "I used it [her role as a politician] as a direct advantage, because I think that as a politician I have a duty to work for the people." While this might have been the case, the reverse argument can also be made: that Ratka conducted favors in order to generate power and become a politician. By giving away parts of her personality through *veze/štele,* Ratka managed to get an official political position. *Veze/štele* were not just reciprocal relations of mutual help among equally positioned persons. Under certain conditions, they reproduced power and hierarchy.

Discussing the paradox of keeping-while-giving in various contexts in Oceania, Weiner (1992) argues that certain practices of exchange that seem to be reciprocal in fact reproduce hierarchies between people. This is because, sometimes, actors in an exchange can keep aside the objects that are considered too valuable, since they materialize the senses of belonging, cosmologies, and ideologies. Keeping aside the objects important for the social survival of the group, while giving away others, becomes a way of transforming differences between people into hierarchy and rank. Those who can keep "inalienable possessions" (difference), while reciprocally exchanging other objects, become those with an elevated status (hierarchy).

Weiner's account of small-scale communities in Oceania is positioned as a criticism of the anthropological understanding of exchange practices as primarily reciprocal. Despite the vast differences between the Oceanic and the Balkan social contexts, some elements of the paradox of keeping-while-giving are useful for understanding the mechanisms of power in the neoliberalizing Bosnian welfare arrangements. Pursuing and granting favors may have seemed to be a practice of reciprocity, a deposit in a "bank" of favors (Caldwell 2004). Indeed, for many people in the Town, pursuits of *veze/štele* included a strong coerciveness regarding reciprocity: I do a favor for you, placing an obligation upon you to do a favor for me in the future. However, Ratka managed to use this outward appearance of reciprocity to gather power by keeping something aside.

As she functioned as a *veza/štela* for many different things, Ratka gave help while keeping aside the ability to decide who would get things done, when, and in what way. Her invaluable possession was her multiple public and private roles that enabled her to manage ambiguity on different scales and to decide if particular support was more like a legal entitlement or a compassionate gift. The principle of keeping (an ability to manage ambiguity) while giving (help to others) meant that the more diverse *veze/štele* one could provide, the greater power one had, and vice versa: the greater power one had, the more *veze/štele* one could provide of a different kind. In order to generate power, one had to be able to provide favors in different domains: in healthcare, municipal administrations, social protection, and so forth.

Ratka's flexible power was both institutional and personal. To put it more precisely, it was a form of power that was created by the successful translation of institutionalized into personalized relations and back. In order to be an active member of the municipal parliament, to run state bodies for social protection, and to participate in elections—in order to become a politically powerful woman—Ratka had to help people to find employment, receive medical treatment, or pay their rent and vice versa. Her power emerged through keeping, giving, and taking across multiple and shifting public and private arenas. This flexible form of power was in some sense also fragile, since there was the looming possibility of being "eaten up" by it.

We should keep in mind that women who want to do political work in BiH "must continue to be perceived *as women,* and moral women at that" (Helms 2007: 237). Politics in BiH is a thoroughly gendered practice, often understood as a "whore," that is, as a corrupt, immoral, and manipulative activity. As Helms suggests, "While politics is in this way feminized, it is nonetheless understood and portrayed in everyday and official discourses alike as a male arena where women, especially respectable women, have no place" (ibid.: 236). Therefore, in order to be recognized as a politician, Ratka strived to be seen as a "moral woman." However, notice that Ratka worked in social protection—rather than in programs of peace reconciliation, democracy building, or any other field where she could present herself as a moral woman. Social protection provided a fine ground for the managers of ambiguity because it was undergoing a neoliberally informed reform, which made personal goodness and compassion—and, by extension, favors—important.

People who occupied a single role within an institution could not accumulate power in this way. They also provided favors, but they could do so only within the specific context of where they worked. For instance, Branko was a man who helped one family obtain passports to take their son across the border for medical treatment. He could help access the municipal government administration, but he had no influence in other public or private institutions. The parents from the Sun often criticized random acts of people like Branko, those who had no other role than that of, for example, a municipal or a social worker. However, I never heard them voicing any direct complaint for the same kind of acts about Ratka or other people who occupied multiple public and private positions.

In the face of widespread dissatisfaction with the randomness of welfare, this absence of open criticism of people with multiple roles for redistributing resources via *veze/štele* is important because it suggests that power emerged from granting favors, while keeping aside an ability to manage the ambiguity. Power emerged from the awareness that a petty sovereign who helps you to meet a doctor is also someone who might decide whether to help you get a job, whether to pay your electricity bill, and whether to open a daycare center for your child (or whether to accept your child in the daycare center).

Flexibility and Ambiguity: Slippages of Influence and Meaning

In Ratka's work, meanings and practices slipped over the provisional boundaries of institutions. It was impossible to distinguish what exactly increased her own influence, wealth, and power—and what increased the influence and power of her political party (the SDS), the Serbian Orthodox Church, "her people" (that is, the Serbs), and BiH citizens. Discussing the institution of Big Men in Melanesia, Wagner suggests that a dichotomy between helping oneself and helping one's group is false, because "the big man aspires to something that is both at once" (1991: 162). Ratka's actions can perhaps be understood in the same way. Initiatives that could be analytically separated as "charitable work," "parliamentary politics," or "religious and nationalist proselytizing" affected one another in a way that enabled Ratka to aspire to several things at once.

Ambiguities between personal and public responsibilities make it impossible to claim that the support coming from Ratka were clearcut instances of nationalist and religious proselytizing, although it is also impossible to claim this support was neutral in terms of ethnonational belonging and party politics. For instance, when she stated, "As a politician I have a duty to work for the people," she used the word *narod* (the people), which is a "discursive, transient category without a politically articulated essence" that can "capture both ethnic (exclusionary, homogenising) belonging and trans-ethnic (inclusionary, heterogeneous) identifications" (Hromadžić 2013: 260). In this way, she discursively left ambiguous whether her duty was to work for the ethnonational category of the Serbs to which she personally belonged or for the Bosnian citizens, which she was supposed to officially represent as a municipal politician.

The same ambiguities were present in her practice. Through myriad public and private roles, Ratka personally helped some Croats and Bosniaks living in the Town, and a few Muslim families occasionally received support from her Orthodox Christian charity. And yet, Ratka's personal actions (her religious charitable work and providing favors to others) bore the mark of all of her institutional roles, including that of being an SDS party member—and vice versa. For instance, a couple of weeks before the elections for the entity's parliament, one of the parents from the Sun suggested to other parents that they vote for Ratka. This was not because she particularly supported, or was even aware of, the political program of the SDS but because she thought that if Ratka was in the parliament, they would have a direct *veza* to the highest political body in the entity—and their situation would stand a greater chance of improving.

This slippage of influence and meaning from charitable work to parliamentary politics, to state-supported projects of social protection, to religious and nationalist proselytizing was possible because Ratka's flexible power worked within a political and social framework in which there was an increasing emphasis on blurring the boundaries between the state and society. Such conflations of public and personal made it irrelevant—and perhaps impossible to say—whether Ratka was really a good person or whether she was cynically helping others while knowing full well that she was keeping-while-giving. The more important thing for me here is that ambiguity can be oppressive, as the frequent complaints about social protection suggest, and that its management reproduced—rather than challenged—the existing inequalities and power arrangements in the Town.

The Emergence of a Flexian
in the Midst of Sociopolitical Transformations

Ratka's biography reveals how she assumed a position from which she could manage ambiguity with ease. Before the 1992–95 war, Ratka had lived and worked in social protection in a town close to Sarajevo. During the war, she became a displaced person and lived in a nearby village for some time before moving to the Town. Since the Bosniak population of that village had been violently expelled, the village was used at the time to house Serbs displaced from other places in BiH. While in the village, Ratka helped other displaced persons sort out the documentation they needed to apply for healthcare ID cards, wrote legal pleas for women who needed to communicate with institutions across the Inter Entity Boundary Line (which separates the two BiH postwar entities), and so forth. In one of our discussions, she told me this was her own "personal, unorganized way of helping people." Soon after moving to the Town, Ratka became the president of the local Red Cross, a position she left when she was elected as a member of municipal parliament.

This means that, after offering personal, unorganized help during the war and during the early postwar years, Ratka gained official legitimacy as a "moral woman" through being part of a well-established humanitarian organization. A Red Cross office (later Red Cross and Red Crescent) was registered for the first time in the Town in the 1930s. It was closed during World War II and reopened in 1945. During the 1992–95 war, the office worked mainly with refugees. Being part of the Red Cross and Red Crescent meant being a part of an already recognized and influential organization. After winning a second mandate in the local parliament, Ratka became involved in founding the Holy Mother. A new organization opened up the possibility of defining new rules of the game.

Importantly, these were the years in which the Town—and the whole of BiH—was undergoing profound transformation. If Ratka was successfully moving across different orders of knowledge and experience when pursuing and granting *veze/štele,* the relationship between these orders was shifting while she was moving—and she was in a position in which she could manage how it would shift, up to a point. In the Town, the postsocialist and postwar conflation of understanding what constitutes personal humanitarian work and what constitutes legal obligation in social protection has been a consequence of her work in this field, at least in part.

The SDS—Ratka's and the mayor's party—had been in power in the Town since the early 1990s, a period in which housing, roads and sewage systems had to be, and had been, built and renewed, as well as hospitals, schools, kindergartens, daycare centers, cafés, and cinemas, and so on. This presented a perfect testing ground in which Ratka and other members of the SDS could define new rules of the game in a number of fields. They had the opportunity to insert themselves where needed and to become "big people" (*veliki ljudi*) or "strong people" (*jaki ljudi*), as they were occasionally called.[5] They were in a position to organize social and political space in particular ways.

Ratka's new religious charity, the Holy Mother, played a major role in redefining meanings and practices pertaining to who was responsible for welfare and in what way, particularly with regard to the social protection of people with developmental disabilities. The Holy Mother propagated the importance of compassion, fate, favors, and gatekeepers, conflating ideas about what—in social protection—constitutes legal obligation and what is instead a matter of personal goodwill. The Holy Mother volunteers visited families in the Town who had children with developmental disabilities once a year, typically for each child's birthday, and sometimes on Orthodox Christian holidays. They regularly brought small items of help, such as cake and/or diapers.

Since there were fewer than ten volunteers and more than a hundred families, the volunteers went on the birthday visits a couple of times per week. Ratka went to every house the Holy Mother visited during the first two years of the organization's work in the early 2000s. By doing so, she met every single family listed in the files of her organization. This meant that her phone number quickly spread throughout the Town and municipality, enabling her to be a *veza/štela* for an increasing number of people. After the first two years, Ratka stopped attending the weekly visits, but her other volunteers kept the relationships with the families going. Once she had become a member of the "world of people" of these families, they could contact her when they needed a *veza/štela* for various things.

If we look at parts of Ratka's biography again, we can see a set of successive steps, each leading to a greater ability to manipulate the boundaries of social space. While working at the Red Cross and the Red Crescent, Ratka dedicated her time to accumulating the financial and material resources of other people and distributing them to those who were in greatest need of them in the form of humanitarian help, placing herself at the center of the new and random networks of redistribution. In doing so, she became an influential person and officially involved in party politics, able to control access to different state resources. She skillfully combined personal power with the power of "faceless" bureaucracy. Once her position as a municipal parliament member seemed to be secure, she founded the Holy Mother and became the head of a state body for social welfare. This enabled her to redefine the boundaries of private and public when helping others and thus to manipulate the tension between social protection as a moral duty and a civic right.

Conclusion

Neoliberalizing welfare arrangements produce ambiguous environments that most people can only navigate in their pursuits of social support. Simultaneously, some people can manage ambiguities of welfare, increasing their own power and status along the way. This chapter has looked at how management of ambiguity in social protection generated power, suggesting that differing abilities to engage with ambiguity reflect and reproduce differences in power and status. The goddess of welfare generated "lawless and prerogatory," "rogue" power (Butler 2004), operating across the personal and the institutional, the private and the public. This power was also fragile, since it required continuous personal investment, creating a danger of spending, or exhausting, oneself through it.

Brief references to the mayor indicate that the Town was also inhabited with people who generated political and economic power in more conventional ways. Due to the character of my ethnographic fieldwork, I learned very little about such people. Journalistic and political, as well as everyday, narratives indicate that social protection provides an easy mechanism to buy votes throughout former Yugoslav countries: various think tanks and activists claim that the ruling political parties give one-off support in the preelection period in exchange for political allegiance and a vote. This exchange falls more directly into corruption or dyadic patron–clientelist relations.

If there were such exchanges in the Town, I have no data on it. This is perhaps due to the secrecy of the matter. More importantly, the sorts of exchanges I followed were not tied to the preelection period. The work of favors in everyday life—the reasons for pursuing them and the forms of sociality, obligation, and power reproduced through them—differs in important ways from such presumably straightforward instances of corruption and clientelism.

Did Ratka's practices present a form of patronage? The answer to this question depends on what we mean by "patronage" and "clientelism." Ratka was not a patron who connected a community to the centralized state apparatus or who provided resources and services solely for political loyalty and allegiance through dyadic relations. Yet, if we understand clientelism and favors as an element of the contemporary regimes of flexible governance in which "'norms' in the Foucauldian sense could no longer be specified because any possible point of reference would not stay still long enough" (Martin 2005: 195) and as a way to translate across the personal and the institutional, she was a patron—someone who generated power by managing ambiguities of welfare support when helping others. Throughout the twentieth century, patronage and clientelism were largely understood as long-term, informal, reciprocal, personal (and often dyadic) relations between persons of unequal status and power in which favors are exchanged for political allegiance and loyalty.

The concepts of clientelism and patronage were often grounded in a set of distinctions between the presumably rational system of the center (the nation–state and its centralized administration) and the presumably social and affective systems of rural communities living in the peripheries of a country (Silverman 1965; Galt 1974). Discussions of favors in postsocialist contexts during the 1990s and 2000s rarely revolved around the concepts of "clients" and "patrons" and "centers" and "peripheries." Instead, favors in Eastern Europe are usually discussed through the language of ambiguities, tensions, and negotiations. Favors in socialist and postsocialist contexts usually did not involve discrete local (peripheral) and national (central) communities but exchanges among members of the same polity—many of whom had shared economic and sociopolitical status (Ledeneva 1998). In numerous cases, favors operated within and outside of the state apparatus and there were no obvious patrons, since it seemed that everybody was brokering something for someone else.

This meant that favors were not understood through a distinction between the center and the periphery. However, the systemic deficiency was looked for in the developing states and their markets. Understanding favors primarily as a by-product of deficient national democracies and markets implicitly suggests that once these states are fully developed and modernized, there will be no further need for it, thereby preventing thinking through the ways in which favors may reflect contemporary globalized sociopolitical and economic processes (see Shore 2006). Furthermore, taking processes within a single country as a relevant scale of reference shrouds the ways in which flexibilization and favors may support one another.

This chapter has attempted to intervene in this by suggesting that *veze/štele* reproduced power in the neoliberalizing environment by shifting state and personal relations—and public and private arenas—as points of reference in welfare, especially with regard to the social protection of people with developmental disabilities. One of the basic characteristics of *veze/štele* in BiH is that they loosen the boundaries between the state and society and enable people to move across them.

In his classic account of patronage in a Greek village in the mid-twentieth century, Campbell writes that the system of favors "introduces a flexibility into administrative machinery whose workings are very often directed by persons remote from the people whose fortunes they are affecting" (1964: 247). Although in post-Dayton BiH the problems were the randomness and ambiguity of welfare, rather than the remoteness of the administrative machinery, *veze/štele* similarly encouraged flexibility within the governance of survival and reproduced the tension between what constituted a legitimate public duty and what was to be regulated by personal, humanitarian goodwill.

Veze/štele have a long history in BiH and, as a locally meaningful way of relating, they became important in a new way during the transition of welfare policies. This chapter does not aim to suggest that all *veze/štele* in contemporary BiH reflected such changes: *veze/štele* in education, top business, or party politics might have worked differently. Instead, it suggests that *veze/štele* were not far away from transnational processes and could be approached beyond the framework of a (deficient) state. The shifts in understanding welfare were the result of simultaneous postsocialist and postwar transformations of BiH. However, the lack of sufficiently stable points of reference characterizes new directions in governance of survival across the world.

In global arenas of international consultancy, development, and politics, ambiguity about public and private roles and responsibilities brings certain individuals power (Wedel 2009). Something similar is happening in BiH welfare, in which the successful management of ambiguity brought power. Although state social services and private charitable activities could be distinguished "on paper" by nominally separate budgets, motivations, and mechanisms of work, in practice, people like Ratka merged them and then separated them, as needed. Occupying numerous positions in public and private arenas enabled such people to manage ambiguity between these arenas, while providing different kinds of favors to others. Through such keeping (of an ability to manage ambiguity)-while-giving (offering help), power emerged.

Notes

1. Busch, however, suggests that the origins of neoliberalism can be traced back to a 1938 Paris meeting of a group of intellectuals advocating liberalism, bankers, lawyers, and industrialists, including F.A. Hayek, Michael Polanyi, Raymond Aron, and Alfred Schütz. Discussing the problems of fascism, Stalinism, and liberalism in France, the United Kingdom, and the United States, they concluded, "If left unchecked, the nation–state would stifle all liberty and freedom," so "what was needed was a new liberalism—a *neo*liberalism—in which an activist state would be always and everywhere at the service of the market … The end result would be greater individual liberty—liberty bounded not by arbitrary rules of nation–states but by competition in the marketplace" (2010: 332).

2. Bockman mentions other such transnational academic places: "During the 1960s and early 1970s, the Praxis Group in Yugoslavia brought together East European and Western intellectuals at the Korcula Summer School to discuss Marxism and critically analyze both Soviet socialist and Western capitalist societies … From the late 1970s through the 1980s, Western intellectuals, including Jacques Derrida, Jürgen Haber-

mas, and Richard Rorty, participated in independent seminars organized by Czech dissidents in Prague … similar collaborations based on an interest in convergence also took place between intellectuals in the USA, Western Europe, and the Third World" (2007: 346).

3. Hickel.

4. Marko Ilić described Ratka's response in almost the same way. He asked her to register a humanitarian telephone number for his son and said that her response was "Wait, don't move, I'll be there in a minute" (see chapter one).

5. The mayor also exploited the rhetorical strategy of being a "powerful man who cares." For example, in a New Year interview for the local newspaper, he said, "I go to bed and wake up with municipal problems [in my mind] and that is my choice … I try to be among my people as much as possible and I am glad when others say I am a people's man (*narodni čovjek*). While talking with people, I try to get a sense of what their difficulties are. Often a kind word alone can help people. I try to always, as much as possible, help the common man … I have never had a security man or a bodyguard, and I never will. If I ever have to defend myself from my people, I would rather not do this job anymore." The mayor used notions of "*help,*" "*a kind word,*" and "being a *people's man*" to represent his public role as inseparable from his private personhood. After all, he claims that he goes to bed and wakes up thinking about municipal issues.

Chapter 6

Navigating Ambiguity

The Moveopticon

> Neoliberal biopower is not about making die, it's not,
> either, about making live. So it's not the old sovereignty,
> but it's not the new biopower. It's something else. What
> I would argue is that it's about not letting live, without
> making die. That is, making life unliveable.
> —Éric Fassin, "The Politics of Actuality: Biopower,
> Racial Democracy, and the Racialization of Sex"

Two children and a young woman needed medical treatment abroad
during 2009–10 in the Town. With more or less average salaries, their
families could not afford the overall costs, which included medical
tests, surgery and postoperative treatment, a trip to Moscow or Vienna, the visa and accommodation for the patient and an accompa-
nying family member, and so forth. The public healthcare system
covered only part of the medical expenses abroad and it did so ret-
roactively. In order to access treatment, these three families initiated
humanitarian actions (*humanitarne akcije*).

A humanitarian action is a grassroots humanitarian assemblage
in which hundreds, and sometimes thousands, of actors donate small
amounts of money to a person who needs a medical treatment abroad.
A humanitarian action is usually initiated by the family of a person
needing the treatment. The donors include persons, welfare institutions, municipalities, nongovernmental organizations (NGOs), private firms, and many other types of actors. This form of help emerged
in former Yugoslav countries in the 1990s. The need for humanitarian
actions in BiH probably increased with the reforms that left more

than 20 percent of citizens without public healthcare insurance (Salihbašić 2008). So many were organized in the country in 2009 and 2010 that a TV and radio show dedicated solely to humanitarian actions was live streamed every working day for two hours.[1]

All three families with whom I worked managed to raise enough money for the trip and the treatment. They raised thousands of euros from donations consisting of several euros each. Many donations came from people the families knew personally: friends, acquaintances, neighbors, work colleagues or fellow students. Many more donations came from friends of friends, people who those close to the family knew personally. Larger donations were given in the name of NGOs, associations, schools, or private firms in which people self-organized and collected money for a family. Furthermore, the state was a donor. The municipal Committee for One-Off Support and the mayor had discretionary power to distribute state funds as humanitarian support to individuals in urgent need. State donations were paid to the private account of the patient or a member of the patient's family. This indicates that some parts of the BiH state apparatus relied on humanitarian principles.

Such principles assume that human life ought to be saved simply because it is human life: nationality, citizenship, gender, and the age of the person needing help are considered irrelevant. However, ethnographic studies indicate that humanitarian aspirations are rarely achieved in practice. Humanitarian actors evaluate lives differently depending on citizenship and/or nationality (Fassin 2007), health, and medical status (Ticktin 2011), and they often increase vulnerability, chaos, and disorder along the way (Dunn 2012). A sociopolitical distinction particularly relevant in humanitarian actions in the Town was between those who knew the "right" people and those who did not. For instance, Petar Božović, an organizer of a humanitarian action in the Town, told me that his son received money for a treatment through the "system of someone who knows someone else" (*sistem ko zna koga*). *Veze* and *štele* significantly affected the success of humanitarian actions. Those who raised money for healthcare abroad were those who pursued *veze* and *štele* in all possible directions.

During humanitarian actions, survival and well-being largely depended on personal agency—on one's ability to navigate social worlds. As we saw in chapters three and four, the postsocialist and postwar reforms of welfare in BiH stressed the need to be flexible and managerial. The reforms did not quite produce subjects who took care of their own biology through self-education, civic associations and self-help groups, responsible lifestyles, and so forth. Bosnians can hardly be understood through the prism of a "regime of self as a prudent yet enterprising individual, actively shaping his or her life course through acts of choice" (Rose and Novas 2007: 441). Instead, the reforms created a need for humanitarian actions.

Humanitarna akcija (singular, literally: "a humanitarian action") is a practice in which a Foucauldian relationship between power and knowledge is organized in a particular way. In this arrangement, there is no dominant institutional gaze, no "tower" where knowledge is gathered, as there is in "panopticons." Neither is there a body of expert knowledge that spreads in a capillary and even manner throughout the society/local community, producing normal and abnormal subjects. Instead, life depends on a combination of local and state forms of knowledge, randomly and unevenly spread across the state and society.

In moveopticons, as I am calling these arrangements, people had to move to survive; they had to navigate relations across state, civic, and private arenas, making themselves known and knowable to a heterogeneous assembly of actors. In order to access healthcare treatment abroad, people were supposed to ask many different actors for donations and thus to make their own paths through the local social worlds. Humanitarian actions are a fine example of the flexible navigation of social relations; although the particular form this flexibility took was far from what development experts and policy advisors would have expected. The flexibility of people who organized humanitarian actions consisted in finding their own paths in order to ensure the survival of their loved ones. Those who needed support through humanitarian actions navigated institutional rules as well as personal wills, without knowing in advance what path would turn out to be productive. Let us take a closer look at how a humanitarian action was organized.

A Humanitarian Action

Vana Žarković, a student of pedagogy in the Town, found out she had leukemia almost by accident. Her neighbor, a medical doctor, met her on the street and, after she complained she was not feeling well, he looked at her glands. The neighbor said she immediately had to go to a cardiac center for an examination. There, Vana learned that she needed a bone marrow transplant. She was sent to Belgrade, the capital of Serbia, for blood infusion therapy that would keep her alive until the bone marrow transplant. The bone marrow transplant could not be performed in BiH. Vana's sister Milica decided to start a humanitarian action to raise money for surgery abroad in two places—the Town (where Vana studied) and in Brčko (where Vana's family lives).

Over the course of several months, Milica organized more than twenty humanitarian parties. She also raised donations from public institutions and local private companies. Milica managed to open a "humanitarian telephone number"[2] and initiated two large concerts with post-Yugoslav pop stars. Milica spoke for local newspapers and TV shows, distributed flyers, and put advertisements up about the humanitarian events for her sister. As the word spread throughout the two towns and beyond, she received some direct payments to her bank account. Milica raised 50,000 euros. The municipality of Brčko, or more precisely, the mayor, paid the rest from the municipal budget to the hospital in Vienna where the transplant was to be performed. Vana underwent surgery that was successful.

Many people helped Milica in various ways. The most important thing for her was to raise money for Vana's surgery, but in order to do that, Milica had to take care of many other things. Milica found eight young men who were willing to donate blood for Vana's regular blood transfusions. She secured a free apartment in Belgrade through a friend, so that Vana could be close to the transfusions. She found a "strong man" (*jak čovjek*) in Brčko who helped her to get posters and invitations for the parties printed for free. After I inquired about his social position, including his ethnonational identification, it turned out that the man identified as Bosniak. For Milica, who identified as a Bosnian Serb, his ethnonationality was less important than the fact that he was well connected in the town of Brčko and able to provide Milica with cost-free printing through his *veze* and *štele*. Overall, she actively worked on forging a relationship with the greatest possible number of people in order to secure help for her sister.

Navigating Social Worlds

On one occasion, I asked Milica to draw the beginnings of the humanitarian action. She first wrote her own name and then linked it to the people with whom she made a decision to start the humanitarian action: her aunt and her boyfriend, Marko:

$$\text{aunt} \longleftarrow \text{Milica} \longrightarrow \text{Marko}$$

Figure 6.1. *Milica's drawing, phase 1*

Milica's aunt told the people at the store where she worked about the action, so Milica continued drawing:

work colleagues

$\uparrow$

$$\text{aunt} \longleftarrow \text{Milica} \longrightarrow \text{Marko}$$

Figure 6.2. *Milica's drawing, phase 2*

The mother of Milica's boyfriend worked in a technical department at the hospital and she received support from her colleagues. The spouse of Marko's brother worked in a local radio broadcasting company and, in addition to telling her colleagues about the humanitarian action, they broadcast information about the action regularly. Marko's brother worked in a firm and he told his colleagues there about the action. As Milica was explaining these relations, she also drew them this way:

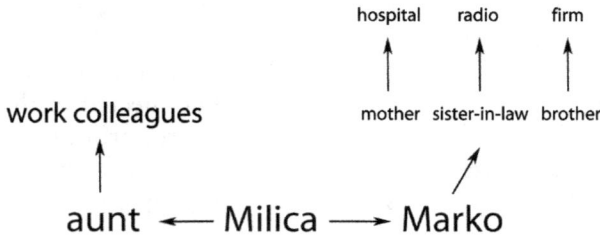

hospital   radio   firm

$\uparrow$ $\uparrow$ $\uparrow$

work colleagues   mother sister-in-law brother

$\uparrow$ $\nearrow$

$$\text{aunt} \longleftarrow \text{Milica} \longrightarrow \text{Marko}$$

Figure 6.3. *Milica's drawing, phase 3*

Milica also added "friends," and "further friends" below her name. Many of these people—friends and colleagues from the hospital, the firm, the radio—told their friends and families about the action, and the drawing extended further:

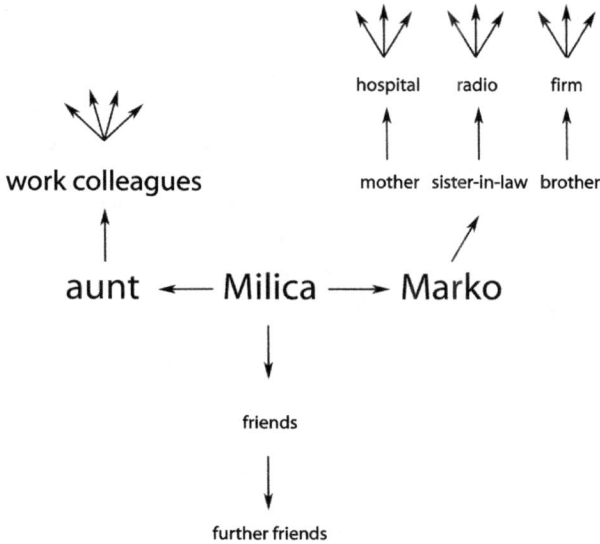

Figure 6.4. *Milica's drawing, final phase*

Milica's drawing indicates that she first had to evoke the responsibility of the people who constituted her *svijet:* her boyfriend, her aunt, and her friends (as we have seen in chapter one, *svijet* refers to the social world that someone inhabits). If evoking reciprocal relationships of give-and-take within a *svijet* could raise sufficient money, the drawing might have looked just like a bifurcation tree (see Figure 6.5). A bifurcation tree is made using a formula whereby a line is split in half and each new part is further split into two:

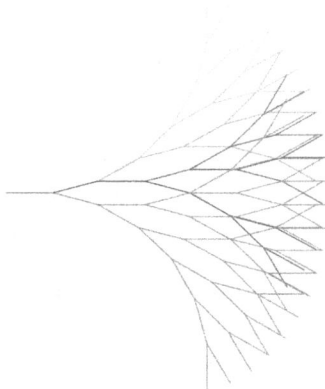

Figure 6.5. *Bifurcation tree, made by Vanja Gagović*[3]

The bifurcation tree is a fractal diagram generated by repeating a set of instructions over and over again. While this repetition provides a common way of thinking about how organisms grow, Strathern (2004) suggests that the social is organized through much more irregular, partial iterations. The not quite replication of the social relations across different scales may be illustrated by the irregular coastline: "Whether one looks at a large-scale map or investigates every inlet and rock on a beach, the scale changes make no difference to the amount of irregularity. It is as though increase in the length of coastline does not increase the area it encloses: the two do not map on to each other" (Strathern 2004: xx).

Humanitarian actions worked through such partial replications. Since there was no existing formula, no clear procedures, no set of instructions to follow, Milica had to invent her own path until enough money was raised to send Vana to Vienna. After asking favors from close friends and family, Milica forged new social relationships and navigated the new paths that opened in front of her, multiplying and branching off in different directions—those leading to a hospital, radio, firm, further friends, and beyond. This is where Milica had to be flexible, adaptable, and inventive. Those who initiated humanitarian actions navigated unknown, yet predictably irregular paths, until they raised sufficient funds.[4] The network that donated money to Milica was composed of social relationships, which were repeated almost recursively across public, private, and state arenas—but not quite. Let us take a closer look at what sorts of social relations got entangled within a humanitarian action.

Who Donated and How?

In humanitarian actions, people donated small amounts of money for various reasons. Some of the people who helped probably simply wanted to support a friend playing football at a humanitarian sports game or to attend a party or a pop concert. Others helped for religious reasons. Some people helped because it was suggested they do so by someone positioned hierarchically above them—such as a company director or a school head teacher. There were those who helped out of a sense of neighborly duty. Although incentives to give were so heterogeneous, most donors personally knew the family that raised money or someone who was somehow connected to them. Local forms of knowledge deeply shaped the donors decisions of whether to help or not.[5]

For instance, Milica wanted to organize a small humanitarian concert. Her friend Ivana asked the director of a hotel in Brčko (who was also Ivana's friend) whether they could use the hotel's stage for free. The director agreed. A couple of weeks later, Ivana got a call from Ana Bekuta, a famous ex-Yugoslav pop singer. It turned out that Bekuta frequently stayed at this hotel. The hotel director asked Bekuta to sing at a humanitarian concert for Milica's sister free of charge.

This action further expanded in scope. Bekuta asked her colleagues to join her. As a result of Ana Bekuta's calls, a concert with ten famous pop singers was held in the Town, including the ex-Yugoslav pop stars Neda Ukraden and Željko Samardžić from Serbia. A couple of thousand people attended the concert. During the concert, the host of the evening took a mobile phone and asked the audience to call the humanitarian number. The following few minutes were spent in silence, while people dialed on their phones. This meant that, in addition to the money raised from the ten convertible marks (five euros) ticket for the concert, at least a couple more hundreds or thousands were raised that evening for Vana through calls made to the humanitarian phone line.

In this case, a single segment of the humanitarian action—the pop concert—entangled multiple ways of relating: kinship, friendship, a business relation between the hotel director and her frequent guest, collegial relationships between pop singers, and so forth. Each segment of the humanitarian action had similarly developed in its own direction, initiated by Milica's efforts. That which enabled survival through humanitarian actions was not citizenship, ethnicity/nationality, residence, or some other category of identity. Rather, it was luck and the skill one had to generate a large network of partial connections across public, private, and state arenas.

Importantly, the organizers of humanitarian actions were not quite left without state support—although BiH's thirteen public healthcare systems did not cover the full price of medical treatments outside of their boundaries. While one might expect the state welfare system to be qualitatively different from humanitarian, charitable, and compassionate forms of helping, support from the state was as arbitrary and grounded in humanitarian reasoning as was the support coming from friends, kin, and other private and civic actors.

Humanitarian Support from the State:
The Municipal Government

The state was one of the humanitarian donors to families who initiated humanitarian actions. The budget of most BiH municipalities
reserved some funds for one-off welfare support. The municipality
of the Town had a Committee for One-Off Support to which people submitted applications for help of up to two hundred euros. The
mayor personally made decisions granting larger sums to individuals
on the basis of medical or welfare needs. Let us take a look at who
received humanitarian support from the municipal government in
order to explore the reasoning behind the municipal decisions.

The Božović family had a son with multiple developmental difficulties who was undergoing expensive long-term treatment in Serbia.
The parents were raising money to send him to Russia for an experimental treatment. The Božovićs were formally eligible for the one-
off humanitarian support fund from the municipality. Nevertheless,
Petar, the father, looked for a *veza/štela*. Petar told me that he had a
sculptor friend who took care of the municipal donation. This friend
had earlier organized a humanitarian art auction for Petar's son and
he was also a friend of the Town's mayor. Petar submitted the application to the municipal government. The mayor made decisions regarding the granting of larger sums and he approved 750 euros (KM
1500) for the Božović family.

In Petar's eyes, knowing someone who knew someone else—that
is, knowing the sculptor who knew the mayor—was decisive for getting the municipal donation. After this, Petar praised the mayor's
kindness of heart and personal willingness to help his family. Although the money for the Božovićs came from the municipal budget,
it was understood as a personal gift from the mayor.

The Ilić family, on the other hand, did not receive any help from
the Town's mayor and the municipality. In their opinion, this was because they did not know the right people. Marko and Ana Ilić raised
money through a humanitarian action to send their baby son, who
had an eye condition called "premature retinopathy," to Russia. The
official reason for declining the Ilićs plea for financial assistance was
that the municipal funds for that year had been spent. However,
Marko Ilić thought that his family would have received support from
the committee had he had a *veza/štela* within the municipality. Marko
submitted the application to the municipality in September 2009 and
was convinced that—even if the money had really been spent—with a
strong *veza/štela* to the mayor, he would have received the money as a

refund or would have been told to resubmit the application in January the following year. Marko knew Ratka by sight, but their connection did not result in gaining municipal support. Instead, Ratka helped the Ilićs with a private donation from her Orthodox Christian charity.

Milica Žarković received a huge amount of financial support from the municipal government from the mayor of Brčko. As we have seen, her sister Vana studied in the Town, while their family lived in Brčko, which is why Milica organized the humanitarian action for Vana in these two towns. Milica got to know the mayor of Brčko through a friend of a friend. No one in her family knew the mayor personally, but Milica managed to find a link to him through other people. The mayor decided to cover two thirds of her sister's extremely expensive surgery from the municipal funds. He even gave advice concerning a hospital in Vienna where Milica's sister could undergo the bone marrow transplant. Milica said her family accepted this advice because the mayor was a trained physician and had experience in "these things"; a couple of years earlier he had helped another family receive a bone marrow transplant in the same hospital in Vienna.

Why did Milica's sister get (generous) municipal help and the Ilićs did not? Perhaps the mayor of Brčko was personally more generous or felt personally more responsible for healthcare abroad than the mayor of the Town did. If humanitarian logic occasionally shaped the redistribution of public resources in BiH, maybe Milica simply had more luck with the mayor than the Ilićs.

If so, why and how did the Town's mayor decide to offer humanitarian aid to the Božović family but not to the Ilić family? The same mayor, in the same year, decided to help one family receive healthcare treatment abroad, but not the other family. In both cases the injured party was a young boy; both families considered themselves to be Bosnian Serbs; both families were conventional, married, consisting of a husband, a wife, and their offspring; both treatments were uncertain and risky and conducted in Russia (the Božovićs wanted to try an experimental treatment, while the Ilićs could not know whether their son's condition was operable until they were at the Russian clinic and their son was examined there).

In the face of all these similarities, there was an important difference. The Božovićs were older, engaged in jobs that linked them with more influential people, and had lived in the Town much longer than the Ilićs. Thus, the key difference, I suggest, was that the Božovićs knew more people and were themselves known to more people than the Ilićs. Being able to generate social connections and relations widely throughout the Town also affected people's struggle to survive. If the Božovićs' and the Ilićs' nationalities, salaries, and citizenship were more or less the same, their social positions in the Town were not.

Marko Ilić worked as a waiter and Ana Ilić was a retail worker before her pregnancy. Petar used to be a specialist construction worker and Milena was a music teacher. The character of their jobs enabled them to circulate among different groups of people. Furthermore, since people were becoming known and knowable to others by being there—exchanging greetings in the same places, walking the same paths every day, and so forth—there were more stories traveling throughout the Town about those who had been living there for a long time. The decision of the Town's mayor is a reflection of all these things put together; Petar had found a sculptor friend who was a direct *veza* to the mayor, while the Ilićs could not do that.

In all humanitarian actions, people engaged in similar activities: they could not know who might help, so they had to move through their social worlds in order to survive and improve their well-being. What made one humanitarian action easier or more successful than the other were the paths a family could take throughout the Town. This difference reveals the importance of *veze* and *štele* for survival and well-being. When one did not personally know the right people, survival and well-being depended on getting to know as many people as possible—in the hope of meeting the right people along the way.

Humanitarian Support from the State: The Public Fund for Children's Protection

Before the municipal government in the Town initiated the Committee for One-Off Support, a similar committee was organized by the Public Fund for Children's Protection. The fund is an entity-level institution. Its humanitarian support did not have a clear starting point, according to my interlocutors. Initially, a few people requested small amounts of financial help, the fund's governing board approved several such requests, and more and more people started asking for help. In 2004, when the number of applications for humanitarian support became unmanageable, the fund formed the Committee for One-Off Support. The fund's committee had to stop working in 2006, because the Audit Committee forbade it.

One of the former members of the fund's committee told me that the number of applications from the same villages or neighborhoods increased over time as people spread the word. There were between ten and twenty applications every month from 2004 onward. On many occasions the same names appeared time and time again, with the same people from the same places applying for it. The committee therefore subsequently introduced a rule wherein any given person could only receive one grant per year. The grants were usually between five hundred and one thousand convertible marks (approximately 250 to 500 euros). The support was given to what are referred to as "social cases" (*socijala,* or *socijalni slučajevi*) in BiH, that is, to very poor families; families whose child had a chronic condition of some kind; families who needed to send their child abroad for medical treatment; families in which the parents' illness diminished their parental abilities; humanitarian organizations and associations, such as the Red Cross and the Red Crescent; and so forth.

The committee consisted of several experts, including a sociologist, a psychologist, and a legal practitioner. It controlled the distribution of the state funds by reviewing applications and checking with the local Center for Social Work to ensure that the claims were true and justifiable. The committee refused many applications when they thought that people misrepresented the facts or when they did not really need urgent help.

Its members formed an official opinion on the basis of the supporting documentation, the formal structure of the application, and the information they received from the Center for Social Work. While their personal relationships with the applicants might have been of less importance when granting money than at the municipal government, the humanitarian, charitable, and compassionate logic of both the municipal and the fund's committee was very similar. For both committees, there were no strict deadlines and no visible public announcements of the application procedure. As a matter of fact, people could learn about the very existence of this one-off form of state support almost exclusively on the grapevine. Personal relationships, phone calls, and face-to-face contacts were thus, once again, constitutive elements of state support.

The committee was shut down at the moment when it was on the verge of increasing bureaucratization. The amount of applications kept growing in size and it took the committee members more and more time each month to check through all the documentation. Instead of widening the program, or transforming it into something less personal and random, it was closed. Still, the director of the fund retained the discretionary right to offer one-off humanitarian support to individuals.

Interestingly enough, the Audit Committee did not seem to have a problem with the humanitarian character of the program; during my fieldwork the municipal government had its own committee with practically the same function. Furthermore, both the mayor and the fund's director retained the discretionary right to offer one-off humanitarian support. The shutting down of the fund's committee reflected the wider dispersion of responsibility for welfare in BiH. A distrustful commentator might say that the problem with the fund's committee was not so much that it distributed state funds in the form of a humanitarian donation as that there was a possibility of turning this ambiguous and personalized form of aid into a standardized, predictable, stable source of public support.

Moveopticon: Power Relations in Humanitarian Actions

The perspective of a moveopticon is inversed to that of a panopticon, or an oligopticon. Panopticon (Foucault 1995) presents a nineteenth-century architectural form of surveillance that illustrates mechanisms of power through which institutions discipline "problematic" members of a national polity. "Oligopticon" is a term that illustrates that governing a city does not include an absolute, panoptical viewpoint but instead a large number of places from which one particular aspect of life is known and controlled—such as water services, crime, and road infrastructure. An oligopticon "sees little, but what it does see it sees well" (Latour and Hermant 2006: 48). However, both in the case of the panoptical organization of prisons, factories, schools, or hospitals and in the case of dozens or more oligopticons governing an aspect of life in a city, the gaze is directed to the subjects, irrespective of whether they wish to be observed. The term "moveopticon" captures a relationship of power in which the subjects do want to be seen and known but have to work hard for that to happen.

Moveopticon puts emphasis on the actions of a subject, rather than on the scope or the number of the observatories. In a moveopticon, subjects have to move around and try to make themselves visible in order to survive and maintain well-being, because there is no institutional gaze in place that could regulate their existence. During humanitarian actions, people had to be known and knowable not to a single center or the central registry (a panopticon "tower") where knowledge is accumulated—because there was no such center.[6] Neither was there a control panel in a closed control room from which it was possible to see all the data considered as relevant for a particular issue as in oligopticons. Instead, they had to be known and knowable to many different public and private claimants at the same time, while the relationship between public and private arenas was shifting.

During my fieldwork, organizers of humanitarian actions had to move from one administrative procedure to the next and from one compassionate person to another, without knowing for sure who would help their family member to survive and stay healthy and in what way. This need to navigate a complex social and bureaucratic terrain is what I aim to capture by the term "moveopticon."

When referring to *humanitarne akcije* as an enactment of a move-opticon, I follow the reading of Nancy Fraser (2003), who suggests that today we are seeing the emergence of a new kind of regulatory structure that is flexible, multilayered, and selectively repressive— and whose contours have yet to be fully determined. Fraser argues that the Foucauldian concept of discipline is closely related to the Fordist mode of social regulation: disciplinary power presents an analytical tool best suited for understanding sociopolitical arrangements of (Fordist) welfare states. In her reading, disciplinary power has, or had, three characteristics. First, it was totalizing, which means that it aimed to include every member of a polity within its reach. Second, the polity was defined through the nation–state framework, which means that the reach of disciplinary mechanisms and institutions largely overlapped with state borders. Third, it depended on self-regulation and the willing subjectification of polity members.

These three propositions are no longer fully valid in post-Fordist countries. First, privatization and the deregulation of formerly public welfare services have loosened the aim of including everybody within the reach of disciplinary power. As a result, many people now fall through the gaps of public welfare systems. Second, the increasing scope of transnational practices means that the framework of nation–states has been decentered. Social regulation today occurs on international and transnational, as well as national, scales. Third, the decentering of the nation–state framework has created new forms of control and surveillance regarding lawful members of a polity, in which the management of prisons is often subcontracted to corporations working for profit and racialized and sexualized violence tend to replace attempts at discipline (Fraser 2003).

The decentering of the national frame has also led to new architectural arrangements of control and surveillance. For instance, Bigo (2008) suggests that this emerging form of social regulation can be understood as a "banopticon," a setting in which arbitrariness becomes the norm. The banopticon materializes in detention camps for foreigners, understood as outsiders considered as a threat to a nation-state. The logic of the banopticon is one of "permanent exceptionalism" or of "derogation by the government of the basic rule of law in the name of emergency" (ibid.: 3). In contemporary regimes of globalized governance, surveillance and control are not executed just through discipline and the punishment of "insiders," that is, the citizens of a country. Instead, control in a banopticon means keeping "outsiders" at a distance from a certain territory and/or from welfare benefits given to the legal residents of that territory. With more than a hundred detention centers for asylum applicants across Europe outside of penal laws, the banopticon is increasingly transforming arbitrariness into routine.

Camps for refugees and internally displaced persons present another architectural form that condenses emerging forms of social regulation. Dunn argues that such places are governed through adhocracy, "a form of power that creates chaos and vulnerability as much as it creates order" (2012: 2). Discussing the distribution of humanitarian aid to internally displaced persons in Georgia, Dunn demonstrates that humanitarian bureaucracies often operate not just by governmental techniques of "seeing, counting, and managing" but also by guesswork, rules of thumb, and "satisficing" (ibid.).

Making rules along the way, this form of governance creates a disorder that prevents people from planning their future and meaningfully organizing their lives. Camps are places of "aleatory sovereignty," a form of governance that is inherently "fragile, unpredictable and haphazard" (Dunn and Cons 2014: 94). In humanitarian actions in the Town, power was similarly arbitrary, unpredictable, and fragile. State officials distributed public funds to individual families on the basis of compassion and personal connections. Humanitarian actions transformed arbitrariness into a routine for the insiders (BiH citizens), rather than for the outsiders (refugees and asylum applicants, for instance).

People who raised humanitarian funds to enable the survival of their family member had to be more than citizens in order to receive aid. They had to be citizens (and thus eligible for various forms of public and private support) as well as fathers, mothers, former colleagues, companions, or friends. In addition to citizens, they also had to be socially and personally located human beings. I cannot say who exactly had responsibility over securing survival in a moveopticon, since no direction of the humanitarian actions and no donor could be separated out as *the* most important. When compassion and empathy become a constitutive part of the administrative apparatus, survival and well-being become a matter of merit judged personally; the issue here is who *deserves* to access healthcare and social protection—and *according to whom*. As we saw in chapter five, bureaucrats who are in a position to make such judgments rely on their personal relations and local knowledge, increasing their power with each decision they make and elevating their social status in the Town's social networks.

Milica and other organizers of humanitarian action could not predict that contact would be useful and that that avenue would be worth pursuing in order to obtain access to the required medical treatment. There was no homogeneity of the capillary distribution of power throughout the "body politic," as is the case with biopower, and no single sovereign who had the right to make decisions over death or life. There were, rather, numerous "petty sovereigns" (Butler 2004) among whom the right to "take life" or "let live" was dispersed (cf. Foucault 2003). This was interspersed with the power of the state apparatus—in which sometimes those actors were employed and in which they made their decisions. Thus, the right of the state apparatus to "make live and to let die" (ibid.: 241) was present, alongside "the resurgence of sovereignty within the field of governmentality" (Butler 2004: 56). As Éric Fassin's quotation at the beginning of the chapter suggests, contemporary global experiments in governance create forms of power that make life unlivable. The BiH welfare systems also did not let many people live, but they did not make them die either.

This is illustrated by the fact that no one could live off the ridiculously low amount of elementary social protection provision (see chapter three) or by the administrative conundrums over healthcare abroad. Submitting welfare documentation to the municipal Committee for One-Off Support could have been as important as evoking shared past and mutual friends. However, neither of these practices brought with them any certainties regarding survival and well-being. In the midst of ambiguity over responsibilities, it was the movement, navigation from one gap led by compassion in the field of governmentality to another, that offered the best chance that life would be protected.

A (Non)Deserving Claimant

Humanitarian actions intertwined sociality with pragmatism in a complex manner and they required a lot of personal work. The effect of this work—a particular moral self, enmeshed in different kinds of relations to numerous other people—was not necessarily always welcomed by those who invested in this work. While I argue that a move-opticon condenses a relationship of power in which the subjects *want* to be seen and known and have to work hard for that to happen, this want was not without its tensions. For instance, Milica complained to me because she did not like the way people perceived her:

> I really don't know what to wear and how to dress anymore, or how to behave, or what to do. I like taking care of myself, and there are a lot of people who say, "She has an ill sister, but look at how she dresses up." Brčko is a small town, and everybody knows each other, and everybody knows everything about everybody else.

She told me that a couple of days previously she had received a big donation directly into her bank account. That night, she went out with two friends to celebrate in a local club. She got a bit drunk, sang loudly, and laughed "like crazy" but then felt uncomfortable because she could "feel the gaze of others": "I knew what some of them were thinking: 'Look at her, she is laughing and drinking, and yet she has a sick sister and asks for money.'" This uncomfortable feeling of being looked at and judged, and the idea that "everybody in the Town knows everybody else," was continuously repeated by many people I met. Of course, it could hardly be literally true if a town has tens of thousands of inhabitants. What this sentence expressed was more of a sense that a person you are not very close to can, and indeed often does, know different pieces of information about you.

Milica positioned herself in the midst of these stories. She repeatedly, actively, and purposefully worked on building a relationship with the greatest possible number of people. She became a particular person along the way: one that "everybody knows" and one "with a problem but smiling," that is, a person worthy of humanitarian support. When asking different people for help, Milica had to adapt to their perceptions of her and to flexibly respond to their differing expectations. She had to position herself within the social worlds of an enormous number of people, engaging with their sympathies as well as antipathies, dedications, and suspicions. Milica both wanted and despised the attention attracted this way. Organizing the humanitarian action became her full-time job, which required a continuous investment of time, energy, and emotions. In order to secure as many donations for her sister as possible, Milica accepted parts of her social position that she did not necessarily want, such as the sense of being judged for having an evening out.

This merging of pragmatic self-interest with sociality can be seen as an act of ironic subjects; we could say that Milica behaved *as if* she was interested in building social links to many different people in order to access welfare support, while knowing full well she did not really welcome such a strategy. My interlocutors criticized the state for making them dependent on other people's compassion and personalized knowledge in order to survive and live well, while they simultaneously invested a lot of time and effort in evoking personal connections and empathy to get things done. "To know it, but to do it anyway," to paraphrase Sloterdijk's (2001) interpretation of ideological cynicism (see also Navaro-Yashin 2002; Žižek 2008), would imply that pragmatic interest was the underlying motive for pursuing *veze* and *štele*, hidden under the ideology of social reciprocities and moral duties. However, Milica's position seemed to be more complex.

Perhaps it is possible to think about this sociality with a purpose through the prism of the willing suspension of disbelief. The "willing suspension of disbelief" is a term that describes the mechanism through which people perceive art that includes elements of fantasy.[7] It refers to our ability as readers and viewers to willingly suspend disbelief in order to do something—to gain aesthetic pleasure, knowledge, enjoyment, to end boredom, and so forth. The double negation points to a moment in which the existence of multiple possibilities is allowed for the sake of achieving something. In order to help her sister survive, Milica temporarily occupied a position in which belief and disbelief in how things are, and how they should be, were allowed to exist as simultaneous multiple options, making it impossible to uniformly and permanently differentiate who she was exactly or what she did out of interest and what out of moral duty or social obligation. Depending on the moment and one's point of view, she was a sister, a citizen, a party organizer, a humanitarian recipient, and/or a Bosnian Serb, emphasizing different roles in different situations.

The ethnographic encounters in this book suggest that, while morality, sociality, and pragmatic self-interest can be separated in analytical terms, in the everyday life of the Town they formed an ambiguous knot (cf. Green 2014) whose different strands should be observed together in order to explore the emerging forms of power, (in)equality, and (in)justice. Milica, Samra (chapter two), the parents from the Sun (chapters three and four), and many other people who pursued favors could not permanently and unambiguously separate interest from sociality, and they pursued both, putting a greater emphasis on one or the other in different moments.

Conclusion

Humanitarian actions demonstrate in what way BiH citizens had to be flexible and self-motivating when it came to survival. In the Town, there were almost no activist patient groups built around particular genetic or medical conditions, that is, there was no biosociality (Rose 2006). But there were favors and their sociality with a purpose. People gained extensive knowledge about their neighbors, work colleagues, or doctors, rather than about their biologies. People envisioned their own paths and put their social worlds into action, constantly working on as many interpersonal relationships as possible. There was none of the perceived "passivity" or "disinterestedness" of which Bosnians are so often accused when it comes to elections or voting patterns (Čelebičić 2016).

The state's protection was partial (incomplete and personalized), as was the protection generated by civil society relations. The links between people, institutional resources, and knowledge about who needs whose help and why were often accidental and flexible—forged temporarily on the spot—rather than administered through preexisting categories. The municipality was one among many actors who donated money to a single person. It distributed public resources sometimes on the basis of compassion and sometimes through bureaucratic indifference, depending on personal entanglements, ways of knowing people, or the time of the year. People who raised humanitarian funds had to be more than citizens. They had to be citizens (and thus eligible for various forms of state and private support) as well as siblings, parents, former colleagues, companions, or friends. In addition to citizens, they also had to be socially and personally located human beings.

Ambiguity shaped contemporary struggles to survive in BiH in a way that was not possible before the war. The ad hoc character of humanitarian actions was not just the result of weak statehood, a temporary failure that would diminish over the course of the development of BiH. Rather, it was the result of developmental transformations of the BiH welfare systems in which there was an increasing emphasis on shared, communal responsibility for well-being. This dispersion of responsibility created an arrangement that I call the "moveopticon." In moveopticons, survival is affected not just by citizenship status, nationality, ethnicity, age, or gender. It is also regulated by an ability to navigate a complex social and bureaucratic terrain—to move between many different social and state actors. Moveopticons demonstrate how power operates on and among those who need help to survive in BiH, given its current condition.

Notes

1. The anchor, Batko, introduced various humanitarian actions and talked with the families who initiated them, then he announced publicly the details of their medical needs and their bank accounts and followed this up with details of what happened after the treatment. In doing so, Batko strongly pushed forward the idea that those who help with a humanitarian action are "normal humans" (*normalni ljudi*), or just "humans" (*ljudi*), by which he meant that they were not interested in politics and ethnonational divisions. In addition to its frequency, the very need for such a TV/radio show reveals that humanitarian actions are often taken as a path to solving burning healthcare problems in contemporary BiH.
2. A charitable line provided by the phone company for which every call raised EUR 0.5 or 1.0 + VAT.
3. Reproduced with the author's permission (Gagović 2016).
4. The internet, and especially Facebook, has been used to spread information about humanitarian actions and particular one-off events (e.g., a humanitarian concert), mostly among younger people. However, online relations have not turned out to be especially productive in terms of raising money.
5. I describe this in more detail in Brković 2014, 2016b.
6. The limits of the Foucauldian concept of biopower for understanding the organization of power in BiH are strikingly visible in the fact that state institutions worked on "improving" the population without having elementary statistical data about this population (i.e., knowledge about its gender, age, professional, and ethnonational or any other characteristic). The last BiH population census data during my fieldwork were from 1991. When population statistics were available, they encompassed only a segment of the population at a municipal, cantonal, or district level or were estimates collected by the international organizations. Foucault (2003: 250) writes that biopower is constituted of two modalities of power that work together: discipline (or the management and improvement of bodies) and biopolitics (or the management and improvement of generalized life/the population). In BiH, the form of power "whose highest function was … to invest life through and through" (Foucault 1978: 139) was severely limited by the fact that the first postwar countrywide census in BiH was conducted only in 2013 and its results were published almost three years later, in 2016.
7. The poet Samuel Taylor Coleridge coined the term in the nineteenth century for a project "in which it was agreed, that my endeavours should be directed to persons and characters supernatural, or at least romantic, yet so as to transfer from our inward nature a human interest and a semblance of truth sufficient to procure for these shadows of imagination that willing suspension of disbelief for the moment, which constitutes poetic faith" (Coleridge 1817).

Conclusion

Morality, Interest, and Sociality
in the Global "Postsocialist" Condition

This book has explored how survival and well-being were governed in a context where the boundaries between public and private roles and responsibilities were often made ambiguous. This question is "at once political and moral" (Han 2013: 233). My intention has been to show that people who needed help were not just "suffering subjects," that is, "the figure of humanity united in its shared vulnerability to suffering … [that] has replaced the savage one as the privileged object of our attention" (Robbins 2013: 450). My interlocutors were, rather, subjects who actively and flexibly worked on changing the terms of their suffering (or perhaps, more accurately, the terms of their need) in ways made intelligible and simultaneously constrained by the specific historical conjuncture of Dayton BiH.

Engagements with welfare in the Town invoked different ideas of "the good." For instance, during humanitarian actions (chapter six), donors invoked various frameworks when they discussed their motivations to give. These included universal humanity, ethnonationalism, Islam, Orthodox and Catholic Christianity, personal compassion, neighborly ethics, professional allegiances, and so forth. Furthermore, my interlocutors said that making welfare claims directed at the mayor (chapter four) or other local powerful persons (chapter five) were justified because "There is law, there is morality, there is God, there are facts." They grounded their requests for better social protection both in the language of legal rights (law and facts) and the language of compassion and moral duty (morality and religion). Bits and pieces of different moral traditions merged together in these moral assemblages (Zigon 2011) of welfare that intertwined competing ideas about what may be considered good and how one ought to behave.

Although this moral complexity, and the ways of working one's way through it, is interesting in itself, the focus of this book is on the ways in which the need can be acknowledged and help provided. That welfare was often a matter of personal moral inclinations transformed the good into a key element of the politics of life, within which the boundary between goodness and citizenship rights as grounds for support was produced and kept ambiguous. Struggles over social justice often involve different emic understandings over what is good, proper, or ethical, some of which may inflict more harm than others (Fraser 2010; Venkatesan 2015). As Han suggests:

> Disregarding experiences of suffering in the name of "the good" may make us incapable of acknowledging the fact that states and markets actually do inflict harm on populations and communities, and may create a slippery slope in which some experiences of suffering are more legitimate or authentic than others. (2013: 234)

Different notions of the good are, therefore, a constitutive part of larger discussions about how a polity should be organized, where its boundaries should be drawn, and how its resources should be redistributed. If we decide to focus analytically on morality, understood as an ability to choose what particular moral self to pursue, then many of the oppressions and solidarities surrounding "living together in the world" (Arendt 1998) are made invisible. A new way of living together in the world emerged out of postwar, neoliberalizing reforms of welfare, which placed a major portion of responsibility for social protection on the local community (see chapters three and four). While the historical conjuncture of Dayton BiH has its own important particularities (Jansen et al. 2016), BiH is also a place struck by the postsocialist condition.

Fraser coins this fortuitous term to describe global political trends that became sharply visible after the end of the Cold War and that include

> an absence of any credible overarching emancipatory project despite the proliferation of fronts of struggle; a general decoupling of the cultural politics of recognition from the social politics of redistribution; and a decentering of claims for equality in the face of aggressive marketization and sharply rising material inequality. (Fraser 1997: 3)

While these processes have been well described in the scholarly literature over the past twenty years, the term itself still introduces some confusion into academic debates. Fraser outlines the contours of the postsocialist condition by using examples from the West, particularly from the United States—rather than from BiH or other former socialist countries. To describe sociopolitical processes in the West as postsocialist disturbs the conventional, developmental vision of the East as having to catch up with the West. The term offers a lens for analyzing the sociopolitical changes in both the West and the East as fundamentally similar.

All three elements of this global postsocialist condition were widely present in BiH during my research. First, instead of hope in a utopian emancipatory project, there was a broad sense of resignation and disappointment with the country, often articulated both from the "inside" and by the "international community" (Gilbert and Mujanović 2015). Second, identitarian politics of (ethnonational) recognition has made rising problems with socioeconomic redistribution practically invisible. The hegemony of ethnonational identity in BiH reflected this global move away from "a socialist political imaginary, in which the central problem of justice is redistribution, to a 'postsocialist' political imaginary, in which the central problem of justice is recognition" (Fraser 1997: 2). Finally, the often obscure, semilegal, or semicriminal privatization of former "social property" (*društveno vlasništvo*) swiftly created sharp material inequalities within the country.

It can be analytically and politically paralyzing to think about BiH outside of these transnational, global shifts "in the grammar of political claims-making" (Fraser 1997: 2)—despite the country's specific history and political-administrative structure. Discussing BiH as an exception, a "divided society," an "impossible state," or an "experiment of the international community" creates "abysses of impossibility to once and for all disentangle and reconcile ideological knots and to move towards a 'better future'" (Majstorović and Turjačanin 2011: 8).

Over the past few years, there have been attempts to find a new language to speak about socioeconomic problems that would "leave no room for ambiguity" (Arsenijević 2014: 9). For instance, the 2014 protests and plenums emerged with slogans such as "We are hungry in all three languages," "Reverse corrupt privatization" and "End nationalism," indicating that poverty cuts across ethnonational differences, speaking "clearly about newly re-identified and new political priorities," and articulating "that it is still possible to demand freedom, justice, and better life" (Arsenijević 2014: 9).

These organized attempts to fight the postsocialist condition were not present in the everyday life of my interlocutors in 2009 and 2010. My interlocutors mostly tried to find their way through some of the elements of the postsocialist condition (rather than to oppose them) and struggled to resolve their personal needs (rather than common ones). In this way, their struggles illuminate emergent forms of power and oppression in the European neoliberalizing semiperiphery. The organization of healthcare and social protection in BiH points to the blurring of lines between public and private and the state and that which is not the state.

Welfare relationships during my fieldwork did not fit into discrete categories of friendship, interest, bureaucracy, or expertise—at least not as a rule. The rule was, rather, the selective relevance of personalized knowledge and connections. Citizenship was not the criterion that guaranteed access to desirable healthcare and social protection or that ensured that procedures and rules would be equally applicable to all members of a polity (i.e., the state). However, this does not mean that some other form of community—ethnonational, religious, or local—was crucial in making decisions concerning when to apply procedures and rules. Rather, all of them occasionally became important and occasionally sank into irrelevance. The importance of personal connections in accessing welfare has to be understood in relation to this.

How can we think about reliance on personal connections in welfare? Did my interlocutors pursue favors pragmatically, because institutions were failing them? Or perhaps out of a moral inclination to help one another? Was this just a reflection of widespread, normalized corruption? This book has argued that brokering social relations in welfare systems was not an instrumental tactic of survival, used in the face of an ongoing crisis[1] nor just a way to reproduce oneself as a moral person. Instead, it was a practice in which pragmatically chasing resources was inseparable from reproducing a sense of self as a social person.

A particular modality of power was taking shape in this situation. Neoliberal restructurings of welfare created an environment in which life was governed through a combination of local and state forms of knowledge, randomly and unevenly spread across the state and society. As we saw in chapter six, during humanitarian actions, people had to keep moving throughout their local community, to ask for favors, and to expose themselves to the gaze of others. In this moveopticon, the organizers of humanitarian actions *wanted* to be seen by various local, public, private, and state actors—because otherwise they were left alone, with no support. They wanted to have their need recognized by their local communities in order to raise thousands of euros for a medical trip abroad.

The only way to achieve this was by pursuing *veze/štele* and increasing one's own visibility through becoming a topic of gossip and conversation in the Town. The organizers of humanitarian actions worked on positioning themselves in the midst of such stories on a full-time basis, pursuing social relationships with as many different kinds of people as possible, leaving aside many questions, problems, and (dis)satisfactions. At the same time, the personalization of institutional roles and responsibilities enabled some people to generate power by managing ambiguities between institutional and personal roles and responsibilities, rights and gifts, the state and that which is not the state. Without fully understanding how the management of ambiguity works, it will be difficult to find ways of challenging it.

Notes

1. I should also note that the global financial crisis that started in 2007–8 did not feature prominently in the talks of my interlocutors, because a sense of "crisis" for them "started long before 2007–08, with the war and the collapse of conditions for 'normal lives.' It was *then* that they slid into the swamp" (Jansen et al. 2016: 15).

Bibliography

Agency for Statistics of Bosnia and Herzegovina. 2011. Demography. Thematic Bulletin. Available at: http://www.bhas.ba/tematskibilteni/demogr afija%20konacna%20bh.pdf Accessed 21 March 2017.
———. 2016. "Census of Population, Households and Dwellings in Bosnia and Herzegovina, 2013. Final Results." Sarajevo. Available at: http://www.popis2013.ba/popis2013/doc/Popis2013prvoIzdanje.pdf. Accessed 25 July 2016.
Ajduković, Marina, and Vanja Branica. 2009. "Some Reflections on Social Work in Croatia (1945–1989)." In *Social Care under State Socialism (1945–1989). Ambitions, Ambiguities, and Mismanagement,* ed. Sabine Hering, 249–64. Opladen and Farmington Hills: Barbara Budrich Publishers.
Alexander, Catherine. 2002. *Personal States. Making Connections between People and Bureaucracy in Turkey.* Oxford: Oxford University Press.
Arendt, Hannah. 1998. *The Human Condition.* Chicago and London: University of Chicago Press.
Armakolas, Ioannis. 2001. "Identity and Conflict in Globalizing Times: Experiencing the Global in Areas Ravaged by Conflict and the Case of the Bosnian Serbs." In *Globalization and National Identities. Crisis or Opportunity?,* ed. Paul Kennedy and J. Catherine Danks, 46–63. New York: Palgrave.
———. 2007. "Sarajevo No More? Identity and the Experience of Place among Bosnian Serb Sarajevans in Republika Srpska." In *The New Bosnian Mosaic: Identities, Memories and Moral Claims in a Post-war Society,* ed. Xavier Bougarel, Elissa Helms, and Gerlachlus Duijzings, 79–99. Aldershot and Burlington: Ashgate.
Armakolas, Ioannis, and Maja Maksimović. 2013. "'Babylution': A Civic Awakening in Bosnia and Herzegovina?" ELIAMEP Working Papers. Hellenic Foundation for European and Foreign Policy, July.
Arsenijević, Damir. 2014. *Unbribable Bosnia and Herzegovina. The Fight for the Commons.* Baden-Baden: Nomos.
Augé, Marc. 1998. *A Sense for the Other: The Timeliness and Relevance of Anthropology.* Stanford: Stanford University Press.
Auyero, Javier. 2001. *Poor People's Politics. Peronist Survival Networks and the Legacy of Evita.* Durham and London: Duke University Press.

Baker, Catherine. 2012. "Prosperity without Security: The Precarity of Interpreters in Postsocialist, Postconflict Bosnia-Herzegovina." *Slavic Review* 71(4): 849–72.

———. 2014. "The Local Workforce of International Intervention in the Yugoslav Successor States: 'Precariat' or 'Projectariat'? Towards an Agenda for Future Research." *International Peacekeeping* 21(1): 91–106.

Bakić-Hayden, Milica. 1995. "Nesting Orientalisms: The Case of Former Yugoslavia." *Slavic Review* 54(4): 917–931.

Ballinger, Pamela. 2002. *History in Exile: Memory and Identity at the Borders of the Balkans.* Princeton: Princeton University Press.

———. 2004. "'Authentic Hybrids' in the Balkan Borderlands." *Current Anthropology* 45(1): 31–60.

Bašić, Sanela. 2013. "Izazovi društvenog razvoja i profesija socijalnog rada u postkonfliktnom i tranzicijskom društvu: Iskustva Bosni i Hercegovini." *Ljetopis socijalnog rada* 20(1): 113–38.

Baskar, Bojan. 2012. "Komšiluk and Taking Care of the Neighbor's Shrine in Bosnia-Herzegovina." In *Sharing Sacred Spaces in the Mediterranean,* ed. Dionigi Albera and Maria Couroucli, 51–68. Bloomington: Indiana University Press.

Baym, K. Nancy. 2015. "Connect with Your Audience! The Relational Labor of Connection." *The Communication Review* 18(1): 14–22.

Bear, Laura. 2015. *Navigating Austerity. Currents of Debt along a South Asian River.* Stanford: Stanford University Press.

Bieber, Florian. 2006. *Post-war Bosnia. Ethnicity, Inequality and Public Sector Governance.* New York: Palgrave Macmillan.

Bigo, Didier. 2008. "Detention of Foreigners, States of Exception, and the Social Practices of Control of the Banopticon." In *Borderscapes: Hidden Geographies and Politics at Territory's Edge,* ed. Prem Kumar Rajaram and Carl Grundy-Warr, 3–34. Minneapolis: Minnesota University Press.

Bilić, Bojan. 2012. *We Were Gasping for Air. [Post-]Yugoslav Anti-war Activism and Its Legacy.* Baden-Baden: Nomos.

Blagojević, Marina. 2009. *Knowledge Production at the Semiperiphery. A Gender Perspective.* Belgrade: Institut za kriminološka i sociološka istraživanja.

Bockman, Johanna. 2007. "The Origins of Neoliberalism between Soviet Socialism and Western Capitalism: 'A Galaxy without Borders.'" *Theory and Society* 36(4): 343–71.

Bornstein, Erica. 2009. "The Impulse of Philanthropy." *Cultural Anthropology* 24(4): 622–51.

Bose, Sumantra. 2002. *Bosnia after Dayton: Nationalist Partition and International Intervention.* Oxford and New York: Oxford University Press.

Bougarel, Xavier. 1996. "Bosnia and Herzegovina—State and Communitarianism." In *Yugoslavia and After: A Study in Fragmentation, Despair and Rebirth,* ed. David A. Dyker and Ivan Vejvoda, 87–115. New York: Longman.

Bougarel, Xavier, Elissa Helms, and Gerlachlus Duijzings. 2007. *The New Bosnian Mosaic: Identities, Memories and Moral Claims in a Post-war Society.* Aldershot and Burlington: Ashgate.

Bowman, Glen. 2003. "Constitutive Violence and the Nationalist Imaginary: Antagonism and Defensive Solidarity in 'Palestine' and 'Former Yugoslavia.'" *Social Anthropology* 11(3): 37–58.

Bringa, Tone. 1995. *Being Muslim the Bosnian Way: Identity and Community in a Central Bosnian Village.* Princeton: Princeton University Press.

Brković, Čarna. 2008. "Upravljanje osećanjima pripadanja: Antropološka analiza 'kulture' i 'identiteta' u Ustavu Republike Srbije." *Etnoantropološki problemi* 3(2): 59–76.

———. 2010. "Šta drugi misle o meni?: Protivljenje feminizmu, menopauza i javnost u postsocijalističkom kontekstu." *Genero* 14: 3–23.

———. 2014. "Surviving in a Moveopticon. Humanitarian Actions in Bosnia and Herzegovina." *Contemporary Southeastern Europe* 1(2): 42–60.

———. 2015a. "Brokering the Grey Zones: Pursuits of Favours in a Bosnian Town." In *Ethnographies of Grey Zones in Eastern Europe,* ed. Ida Harboe Knudsen and Martin Demant Frederiksen, 57–72. London: Anthem Press.

———. 2015b. "Management of Ambiguity: Favours and Flexibility in Bosnia and Herzegovina." *Social Anthropology* 23(3): 268–82.

———. 2016a. "Flexibility of *Veze/Štele*: Negotiating Social Protection." In *Negotiating Social Relations in Bosnia and Herzegovina. Semiperipheral Entanglements,* ed. Stef Jansen, Čarna Brković and Vanja Čelebičić, 94–108. New York: Routledge.

———. 2016b. "Scaling Humanitarianism: Humanitarian Actions in a Bosnian Town." *Ethnos* 81(1): 99–124.

Brunnbauer, Ulf. 2011. "The Balkan as Trans-Local Space. Entanglement, Movement and History." *Südosteuropa Mitteilungen* 3: 78–94.

Brunnbauer, Ulf, and Hannes Grandits, eds. 2013. *The Ambiguous Nation. Case Studies from Southeastern Europe in the 20th Century.* München: Oldenbourg Verlag.

Buck, D. Andrew. 2006. "Postsocialist Patronage: Expressions of Resistance and Loyalty." *Studies in Comparative International Development* 41(3): 3–24.

Bugarel, Ksavije. 2004. *Bosna: Anatomija rata.* Beograd: Fabrika knjiga.

Busch, Lawrence. 2010. "Can Fairy Tales Come True? The Surprising Story of Neoliberalism and World Agriculture." *Sociologia Ruralis* 50(4): 331–51.

Butler, Judith. 2004. *Precarious Life: The Powers of Mourning and Violence.* London: Verso.

Caldwell, L. Melissa. 2004. *Not by Bread Alone: Social Support in the New Russia.* Berkeley: University of California Press.

Campbell, John Kenedy. 1964. *Honour, Family and Patronage. A Study of Institutions and Moral Values in a Greek Mountain Community.* Oxford: Clarendon Press.

Candea, Matei. 2010. "Anonymous Introductions: Identity and Belonging in Corsica." *Journal of the Royal Anthropological Institute* 16(1): 119–37.

Čelebičić, Vanja. 2013. "'Waiting Is Hoping': Future and Youth in a Bosnian Border Town." PhD diss., University of Manchester.

Čelebičić, Vanja. 2016. "Beyond to Vote or Not to Vote: How Youth Engage with Politics." In *Negotiating Social Relations in Bosnia and Herzegovina. Semiperipheral Entanglements*, ed. Stef Jansen, Čarna Brković, and Vanja Čelebičić, 127–41. New York: Routledge.

Chari, Sharad, and Katherine Verdery. 2009. "Thinking between the Posts: Postcolonialism, Postsocialism, and Ethnography after the Cold War." *Comparative Studies in Society and History* 51(1): 6–34.

Clarke, John. 2008. "Living with/in and without Neo-liberalism." *Focaal* 51: 135–47.

Clarke, John, Dave Bainton, Noémi Lendvai, and Paul Stubbs. 2015. *Making Policy Move. Towards a Politics of Translation and Assemblage*. Bristol: Policy Press.

Cohen, Susanne. 2015. "The New Communication Order: Management, Language, and Morality in a Multinational Corporation." *American Ethnologist* 42(2): 324–39.

Coleridge, Samuel Taylor. 1817. "Samuel Taylor Coleridge: Biographia Literaria (1817)." Available at: http://www.english.upenn.edu/~mgamer/Etexts/biographia.html. Accessed 29 November 2015.

Coles, Kimberley. 2007. *Democratic Designs: International Intervention and Electoral Practices in Post-war Bosnia-Herzegovina*. Ann Arbor: University of Michigan Press.

Collier, J. Stephen. 2011. *Post-Soviet Social. Neoliberalism, Social Modernity, Biopolitics*. Princeton and Oxford: Princeton University Press.

Collier, J. Stephen, and Lucan Way. 2004. "Beyond the Deficit Model: Social Welfare in Post-Soviet Georgia." *Post-Soviet Affairs* 20(3): 258–84.

Čolović, Ivan. 2013. "Balkanist Discourse and Its Critics." *Hungarian Review* 4(2): 70–79.

Comaroff, Jean, and L. John Comaroff. 2012. "Theory from the South: Or, How Euro-America Is Evolving toward Africa." *Anthropological Forum* 22(2): 113–31.

Constitutional Court of Bosnia and Herzegovina. 1995. "The Constitution of Bosnia and Herzegovina." Available at: http://www.ccbh.ba/public/down/USTAV_BOSNE_I_HERCEGOVINE_engl.pdf. Accessed 21 March 2017.

Council of Ministers of BiH, Government of Federation of BiH, Government of Republika Srpska, Office of the BiH Coordinator for PRSP. 2004. "The Medium Term Development Strategy." Available at: https://www.imf.org/external/pubs/ft/scr/2004/cr04114.pdf. Accessed 21 March 2017.

Dahlman, Carl, and Gearóid Ó Tuathail. 2005. "Broken Bosnia: The Localized Geopolitics of Displacement and Return in Two Bosnian Places." *Annals of the Association of American Geographers* 95(3), 644–62.

Danielsson, Anna. 2014. *On the Power of Informal Economies and the Informal Economies of Power. Rethinking Informality, Resilience and Violence in Kosovo.* Uppsala: Acta Universitatis Upsaliensis.

Deacon, Bob, Noemi Lendvai, and Paul Stubbs. 2007. "Social Policy and International Interventions in South East Europe: Conclusions." In *Social Policy and International Interventions in South East Europe*, ed. Bob Deacon and Paul Stubbs, 221–42. Cheltenham: Edward Elgar.

Deacon, Bob, and Paul Stubbs. 1998. "International Actors and Social Policy Development in Bosnia-Herzegovina: Globalism and the 'New Feudalism.'" *Journal of European Social Policy* 8(2): 99–115.

Du Gay, Paul, ed. 2005. *The Values of Bureaucracy.* New York: Oxford University Press.

———. 2008. "'Without Affection or Enthusiasm.' Problems of Involvement and Attachment in 'Responsive' Public Management." *Organization* 15(3): 335–53.

Duijzings, Ger. 2002. *Geschiedenis en herinnering in Oost-Bosnie: de achtergronden van de val van Srebrenica.* Amsterdam: Boom/NIOD.

Duijzings, Gerlachlus. 2003. "Ethnic Unmixing under the Aegis of the West: A Transnational Approach to the Breakup of Yugoslavia." *Bulletin of the Royal Institute for Inter-Faith Studies* 5(2): 1–16.

———. 2007. "Commemorating Srebrenica: Histories of Violence and the Politics of Memory in Eastern Bosnia." In *The New Bosnian Mosaic: Identities, Memories and Moral Claims in a Post-war Society*, ed. Xavier Bougarel, Elissa Helms, and Gerlachlus Duijzings, 143–66. Aldershot and Burlington: Ashgate.

Dunn, Elizabeth C. 2004. *Privatizing Poland: Baby Food, Big Business, and the Remaking of Labor.* Ithaca: Cornell University Press.

———. 2008. "Postsocialist Spores: Disease, Bodies, and the State in the Republic of Georgia." *American Ethnologist* 35(2): 243–58.

———. 2012. "The Chaos of Humanitarian Aid: Adhocracy in the Republic of Georgia." *Humanity* 3(1): 1–23.

Dunn, Elizabeth C., and Jason Cons. 2014. "Aleatory Sovereignty and the Rule of Sensitive Spaces." *Antipode* 46(1): 92–109.

Dzenovska, Dace. 2014. "Bordering Encounters, Sociality and Distribution of the Ability to Live a 'Normal Life.'" *Social Anthropology* 22(3): 271–87.

Džumhur, Jasminka, Nives Jukić, and Ljubomir Sandić. 2010. *Specijalni izvještaj o stanju prava djece s posebnim potrebama/smetnjama u psihofizičkom razvoju.* Sarajevo: Institucija ombudsmena za ljudska prava Bosne i Hercegovine.

Eisenstadt, Shmuel Noah, and Louis Roniger. 1984. *Patrons, Clients and Friends. Interpersonal Relations and the Structure of Trust in Society.* Cambridge, UK: Cambridge University Press.

Fassin, Didier. 2005. "Compassion and Repression: The Moral Economy of Immigration Policies in France." *Cultural Anthropology* 20(3): 362–87.

———. 2007. "Humanitarianism as a Politics of Life." *Public Culture* 19(3): 499–520.

Fassin, Éric. 2015. "The Politics of Actuality: Biopower, Racial Democracy, and the Racialization of Sex. Key Note Talk at the Conference Engaging Foucault, 5 December 2014." Institute for Philosophy and Social Theory, Belgrade, Serbia. Available at: https://www.youtube.com/watch?v=rpm8srP2Fyg (55'). Accessed 6 August 2016.

Fink, Janet, Gail Lewis, and John Clarke. 2001. *Rethinking European Welfare. Transformations of Europe and Social Policy.* London: Open University and SAGE.

Foster, John. 2017. "Engagement and Alienation among Manchester's Unemployed." *Anthropology Matters* 17(1): 1–19.

Foucault, Michel. 1978. *The History of Sexuality. Vol 1: An Introduction.* New York: Pantheon Books.

———. 1984. "Practices and Sciences of the Self." In *The Foucault Reader*, ed. Paul Rabinow, 331–90. New York: Pantheon Books.

———. 1990. *The Use of Pleasure. The History of Sexuality, Vol. 2.* New York: Vintage Books.

———. 1995. *Discipline and Punish: The Birth of the Prison.* New York: Vintage.

———. 2003. *"Society Must Be Defended." Lectures at the Collège de France, 1975–1976.* New York: Picador.

Fraser, Nancy. 1997. *Justice Interruptus.* New York: Routledge.

———. 2003. "From Discipline to Flexibilization? Rereading Foucault in the Shadow of Globalization." *Constellations* 10(2): 160–71.

Fraser, Nancy. 2010. *Scales of Justice. Reimagining Political Space in a Globalizing World.* New York: Columbia University Press.

Galt, H. Anthony. 1974. "Rethinking Patron-Client Relationships: The Real System and the Official System in Southern Italy." *Anthropological Quarterly* 47(2): 182–202.

Gershon, Ilana. 2011. "Neoliberal Agency." *Current Anthropology* 52(4): 537–55.

Geršković, Leon. 1974. "Samoupravne interesne zajednice u socijalističkom samoupravnom društvu." *Politička misao: časopis za političke znanosti* 11(3): 3–15.

Gilbert, Andrew. 2006. "The Past in Parenthesis: (Non)Post-Socialism in Post-war Bosnia-Herzegovina." *Anthropology Today* 22(4): 14–18.

———. 2012. "Legitimacy Matters: Managing the Democratisation Paradox of Foreign State-Building in Bosnia and Herzegovina." *Südosteuropa* 60(4): 483–96.

Gilbert, Andrew, and Jasmin Mujanović. 2015. "Dayton at Twenty: Towards New Politics in Bosnia-Herzegovina." *Southeast European and Black Sea Studies* 15(4): 605–10.

Giordano, Christian. 2012. "The Anthropology of Mediterranean Societies." In *A Companion to the Anthropology of Europe*, ed. Ullrich Kockel, Máiréad Nic Craith, and Jonas Frykman, 13–30. Chichester: Willey-Blackwell.

Giroux, Henry A. 2011. "Neoliberal Politics as Failed Sociality: Youth and the Crisis of Higher Education." *Logos* 10(2). Available at: http://logosjour

nal.com/2011/neoliberal-politics-as-failed-sociality-youth-and-the-cri sis-of-higher-education. Accessed 21 March 2017.

Grandits, Hannes. 2007. "The Power of 'Armchair Politicians': Ethnic Loyalty and Political Factionalism among Herzegovinian Croats." In *The New Bosnian Mosaic. Identities, Memories and Moral Claims in a Postwar Society,* ed. Xavier Bougarel, Elissa Helms, and Gerlachlus Duijzings, 101–22. Aldershot and Burlington: Ashgate.

Green, Sarah. 2014. "Anthropological Knots. Conditions of Possibilities and Interventions." *HAU* 4(3): 1–21.

Green, Sarah F. 2005. *Notes from the Balkans: Locating Marginality and Ambiguity on the Greek-Albanian Border.* Princeton: Princeton University Press.

——. 2012. "A Sense of Border." In *A Companion to Border Studies,* ed. Thomas M. Wilson and Hastings Donnan, 573–92. Wiley-Blackwell Companions to Anthropology. Chichester: Willey-Blackwell.

Greenberg, Jessica. 2011. "On the Road to Normal: Negotiating Agency and State Sovereignty in Postsocialist Serbia." *American Anthropologist* 113(1): 88–100.

——. 2014. *After the Revolution. Youth, Democracy, and the Politics of Disappointment in Serbia.* Stanford: Stanford University Press.

Gupta, Akhil. 1995. "Blurred Boundaries: The Discourse of Corruption, the Culture of Politics, and the Imagined State." *American Ethnologist* 22(2): 375–402.

Hammel, Eugene A. 1968. *Alternative Social Structures and Ritual Relations in the Balkans.* Englewood Cliffs: Prentice-Hall.

Hanks, F. William, and Carlo Severi. 2014. "Translating Worlds: The Epistemological Space of Translation." *HAU* 4(2): 1–16.

Han, Clara. 2013. "Suffering and Pictures of Anthropological Inquiry. A Response to Comments on Life in Debt." *HAU* 3(1): 231–40.

Hann, Chris, ed. 2002. *Postsocialism: Ideals, Ideologies and Practices in Eurasia.* London and New York: Routledge.

——. 2003. "Is Balkan Civil Society an Oxymoron? From Königsberg to Sarajevo, via Przemyśl." *Ethnologia Balkanica* 7: 63–78.

Hann, Chris, and Elizabeth C. Dunn. 1996. *Civil Society. Challenging Western Models.* London and New York: Routledge.

Harboe Knudsen, Ida. 2014. "Grey Zones of Welfare. Normative Coping Strategies in Rural Lithuania." *Journal of Eurasian Studies* 6(1): 17–23.

Harboe Knudsen, Ida, and Martin Frederiksen, eds. 2015. *Ethnographies of Grey Zones in Eastern Europe.* London: Anthem Press.

Hart, Barry, and Edita Colo. 2014. "Psychosocial Peacebuilding in Bosnia and Herzegovina: Approaches to Relational and Social Change." *Intervention* 12(1): 76–87.

Haukanes, Haldis, and Frances Pine, eds. 2005. *Generations, Kinship and Care. Gendered Provisions of Social Security in Central Eastern Europe.* Centre for Women's and Gender Research Series, vol. 17. Bergen: University of Bergen.

Hayden, M. Robert. 1993. "The Partition of Bosnia and Herzegovina." The National Council for Soviet and East European Research. Available at: https://www.ucis.pitt.edu/nceeer/pre1998/1993-807-20-3-Hayden.pdf. Accessed 7 August 2016.

Hayden, M. Robert. 1999. *Blueprints for a House Divided. The Constitutional Logic of the Yugoslav Conflicts.* Ann Arbor: University of Michigan Press.

Hayden, M. Robert. 2002. "Antagonistic Tolerance: Competitive Sharing of Religious Sites in South Asia and the Balkans." *Current Anthropology* 43(2): 205–31.

Hayden, M. Robert. 2005. "'Democracy' without a Demos? The Bosnian Constitutional Experiment and the Intentional Construction of Nonfunctioning States." *East European Politics and Societies* 19(2): 226–59.

Hayden, M. Robert. 2007. "Moral Vision and Impaired Insight: Or the Imagination of Other People's Communities in Bosnia." *Current Anthropology* 48: 105–31.

Helms, Elissa. 2003. "Women as Agents of Ethnic Reconciliation? Women's NGOs and International Intervention in Postwar Bosnia-Herzegovina." *Women's Studies International Forum* 26(1): 15–34.

Helms, Elissa. 2006. "Gendered Transformations of State Power: Masculinity, International Intervention, and the Bosnian Police." *Nationalities Papers* 34(3): 343–61.

Helms, Elissa. 2007. "'Politics Is a Whore': Women, Morality and Victimhood in Post-War Bosnia-Herzegovina." In *The New Bosnian Mosaic: Identities, Memories and Moral Claims in a Post-war Society,* ed. Xavier Bougarel, Elissa Helms, and Gerlachlus Duijzings, 235–53. Aldershot and Burlington: Ashgate.

Helms, Elissa. 2008. "East and West Kiss: Gender, Orientalism, and Balkanism in Muslim-Majority Bosnia-Herzegovina." *Slavic Review* 67(1): 88–119.

Helms, Elissa. 2010. "The Gender of Coffee: Women and Reconciliation Initiatives in Post-war Bosnia and Herzegovina." *Focaal* 57: 17–32.

Helms, Elissa. 2013. *Innocence and Victimhood. Gender, Nation, and Women's Activism in Postwar Bosnia-Herzegovina.* Madison: University of Wisconsin Press.

Henig, David. 2012. "'Knocking on My Neighbour's Door': On Metamorphoses of Sociality in Rural Bosnia." *Critique of Anthropology* 32(3): 3–19.

Henig, David. 2017. "A Good Deed Is Not a Crime: Moral Cosmologies of Favours in Muslim Bosnia." In *Economies of Favour after Socialism,* ed. David Henig and Nicolette Makovicky, 181–202. Oxford: Oxford University Press.

Hering, Sabine, ed. 2009. *Social Care under State Socialism (1945–1989). Ambitions, Ambiguities, and Mismanagement.* Opladen and Farmington Hills: Barbara Budrich Publishers.

Herzfeld, Michael. 1993. *The Social Production of Indifference. Exploring the Symbolic Roots of Western Bureaucracy.* Chicago and London: University of Chicago Press.

Herzfeld, Michael. 1999. *Anthropology through the Looking-Glass. Critical Ethnography in the Margins of Europe.* Cambridge, UK: Cambridge University Press.

———. 2005. *Cultural Intimacy: Social Poetics in the Nation-State.* New York and Abingdon: Routledge.

Hickel, Jason. "A Short History of Neoliberalism (and How We Can Fix It)." Available at: http://www.newleftproject.org/index.php/site/article_comments/a_short_history_of_neoliberalism_and_how_we_can_fix_it. Accessed 4 August 2016.

Hodges, Andrew. 2014. "The Scientific Community: Creating a Language to Deal with the 'Everyday Geopolitics' of Neoliberal 'Transition' in Post-Socialist Serbia." *Anthropology Matters* 15(1): 91–113.

———. 2016. "Croatian Language Standardization and the Production of Nationalized Political Subjects through Language? Perspectives from the Social Sciences and Humanities." *Etnološka tribina* 46(39): 3–91.

Hrelja, Kemal. 2002. *UNDP Human Development Report.* Sarajevo: United Nations Development Program.

Hromadžić, Azra. 2011. "Bathroom Mixing: Youth Negotiate Democracy in Postconflict Bosnia and Herzegovina." *Political and Legal Anthropology Review* 34(2): 268–89.

Hromadžić, Azra. 2013. "Discourses of Trans-ethnic Narod in Postwar Bosnia and Herzegovina." *Nationalities Papers* 41(2): 259–75.

Hughes, Caroline, and Vanessa Pupavac. 2005. "Framing Post-conflict Societies: International Pathologisation of Cambodia and the Post-Yugoslav States." *Third World Quarterly* 26(6): 873–89.

Human Rights Watch. 2000. *"Unfinished Business."* Available at: http://www.refworld.org/docid/3ae6a87b0.html. Accessed 28 August 2014.

Humphrey, Caroline. 2012. "Favors and 'Normal Heroes.' The Case of Postsocialist Higher Education." *HAU* 2(2): 22–41.

Huntington, Samuel. 1965. "Political Development and Political Decay." *World Politics* 17(3): 386–430.

Hutchins, Edwin. 1993. "Learning to Navigate." In *Understanding Practice. Perspectives on Activity and Context,* ed. Seth Chaiklin and Jean Lave, 35–63. Cambridge, UK: Cambridge University Press.

Husanović, Jasmina. 2011. "Upravljanje životom kroz biopolitičke/tanatopolitičke režime u Bosni i Hercegovini: bauci emancipativne politike." In *U okrilju nacije. Etnički i državni identitet kod mladih u Bosni i Hercegovini,* ed. Danijela Majstorović and Vladimir Turjačanin, 266–78. Banja Luka: Centar za kulturni i socijalni popravak.

Jansen, Stef. 2003. "'Why Do They Hate Us?' Everyday Serbian Nationalist Knowledge of Muslim Hatred." *Journal of Mediterranean Studies* 13(2): 215–37.

———. 2005a. *Antinacionalizam. Etnografija otpora u Beogradu i Zagrebu.* Beograd: XX vek.

———. 2005b. "National Numbers in Context: Maps and Stats in Representations of the Post-Yugoslav Wars." *Identities* 12(1): 45–68.

———. 2006. "The Privatisation of Home and Hope: Return, Reforms and the Foreign Intervention in Bosnia-Herzegovina." *Dialectical Anthropology* 30: 177–99.

———. 2009a. "After the Red Passport: Towards an Anthropology of the Everyday Geopolitics of Entrapment in the EU's Immediate Outside." *Journal of the Royal Anthropological Institute* 15(4): 815–32.

———. 2009b. "Hope and the State in the Anthropology of Home: Preliminary Notes." *Ethnologia Europaeana* 39(1): 54–60.

———. 2011. "Refuchess: Locating Bosniac Repatriates after the War in Bosnia-Herzegovina." *Population, Space and Place* 17(2): 140–52.

———. 2015. *Yearnings in the Meantime: 'Normal Lives' and the State in a Sarajevo Apartment Complex.* Oxford: Berghahn Books.

Jansen, Stef, Čarna Brković, and Vanja Čelebičić, eds. 2016. *Negotiating Social Relations in Bosnia and Herzegovina. Semiperipheral Entanglements.* New York: Routledge.

Službeni glasnik Republike Srpske. 2004. "Službeni glasnik Republike Srpske" 101/04.

Jouhanneau, Cécile. 2016. "The Discretion of Witnesses. War Camp Memories between Politicization and Civility." In *Negotiating Social Relations in Bosnia and Herzegovina. Semiperipheral Entanglements,* ed. Stef Jansen, Čarna Brković and Vanja Čelebičić, 31–45. New York: Routledge.

Kalb, Don. 2009. "Conversations with a Polish Populist: Tracing Hidden Histories of Globalization, Class, and Dispossession in Postsocialism (and Beyond)." *American Ethnologist* 36(2): 207–23.

Kingfisher, Catherine. 2016. *A Policy Travelogue. Tracing Welfare Reform in Aotearoa/New Zealand and Canada.* New York and Oxford: Berghahn Books.

Knaus, Gerald, and Felix Martin. 2003. "Lessons from Bosnia and Herzegovina. Travails of the European Raj." *Journal of Democracy* 14(3): 60–74.

Kolind, Torsten. 2008. *Post-war Identification: Everyday Muslim Counter-discourse in Bosnia Herzegovina.* Aarhus: Aarhus University Press.

Kolstrup, Henrik. 2002. "Foreword." In *UNDP Human Development Report,* ed. Kemal Hrelja, 3–4. Sarajevo: United Nations Development Program.

Kordić, Snježana. 2010. *Jezik i nacionalizam.* Zagreb: Durieux.

Kostovicova, Denisa. 2004. "Republika Srpska and Its Boundaries in Bosnian Serb Geographical Narratives in the Post-Dayton Period." *Space and Polity* 8(3): 267–87.

Koutkova, Karla. 2016. "'The King Is Naked': Internationality, Informality and Ko Fol State-Building in Bosnia." In *Negotiating Social Relations in Bosnia and Herzegovina. Semiperipheral Entanglements,* ed. Stef Jansen, Čarna Brković, and Vanja Čelebičić, 109–21. New York: Routledge.

Kuper, Adam. 1999. *Culture—the Anthropologists' Account.* Cambridge, MA and London: Harvard University Press.

Kurtović, Larisa. 2011. "What Is a Nationalist? Some Thoughts on the Question from Bosnia-Herzegovina." *The Anthropology of East Europe Review* 29(2): 242–53.

Kurtović, Larisa. 2015. "'Who Sows Hunger, Reaps Rage': On Protest, Indignation and Redistributive Justice in Post-Dayton Bosnia-Herzegovina." *Southeast European and Black Sea Studies* 15(4): 639–59.

Laidlaw, James. 2002. "For an Anthropology of Ethics and Freedom." *Journal of the Royal Anthropological Institute* 8(2): 311–32.

Lampland, Martha. 2002. "The Advantages of Being Collectivized: Cooperative Farm Managers in the Postsocialist Economy." In *Postsocialism. Ideals, Ideologies and Practices in Eurasia,* ed. Chris Hann, 31–56. London and New York: Routledge.

Latour, Bruno, and Hermant Emilie. 2006. *Paris: Invisible City* [Bruno Latour and Emilie Hermant. 1998. Paris: *ville invisible.* Paris: La Découverte-Les Empêcheurs de penser en rond. Trans. Liz Carey-Libbrecht.] Available at: http://www.bruno-latour.fr/sites/default/files/downloads/viii_paris-city-gb.pdf. Accessed 8 August 2016.

Leach, Edmund. 1993. *Culture and Communication. The Logic by Which Symbols Are Connected.* Cambridge, UK: Cambridge University Press.

Ledeneva, Alena. 1998. *Russia's Economy of Favours. Blat, Networking and Informal Exchange.* Cambridge, UK: Cambridge University Press.

———. 2006. *How Russia Really Works: The Informal Practices That Shaped Post-Soviet Politics and Business.* New York: Cornell University Press.

———. 2009. "From Russia with Blat: Can Informal Networks Help Modernize Russia?" *Social Research* 76(1): 257–88.

———. 2011. "Open Secrets and Knowing Smiles." *East European Politics and Societies* 25(4): 720–36.

Lendvai, Noémi, and Paul Stubbs. 2009. "Assemblages, Translation, and Intermediaries in South East Europe." *European Societies* 11(5): 673–95.

Leskošek, Vesna. 2009. "Social Policy in Yugoslavia between Socialism and Capitalism." In *Social Care under State Socialism (1945–1989). Ambitions, Ambiguities, and Mismanagement,* ed. Sabine Hering, 239–47. Opladen and Farmington Hills: Barbara Budrich Publishers.

Li Causi, Luciano. 1975. "Anthropology and Ideology. The Case of Patronage in Mediterranean Societies." *Critique of Anthropology* 2(4–5): 90–109.

Maček, Ivana. 2007. "'Imitation of life': Negotiating Normality in Sarajevo under Siege." In *The New Bosnian Mosaic: Identities, Memories and Moral Claims in a Post-War Society,* ed. Xavier Bougarel, Elissa Helms, and Gerlachlus Duijzings, 39–57. Aldershot and Burlington: Ashgate.

Maglajlić-Holiček, Reima Ana, and Ešref Kenan Rašidagić. 2007. "Bosnia-Herzegovina." In *Social Policy and International Interventions in South East Europe,* ed. Bob Deacon and Paul Stubbs, 149–66. Cheltenham: Edward Elgar.

Majstorović, Danijela. 2015. "What Remains 'after Plenums': Activist Citizenship and the Language of the 'New Political.'" Available at: http://www.artsrn.ualberta.ca/direct-democracy/?p=131. Accessed 4 April 2015.

Majstorović, Danijela, and Vladimir Turjačanin. 2011. *U okrilju nacije. Etnički i državni identitet kod mladih u Bosni i Hercegovini.* Banja Luka: Centar za kulturni i socijalni popravak.

Makovicky, Nicolette, ed. 2014. *Neoliberalism, Personhood, and Postsocialism. Enterprising Selves in Changing Economies.* Burlington: Ashgate.

Malkki, Liisa. 1992. "National Geographic: The Rooting of Peoples and the Territorialization of National Identity among Scholars and Refugees." *Cultural Anthropology* 7(1): 24–45.

Martin, Emily. 1994. *Flexible Bodies: Tracking Immunity in American Culture from the Days of Polio to the Age of AIDS.* Boston: Beacon Press.

———. 2005. "Managing Americans. Policy and Changes in the Meanings of Work and the Self." In *Anthropology of Policy. Critical Perspectives on Governance and Power,* ed. Cris Shore and Susan Wright, 183–97. New York: Routledge.

Matza, Tomas. 2012. "'Good Individualism?' Psychology, Ethics, and Neoliberalism in Postsocialist Russia." *American Ethnologist* 39(4): 804–18.

McCall, Leslie. 2005. "The Complexity of Intersectionality." *Signs* 30(3): 1771–800.

Miković, Milanka. 2006. "Historija socijalnog rada i obrazovanja socijalnih radnika u Bosni i Hercegovini." *Godišnjak Fakulteta političkih nauka* 1: 447–56.

Mikuš, Marek. 2016. "The Justice of Neoliberalism: Moral Ideology and Redistributive Politics of Public-Sector Retrenchment in Serbia." *Social Anthropology* 24(2): 211–27.

Milenković, Miloš. 2008. "Problemi konstitucionalizacije multikulturalizma—pogled iz antropologije." *Etnoantropološki problemi* 3(2): 45–57.

Mitchell, Timothy. 2004. "The Middle East in the Past and Future of Social Science." In *The Politics of Knowledge: Area Studies and the Disciplines,* ed. David L. Szanton, 74–118. Berkeley and Los Angeles: University of California Press.

Montoya, Ainhoa. 2014. "Ethnographies of the Opportunities and Risks of Neoliberalisation." *Anthropology Matters* 15(1): 1–15.

Morris, Jeremy, and Abel Polese, eds. 2014. *The Informal Post-Socialist Economy: Embedded Practices and Livelihoods.* London and New York: Routledge.

Muehlebach, Andrea. 2011. "On Affective Labor in Post-Fordist Italy." *Cultural Anthropology* 26(1): 59–82.

———. 2012. *The Moral Neoliberal. Welfare and Citizenship in Italy.* Chicago: University of Chicago Press.

Mujačić, Mahmut. 1973. "Susjedski odnosi u jednoj lokalnoj zajednici." *Sociologija i prostor* 39: 39–53.

Mujkić, Asim. 2007. "We, the Citizens of Ethnopolis." *Constellations* 14(1): 112–28.

Narayan, Kirin. 1993. "How Native Is a 'Native' Anthropologist?" *American Anthropologist* 95(3): 671–86.

Navaro-Yashin, Yael. 2002. *Faces of the State. Secularism and Public Life in Turkey.* Princeton: Princeton University Press.

Navaro-Yashin, Yael. 2007. "Make-Believe Papers, Legal Forms and the Counterfeit: Affective Interactions between Documents and People in Britain and Cyprus." *Anthropological Theory* 7(1): 79–98.

NIOD [Nederlands Instituut voor Oorlogsdocumentatie]. 2002. Srebrenica. A "Safe" Area: Reconstruction, Background, Consequences and Analyses of the Fall of a Safe Area. Amsterdam: NIOD Institute for War, Holocaust and Genocide Studies.

Nixon, Nicola. 2009. Veze među nama: Društveni kapital u Bosni i Hercegovini. Sarajevo: Razvojni program Ujedinjenih nacija (UNDP) u Bosni i Hercegovini.

Njaradi, Dunja. 2012. "The Balkan Studies: History, Post-Colonialism and Critical Regionalism." *Journal of Contemporary Central and Eastern Europe* 20(2–3): 185–201.

Norris, David. 1999. *In the Wake of the Balkan Myth.* Basingstoke: Macmillan.

Obad, Orlanda. 2014. "On the Privilege of the Peripheral Point of View: A Beginner's Guide to the Study and Practice of Balkanism." In *Mirroring Europe: Ideas of Europe and Europeanization in Balkan Societies,* ed. Tanja Petrović, 20–38. Boston: Brill.

Ong, Aihwa. 1999. *Flexible Citizenship. The Cultural Logics of Transnationality.* Durham and London: Duke University Press.

———. 2006. *Neoliberalism as Exception: Mutations in Citizenship and Sovereignty.* Durham: Duke University Press.

Palmberger, Monika. 2010. "Distancing Personal Experiences from the Collective: Discursive Tactics among Youth in Post-war Mostar." *L'Europe en formation* 357: 107–24.

Peirano, G.S. Mariza. 1998. "When Anthropology Is at Home: The Different Contexts of a Single Discipline." *Annual Review of Anthropology* 27: 105–28.

Petrović, Jelena. 2014. "551.35 Geometry of Time." Available at: http://www.lanacmajcanin.com/projects/item/132-551-35-geometry-of-time. Accessed 8 December 2015.

Petryna, Adriana. 2002. *Life Exposed. Biological Citizenship after Chernobyl.* Princeton and Oxford: Princeton University Press.

Phillips, Sarah. 2008. *Women's Social Activism in the New Ukraine.* Bloomington and Indianapolis: Indiana University Press.

———. 2011. *Disability and Mobile Citizenship in Postsocialist Ukraine.* Bloomington and Indianapolis: Indiana University Press.

Pine, Frances. 2015. "Living in the Grey Zones: When Ambiguity and Uncertainty Are the Ordinary." In *Ethnographies of Grey Zones in Eastern Europe. Relations, Borders and Invisibilities,* ed. Ida Harboe Knudsen and Martin Frederiksen, 25–40. London: Anthem Press.

Pugh, Michael. 2002. "Postwar Political Economy in Bosnia and Herzego-vina: The Spoils of Peace." *Global Governance* 8(4): 467–82.

———. 2005. "Transformation in the Political Economy of Bosnia since Day-ton." *International Peacekeeping* 12(3): 448–62.

Pugh, Michael, Neil Cooper, and Mandy Turner. 2008. *Whose Peace? Critical Perspectives on the Political Economy of Peacebuilding*. Basingstoke and New York: Palgrave Macmillan.

Read, Rosie. 2007. "Labour and Love: Competing Constructions of 'Care' in a Czech Nursing Home." *Critique of Anthropology* 27(2): 203–22.

Read, Rosie, and Tatjana Thelen. 2007. "Introduction: Social Security and Care after Socialism: Reconfigurations of Public and Private." *Focaal* 50: 3–18.

Reeves, Madeleine. 2013. "Clean Fake: Authenticating Documents and Persons in Migrant Moscow." *American Ethnologist* 40(3): 508–24.

———. 2014. *Border Work. Spatial Lives of the State in Rural Central Asia*. Ithaca: Cornell University Press.

Rivkin-Fish, Michele. 2005. "Bribes, Gifts and Unofficial Payments: Rethinking Corruption in Post-Soviet Russian Health Care." In *Corruption: Anthropological Perspectives*, ed. Dieter Haller and Chris Shore, 47–64. London: Pluto Press.

Robbins, Joel. 2013. "Beyond the Suffering Subject: Toward an Anthropology of the Good." *Journal of the Royal Anthropological Institute* 19(3): 447–62.

Rogers, Douglas. 2010. "Postsocialisms Unbound: Connections, Critiques, Comparisons." *Slavic Review* 69(1): 1–15.

Rose, Nikolas. 2000. "Community, Citizenship, and the Third Way." *American Behavioral Scientist* 43(9): 1395–411.

———. 2006. *The Politics of Life Itself*. Princeton: Princeton University Press.

Rose, Nikolas, and Carlos Novas. 2007. "Biological Citizenship." In *Global Assemblages. Technology, Politics, and Ethics as Anthropological Problems*, ed. Aihwa Ong and Stephen J. Collier, 439–65. Malden: Blackwell Publishing.

Roth, Klaus. 2006. "Living Together or Living Side by Side? Interethnic Coexistence in Multiethnic Societies." In *Negotiating Culture. Moving, Mixing and Memory in Contemporary Europe*, ed. Reginald Byron and Ullrich Kockel, 18–32. Berlin: Lit Verlag.

Ryang, Sonia. 1997. "Native Anthropology and Other Problems." *Dialectical Anthropology* 22: 23–49.

Sajo, Andras. 2002. "Introduction. Clientelism and Extortion: Corruption in Transition." In *Political Corruption in Transition. A Skeptic's Handbook*, ed. Stephen Kotkin and Andras Sajo, 1–21. Budapest: Central European University Press.

Salihbašić, Šehzada. 2008. Specifičnosti finansiranja zdravstvene zaštite u BiH. Available at: http://www.uptz.ba/index.php?option=com_content&view=article&id=65:specifinosti-finansiranja-zdravstvene-zatite-u-

bih-sehzada-salihbai&catid=41:zdravstvene-usluge-pacijentima&Itemid
=64. Accessed 30 October 2013.

Saller, P. Richard. 1982. *Personal Patronage under the Early Empire*. Cambridge, UK: Cambridge University Press.

Sarajlić, Eldar. 2012. "Conceptualising Citizenship Regime(s) in Post-Dayton Bosnia and Herzegovina." *Citizenship Studies* 16(3–4): 367–81.

Šavija-Valha, Nebojša. 2010. "Ironijski subjekt svakodnevne komunikacije u Bosni i Hercegovini." PhD diss., Institutum Studiorum Humanitatis.

———. 2013. *Raja—Ironijski subjekt svakodnevne komunikacije u Bosni i Hercegovini i raja kao strategija življenja*. Zagreb: Jesenski i Turk.

———. 2016. "Raja: The Ironic Subject of Everyday Life in Sarajevo." In *Negotiating Social Relations in Bosnia and Herzegovina. Semiperipheral Entanglements,* ed. Stef Jansen, Čarna Brković, and Vanja Čelebičić, 163–78. New York: Routledge.

Schmidt, W. Steffen, C. James Scott, Carl Lande, and Laura Guasti, eds. 1977. *Friends, Followers and Factions: A Reader in Political Clientelism*. Berkeley: University of California Press.

Scott, James C. 1998. *Seeing Like a State. How Certain Schemes to Improve the Human Condition Have Failed*. New Haven and London: Yale University Press.

Shaw, Jo, and Igor Štiks, eds. 2012. *Citizenship after Yugoslavia*. New York: Routledge.

Shever, Elana. 2012. *Resources for Reform. Oil and Neoliberalism in Argentina*. Stanford: Stanford University Press.

Shore, Cris. 2000. *Building Europe. The Cultural Politics of European Integration*. London and New York: Routledge.

Shore, Cris. 2006. "The Limits of Ethnography versus the Poverty of Theory: Patron-Client Relations in Europe Re-Visited." *Sites* 3(2): 40–59.

Silverman, F. Sydel. 1965. "Patronage and Community-Nation Relationships in Central Italy." *Ethnology* 4(2): 172–89.

Sloterdijk, Peter. 2001. *Critique of Cynical Reason*. Minneapolis: University of Minnesota Press.

Song, Jesook. 2009. *South Koreans in the Debt Crisis. The Creation of a Neoliberal Welfare Society*. Durham and London: Duke University Press.

Sorabji, Cornelia. 1995. "A Very Modern War: Terror and Territory in Bosnia-Hercegovina." In *War: A Cruel Necessity?*, ed. Robert A. Hinde and Helen E. Watson, 80–95. London: Tauris.

———. 2006. "Managing Memories in Post-war Sarajevo: Individuals, Bad Memories, and New Wars." *Journal of the Royal Anthropological Institute* 12(1): 1–18.

———. 2007. "Bosnian Neighbourhoods Revisited: Tolerance, Commitment and Komšiluk in Sarajevo." In *On the Margins of Religion*, ed. João de Pina Cabral and Frances Pine, 97–113. Oxford: Berghahn Books.

Stambolieva, Marija. 2015. "Welfare State Change and Social Citizenship in the Post-Yugoslav States." *European Politics and Society* 16(3): 379–94.

———. 2016. *Welfare State Transformation in the Yugoslav Successor States: From Social to Unequal.* London and New York: Routledge.

Stan, Sabina. 2012. "Neither Commodities nor Gifts: Post-Socialist Informal Exchanges in the Romanian Healthcare System." *Journal of the Royal Anthropological Institute* 18(1): 65–82.

Republika Srpska Confederation of Trade Unions. "Union Consumer Basket." Available at: http://www.savezsindikatars.org/sindikalna_potrosa cka_korpa.php. Accessed 5 October 2015.

Republički zavod za statistiku Republike Srpske. 2011. Statistički godišnjak Republike Srpske [Statistical Yearbook of Republika Srpska]. Banja Luka: Republički zavod za statistiku Republike Srpske.

Stefansson, Anders. 2006. "Homes in the Making: Property Restitution, Refugee Return, and Senses of Belonging in a Post-war Bosnian Town." *International Migration* 44(3): 115–39.

———. 2010. "Coffee after Cleansing? Co-existence, Co-operation and Communication in Post-conflict Bosnia and Herzegovina." *Focaal* 57: 62–76.

Stenning, Alison, Adrian Smith, Alena Rochovská, and Dariusz Świątek. 2010. *Domesticating Neo-Liberalism. Spaces of Economic Practice and Social Reproduction in Post-Socialist Cities.* Malden: Wiley-Blackwell.

Štiks, Igor. 2013. "A Laboratory of Citizenship: Shifting Conceptions of Citizenship in Yugoslavia and Post-Yugoslav States." In *Citizenship after Yugoslavia,* ed. Jo Shaw and Igor Štiks, 15–38. Oxon and New York: Routledge.

Strathern, Marilyn. 1987. "An Awkward Relationship: The Case of Feminism and Anthropology." *Signs* 12(2): 276–92.

———. 2004. *Partial Connections.* Walnut Creek: Altamira Press.

Stubbs, Paul. 2001. "'Socijalni sektor' ili devalviranje značaja socijalne politike? Regulatorni režim socijalnog blagostanja u Bosni i Hercegovini danas." In *Međunarodne politike podrške zemljama jugoistočne Evrope: Lekcije (ne)naučene u BiH,* ed. Žarana Papić, 125–39. Sarajevo: Müller.

Stubbs, Paul. 2002. "Globalisation, Memory and Welfare Regimes in Transition: Towards an Anthropology of Transnational Policy Transfers." *International Journal of Social Welfare* 11(4): 321–30.

———. 2005. "Stretching Concepts Too Far? Multi-level Governance, Policy Transfer and the Politics of Scale in South East Europe." *Southeast European Politics* 6(2): 66–87.

———. 2007. "Civil Society or Ubleha? Reflections on Flexible Concepts, Meta-NGOs and New Social Energy in the Post-Yugoslav Space." In *20 Pieces of Encouragement for Awakening and Change: Peacebuilding in the Region of the Former Yugoslavia,* ed. Helena Rill, Tamara Šmidling, and Ana Bitoljanu, 215–28. Belgrade: Center for Nonviolent Action.

———. 2013. "Flex Actors and Philanthropy in (Post-)Conflict Arenas: Soros' Open Society Foundations in the Post-Yugoslav Space." *Croatian Political Science Review* 50(5): 114–38.

———. 2014. "Thinking Reform Otherwise in the Semi-periphery: Agency, Flexibility and Translation." Paper presented at the Ninth International Conference of Interpretive Policy Analysis, Wageningen, Netherlands, 3–5 July.

———. 2015. "Performing Reform in South East Europe: Consultancy, Translation and Flexible Agency." In *Making Policy Move. Towards a Politics of Translation and Assemblage,* ed. John Clarke, Dave Bainton, Noemi Lendvai, and Paul Stubbs, 67–95. Bristol: Policy Press.

Stubbs, Paul, and Siniša Zrinščak. 2011. "Rethinking Clientelism, Governance and Citizenship in Social Welfare: The Case of Croatia." Paper presented at the 9th Annual ESPAnet Conference: Sustainability and Transformation in European Social Policy, Valencia, Spain, 8–10 September.

SUMERO [Savez organizacija za podršku osobama s intelektualnim teškoćama FBiH]. 2012. Samoodređenje. Sarajevo: SUMERO.

Švenda Radeljak, Ksenija. 2006. "Časopis Socijalni rad—prvih 10 godina (1960–1969)." *Ljetopis socijalnog rada* 13(1): 115–32.

Taylor, Charles. 2007. *A Secular Age.* Cambridge, MA and London: Belknap Press of Harvard University Press.

Thelen, Tatjana. 2011. "Shortage, Fuzzy Property and Other Dead Ends in the Anthropological Analysis of (Post)Socialism." *Critique of Anthropology* 31(1): 43–61.

Ticktin, Miriam. 2006. "Where Ethics and Politics Meet: The Violence of Humanitarianism in France." *American Ethnologist* 33(1): 33–49.

———. 2011. *Casualties of Care. Immigration and the Politics of Humanitarianism in France.* Berkeley: University of California Press.

Todorova, Maria, ed. 2004. *Balkan Identities. Nation and Memory.* London: C. Hurst.

———. 2009. *Imagining the Balkans.* New York: Oxford University Press.

Tuathail, Gearóid Ó. 2013. "'Republika Srpska Will Have a Referendum': The Rhetorical Politics of Milorad Dodik." *Nationalities Papers* 41(1): 166–204.

Tuathail, Gearóid Ó., and Carl Dahlman. 2006. "The 'West Bank of the Drina': Land Allocation and Ethnic Engineering in Republika Srpska." *Transactions of the Institute of British Geographers* 31(3): 304–22.

Vasiljević, Jelena. 2011. "Ključni elementi transformacije režima državljanstva u Srbiji od 1990. godine." *Filozofija i društvo* 22(4): 63–82.

———. 2012. "Imagining and Managing the Nation: Tracing Citizenship Policies in Serbia." *Citizenship Studies* 16(3–4): 323–36.

Venkatesan, Soumhya. 2009. "Charity: Conversations about Need and Greed." In *Ethnographies of Moral Reasoning. Living Paradoxes of a Global Age,* ed. Karen Sykes, 67–89. New York: Palgrave Macmillan.

———. 2015. "There Is No Such Thing As the Good: The 2013 Meeting of the Group for Debates in Anthropological Theory." *Critique of Anthropology* 35(4): 430–80.

Venneri, Giulio. 2010. "Beyond the Sovereignty Paradox: EU 'Hands-up'

Statebuilding in Bosnia and Herzegovina." *Journal of Intervention and Statebuilding* 4(2): 153–78.

Verdery, Katherine. 1996. *What Was Socialism, and What Comes Next?* Princeton: Princeton University Press.

———. 1999. *The Political Lives of Dead Bodies*. New York: Columbia University Press.

Vetters, Larissa. 2007. "The Power of Administrative Categories: Emerging Notions of Citizenship in the Divided City of Mostar." *Ethnopolitics* 6(2): 187–209.

Vetters, Larissa. 2014. "Contingent Statehood: Clientelism and Civic Engagement as Relational Modalities in Contemporary Bosnia and Herzegovina." *Social Analysis* 58(3): 20–37.

Vigh, Henrik Erdman. 2009. "Motion Squared. A Second Look at the Concept of Social Navigation." *Anthropological Theory* 9(4): 419–38.

Vukajlija. Available at: http://vukajlija.com/socijala?strana=1. Accessed 6 February 2017.

Wagner, Roy. 1991. "The Fractal Person." In *Big Men and Great Men: Personifications of Power in Melanesia*, ed. Maurice Godelier and Marilyn Strathern, 159–96. Cambridge, UK: Cambridge University Press.

Wagner, Sarah. 2008. *To Know Where He Lies: DNA Technology and the Search for Srebrenica's Missing*. Berkeley and Los Angeles: University of California Press.

Wanner, Catherine. 2005. "Money, Morality and New Forms of Exchange in Postsocialist Ukraine." *Ethnos* 70(4): 515–37.

Wedel, Janine. 1986. *The Private Poland*. New York: Facts on File.

———. 2009. *Shadow Elite. How the World's New Power Brokers Undermine Democracy, Government, and the Free Market*. New York: Basic Books.

Weiner, Annette B. 1992. *Inalienable Possessions. The Paradox of Keeping-While-Giving*. Berkeley, Los Angeles, and Oxford: University of California Press.

Wimmer, Andreas, and Nina Glick Schiller. 2002. "Methodological Nationalism and beyond: Nation-State Building, Migration and the Social Sciences." *Global Networks* 2: 301–34.

Wright, Susan. 1998. "The Politicization of Culture." *Anthropology Today* 14(1): 7–15.

Yan, Yunxiang. 2003. *Private Life under Socialism: Love, Intimacy, and Family Change in a Chinese Village, 1949–1999*. Stanford: Stanford University Press.

Yang, Mayfair Mei-hui. 2002. "The Resilience of Guanxi and Its New Deployments: A Critique of Some New Guanxi Scholarship." *China Quarterly* 170: 459–76.

Završek, Darja. 2006. "Spol, socijalna skrb i obrazovanje za socijalni rad u početku socijalističke vlasti u Sloveniji." *Ljetopis socijalnog rada* 13(1): 63–74.

———. 2008. "Engendering Social Work Education under State Socialism in Yugoslavia." *British Journal of Social Work* 38(4): 734–50.

Zigon, Jarret. 2011. "Working on the Self in Russian Orthodox Church Drug Rehabilitation: A Moral and Ethical Assemblage." *Ethos* 39(1): 30–50.

Žižek, Slavoj. 2008. *The Sublime Object of Ideology.* London and New York: Verso.

Index

www.ingramcontent.com/pod-product-compliance
Lightning Source LLC
Chambersburg PA
CBHW070927030426
42336CB00014BA/2571